Thomas Wolfe

THREE DECADES OF CRITICISM

Thomas Wolfe

THREE DECADES OF CRITICISM

edited with an introduction by
LESLIE A. FIELD

1968
NEW YORK
New York University Press
LONDON
University of London Press Limited

". . . the time of rivers, mountains, oceans,
and the earth . . ."

Time

| Joyce | past present future | My mother |

Time Immutable

My father, Aunt Mary, Sylvia

Acknowledgments

FIRST, an acknowledgment of a personal nature: This book could not have been completed without the silence of the study. The door being closed, you turned and walked away. Most of the time. Thus, many thanks to Joyce, Jeffrey, and Linda. . . .

My appreciation must also go to Oscar Cargill and William T. Stafford for their contributions. Finally, it is with great pleasure that I acknowledge the authors and publishers who have granted me permission to reprint their copyright works in this volume. Please note that page references for each entry below refer to pages of original publication.

"Gargantua Fills His Skin," by Oscar Cargill. Originally published in the *University of Kansas City Review*, XVI (Autumn, 1949), 20–30. Copyright © 1949 by the University of Kansas City. Reprinted by permission of the author and the publisher.

" 'The Dark, Ruined Helen of His Blood': Thomas Wolfe and the South," by C. Hugh Holman, pp. 177–97. Reprinted by permission of the author and the copyright owners, from *South: Modern Southern Literature in its Cultural Setting*, ed. Louis D. Rubin, Jr., and Robert Jacobs. New York: Doubleday & Co., Inc., 1961; copyright © 1961 by Louis D. Rubin, Jr. and Robert Jacobs.

"Thomas Wolfe and Death," by J. Russell Reaver and Robert I. Strozier. Originally published in the *Georgia Review*, XVI (Fall, 1962), 330–50. Copyright © 1962 by the University of Georgia. Reprinted by permission of the authors and the publisher.

"Thomas Wolfe: Time and the South," pp. 72–104. From *The Faraway Country: Writers of the Modern South*, by Louis D.

Rubin, Jr. Copyright © 1963 by the University of Washington Press. Reprinted by permission of the author and the University of Washington Press.

"Thomas Wolfe: Dark Time," pp. 207–26. From *Time and Reality: Studies in Contemporary Fiction*, by Margaret Church. Copyright © 1963 by the University of North Carolina Press. Reprinted by permission of the author and the University of North Carolina Press.

"Thomas Wolfe: The Second Cycle," by Robert C. Slack, pp. 41–53. From *Lectures on Modern Novelists* (Carnegie Series in English, Number Seven), Department of English, Carnegie Institute of Technology, Pittsburgh, Pennsylvania, 1963. Reprinted by permission of the publisher and the author. Copyright © 1963 by the Department of English.

Thomas Wolfe's Purdue Speech: "Writing and Living," edited by William Braswell and Leslie A. Field, pp. 47–54. Copyright © 1962 by Paul Gitlin, Administrator CTA of the Estate of Thomas Wolfe; copyright © 1964 by the Purdue Research Foundation. Reprinted by permission of Paul Gitlin for the Estate of Thomas Wolfe, the Purdue Research Foundation, and the editors.

"Genius Is Not Enough," by Bernard DeVoto. Originally published in the *Saturday Review*, XIII (April 25, 1936), 3–4, 14–15. Reprinted by permission of Mrs. Bernard DeVoto, owner of the copyright, and by the *Saturday Review*.

"Thomas Wolfe," by Maxwell E. Perkins. Originally published in the *Harvard Library Bulletin*, I (Autumn, 1947), 269–77. Copyright © 1947 by the President and Fellows of Harvard College. Reprinted by permission of the *Harvard Library Bulletin*.

From "A Note on Thomas Wolfe," by Edward C. Aswell, pp. 354–56 in *The Hills Beyond* by Thomas Wolfe. Copyright © 1941 by Maxwell Perkins as Executor. Reprinted by permission of Harper & Row, Publishers.

"A Study of Semantic States: Thomas Wolfe and the Faustian Sickness," by Martin Maloney, pp. 15–25. Reprinted from *General*

Semantics Bulletin, Nos. 16 and 17 (1955), by permission of the publisher and copyright owner, Institute of General Semantics for Linguistic Epistemologic Scientific Research and Education, Lakeville, Connecticut.

"Rhetoric in Southern Writing: Wolfe," by Floyd C. Watkins. Originally published in the *Georgia Review,* XII (Spring, 1958), 79–82. Copyright © 1958 by the University of Georgia. Reprinted by permission of the author and the publisher.

Thomas Wolfe: An Introduction and Interpretation, by Richard Walser, pp. 3–10. From *Thomas Wolfe: An Introduction and Interpretation,* American Authors and Critics Series, copyright © 1961 by Holt, Rinehart and Winston, Inc. Used by permission. Reprinted by permission of the author and the publisher.

"The Durable Humor of *Look Homeward, Angel,*" by Bruce R. McElderry, Jr. Originally published in the *Arizona Quarterly,* XI (Summer, 1955), 123–28. Copyright © 1955 by the *Arizona Quarterly,* University of Arizona. Reprinted by permission of the author and the publisher.

"Wolfe's *Look Homeward, Angel* as a Novel of Development," by Richard S. Kennedy. Originally published in the *South Atlantic Quarterly,* LXIII (Spring, 1964), 218–26. Copyright © 1964 by the Duke University Press. Reprinted by permission of the author and the publisher.

"A Note on the Hamlet of Thomas Wolfe," by Robert Penn Warren, pp. 170–83. From *Selected Essays of Robert Penn Warren.* Copyright © 1958 by Robert Penn Warren. Reprinted by permission of Random House, Inc.

"Wolfe's *Of Time and the River,*" by Irving Halperin. Originally published in the *Explicator,* XVIII (Nov., 1959), item 9. Copyright © 1959 by the *Explicator.* Reprinted by permission of the author and the publisher.

"Esther Jack as Muse," by Paschal Reeves, pp. 280–85. From "Thomas Wolfe: Notes on Three Characters." Originally published in *Modern Fiction Studies,* XI (Autumn, 1965), 275–85. Copyright

ⓒ 1965 by the Purdue Research Foundation. Reprinted by permission of the author and the Purdue Research Foundation.

"Symbolic Patterns in *You Can't Go Home Again*," by Clyde C. Clements, Jr. Originally published in *Modern Fiction Studies,* XI (Autumn, 1965), 286–96. Copyright ⓒ 1965 by the Purdue Research Foundation. Reprinted by permission of the author and the Purdue Research Foundation.

"*The Hills Beyond*: A Folk Novel of America," by Leslie A. Field. Revision of "Wolfe's Use of Folklore." Originally published in *New York Folklore Quarterly,* XVI (Autumn, 1960), 203–15. Copyright ⓒ 1960 by the New York Folklore Society. Used by permission of the publisher and the author.

Analysis of "The Lost Boy" from *The Writer's Art: A Collection of Short Stories,* 1950. Reprinted with the permission of D. C. Heath and Company. Copyright ⓒ 1950 by D. C. Heath and Company. Appreciation is also expressed to Wallace Stegner, the author of the essay, pp. 178–83, for granting his permission, and to Richard Scowcraft and Boris Ilyin, the other authors of *The Writer's Art.*

"Theme in Thomas Wolfe's 'The Lost Boy' and 'God's Lonely Man,'" by Lois Hartley. Originally published in the *Georgia Review,* XV (Summer, 1961), 230–35. Copyright ⓒ 1961 by the University of Georgia. Reprinted by permission of the author and the publisher.

"Critical Commentary on 'Only the Dead Know Brooklyn,'" pp. 143–46. From *The Order of Fiction: An Introduction,* by Edward A. Bloom. Copyright ⓒ 1964 by the Odyssey Press, Inc. Reprinted by permission of the author and the Odyssey Press, Inc.

"Criticism of Thomas Wolfe: A Selected Checklist," by Maurice Beebe and Leslie A. Field. Originally published in *Modern Fiction Studies,* XI (Autumn, 1965), 315–28. Copyright ⓒ 1965 by the Purdue Research Foundation. Reprinted with some revisions and additions by permission of the compilers and the Purdue Research Foundation.

Introduction

WHO READS Thomas Wolfe? And who writes about him? The latter question properly expanded becomes: Does a respectable body of criticism and scholarship exist on Thomas Wolfe's work? In part, these questions—frequently asked but never resolved—prompted the undertaking of this present collection of critical essays on Thomas Wolfe.

In the light of quantitative evidence one could say that the questions are largely rhetorical. Today, thirty years after Wolfe's death, and almost forty years after the publication of his first novel, Wolfe is, apparently, being read and written about in great abundance. Since Herbert Muller's monograph on Wolfe in 1947, some twenty-five books, including two comprehensive bibliographies, have appeared on Wolfe both in America and abroad.

As for essays on Wolfe, Elmer D. Johnson in his 1959 bibliography listed 522 items under "Periodical Articles About Wolfe." (He categorized another 1136 items under a variety of other headings.) Of the "periodical articles" listed by Johnson, some are little more than obituary notices, bits of puffery, and so on. Nevertheless, it is an impressive list. Since Johnson's bibliography, many more articles on Wolfe have appeared; the checklist at the end of this collection has added about fifty-five critical essays.

Over the years, essays on or by Thomas Wolfe have been printed in almost every conceivable magazine or journal—from *Trains* to *Vogue* to the *Sewanee Review* to *PMLA*. It would be tempting (but perhaps impolitic) to speculate that once upon a time Wolfe provided auspicious beginnings for at least two fledgling journals which today soar in the rarified atmosphere of the "establishment journal heaven." Case Number One: A very early but sagacious (and subsequently much reprinted) essay on Wolfe by John Peale Bishop made its first appearance in the initial issue of *Kenyon Review*. Case Number Two: The two lead-off articles in the first issue of *College English* (the one by William Braswell was also much reprinted in after years) were given over to Thomas Wolfe. If, however, one observes that other journals such as *American Literature* have reached their pinnacles without ever having published articles on Thomas Wolfe, one would be forced to concede that the above speculation is perhaps slighty shaky—but nonetheless intriguing.

During Wolfe's lifetime he was known as the author of a few long, short stories which appeared in magazines, and four books: *Look Homeward, Angel* (1929), *Of Time and the River* (1935), *From Death to Morning* (1935), and *The Story of a Novel* (1936). After his death in 1938, three other major works were published: *The Web and the Rock* (1939), *You Can't Go Home Again* (1940), and *The Hills Beyond* (1941).

Since the publication of his last posthumous work, the following have been edited and published: three volumes of his letters, his play *Mannerhouse* (1948), his notes on the West—*A Western Journal* (1951), poetic passages plucked from the novels and put together as *A Stone, A Leaf, A Door* (1950) (in 1939 *The Face of a Nation* appeared), and Wolfe's last full-length statement about his craft or art of fiction, *Thomas Wolfe's Purdue Speech* (1964). During the years 1961–1962, the distinguished scholar-critic C. Hugh Holman edited three Wolfe books: *The Shorter Novels of Thomas Wolfe, The Thomas Wolfe Reader,* and *The World of Thomas Wolfe.*

Today almost all of Thomas Wolfe's significant writings are in print and, evidently, are being sold; many of them have been translated and are selling abroad. (In 1961 it was somewhat startling to be confronted with about one-fifth of a large window display in a Munich bookstore given over to German editions of Thomas Wolfe's works.) In this country Wolfe's major writings have now all been reprinted in paperback editions.

To return to the twenty-five books about Wolfe mentioned earlier, some, such as *The Strange Case of Thomas Wolfe* (1949) put out by the Chicago Literary Club and Pierre Brodin's *Thomas Wolfe* (1949), which is really a translated chapter taken from Mr. Brodin's French book entitled *American Writers Between Two Wars,* are in a class by themselves. These books and others which fit into a peculiar nonbook genre on the margins of the publishing industry contribute nothing new to an understanding of Wolfe's work. A number of other books, such as *Thomas Wolfe at Washington Square* (1954), *Thomas Wolfe's Characters* (1957), and the Twayne *Thomas Wolfe* (1964), deal heavily with Wolfe biography. Still others, such as the early (1950) *Thomas Wolfe: Carolina Student—A Brief Biography* by Agatha Boyd Adams and the later (1960) *Thomas Wolfe: A Biography* by Elizabeth Nowell are, as their subtitles tell us, straightforward biographies. A handful of the books on Wolfe, however, do stand alone as excellent critical and scholarly treatments of Wolfe's writings. In this category one would have to single out three books published in America—those by Muller, *Thomas Wolfe* (1947); Louis D. Rubin, Jr., *Thomas Wolfe: The Weather of his Youth* (1955); and Richard S. Kennedy, *The Window of Memory: The Literary Career of Thomas Wolfe* (1962).

To sum up, one can say that by many yardsticks Wolfe has retained a large degree of popularity over the years—especially as evidenced by the number and variety of his books in print and the number and variety of books and articles about him.

II

Thus far this survey of Wolfe may have fallen victim to a trap often considered by Wolfe and his critics concerning his own writing in that this essay may very well be a lopsided concern with a quantitative or an "amount and number" approach. If so, a shift to the qualitative may redress the balance. First, a further consideration of Thomas Wolfe and biography. It has often been said that what has been written about Wolfe the man all but dwarfs *that which has been seriously written about his fiction*. As with most truths, this one is not without its rationale and ramifications.

However, the comments here on biography thus far and elsewhere in this essay are not to be taken to mean that a focus on biographical elements of a writer is per se bad. On the contrary, a school of criticism very much in vogue earlier in this century championing the extremes of such an approach has now happily been almost ridiculed out of existence. One must acknowledge that biographical elements are often, pure and simple, quite interesting, and frequently can help elucidate a writer's work. At present Andrew Turnbull, the eminent biographer of Fitzgerald, is at work on what augurs to be the most skillful and knowledgeable biography of Wolfe thus far. Moreover, Richard S. Kennedy and Paschal Reeves are currently editing Wolfe's notebooks for publication. Both undertakings should be edifying and extremely helpful as critical tools for the examination of Wolfe's writings.

Because Wolfe epitomizes that peculiar twentieth-century literary animal, the autobiographical novelist, one can understand that the bulk of writing on Wolfe would focus on biography and critical biography rather than on "pure" criticism. Something of the same approach often appears in writings about Joyce, Proust, and Whitman —writers who are often recognized as having a certain kinship with Wolfe. Unfortunately, Wolfe, more often than not, is considered a sort of poor kin to the above. Thus the reasoning seems to go, he deserves and has received *only* the biographical treatment; the others deserve and thus have received much more.

This line of thinking, however common it is in academic and literary circles, ignores the facts. True, we do not have the multitude of solid critical works on Wolfe as we do on Joyce, Lawrence, Faulkner, Hemingway, and a number of other modern writers. But, despite the heavy emphasis on the biographical in the writings about Wolfe, a small but significant body of Wolfe criticism has emerged, especially in the three decades from 1935 to 1965. It is hoped that this present collection of essays will confirm this view.

III

In his four large novels and two collections of short stories, Wolfe was concerned with a few central themes. In *The Story of a Novel* Wolfe himself pointed out that he had been involved with themes he saw as central to his writing: his various concepts of time, the "Where now?" motif, and man's search for a spiritual father. In his *Purdue Speech* he said that these earlier themes were no longer crucial. He realized that as a beginning writer he had been too egocentric, too much the sensitive artist divorced from his environment. Late in his life he saw the need for looking outside of himself, for looking at the political, social, and economic world, and for trying to understand it, assimilate it, and somehow bring it into his writing. This, in fact, he attempted to do in his last novel, *You Can't Go Home Again*.

If one had to pick a watershed year for Wolfe criticism, 1936 would seem to be the year. At this time, two years before Wolfe's death, *The Story of a Novel* appeared. Then Bernard DeVoto's fiery "Genius Is Not Enough" burst upon the critical scene. DeVoto's indictment focused the lines of argument, and for today's student of Wolfe the charges have become a part of the furniture of Wolfe criticism: Wolfe's writing is formless autobiography, chopped up, renailed, and rearranged by the author's editor and friend Maxwell E. Perkins. The controversy has never been decently interred. But over the years a sober, more reflective kind of criticism has sat up with the corpse. By and large there has been an uneven coming of age in Wolfe criticism over the past three decades in that the critics of the fifties and sixties have been more prone to accept some of DeVoto's charges without using them as pivotal for their own critical treatments of Wolfe.

One can pick out the major concerns of the more serious critics: Wolfe's "discovery" of America; his concepts of time, faith, loneliness, and death; his notions of isolation, alienation, change, and experience; his gusto, vitality, and Faustian qualities; his struggles stemming from his ambivalent views of the city versus the country, the North versus the South; his social awareness; his search for a spiritual father, and his romantic quest; his *use* of autobiography, folklore, language, and rhetoric; his humor; his dramatic qualities; his resemblances to and affinity for other writers.

IV

The essays in this collection address themselves to one or more of these critical concerns. Because of space limitations, many excellent essays could not be included. In a number of instances, difficult editorial decisions had to be made in selecting one rather than four or five other essays addressed to a similar critical problem. For example, at least six first-rate essays on time and Thomas Wolfe were originally considered for this collection. Finally, the essays by Margaret

Church and Louis D. Rubin, Jr. won out. Although this present collection would be much better with the inclusion of all six provocative essays, the allotted space would not permit an all-inclusive approach. But it is hoped that the two essays selected, in addition to their obvious functions, will act as a point of departure. Having studied one or two essays on a significant Wolfeian theme, one may then use the accompanying bibliography and cross references within the essays themselves to follow up other essays on the same general theme.

In certain instances there was such a large number of articles and excerpts on one subject that it soon became apparent that a complete book of essays could be devoted to that area alone. *Look Homeward, Angel* is a case in point. Since most critics and scholars of Wolfe consider this his best work, more has been written on this novel than on any other of his books. Therefore, the two essays on *Look Homeward, Angel* rather than the dozen which could have appeared. When, almost all things being equal, a rule of thumb had to be applied, generally the journal article was chosen rather than the more readily available chapter in a book, the shorter essay rather than the longer.

One could go on attempting to justify this that or the other selection as opposed to many others. Suffice it to say that for each essay appearing in the present book, two or three others could have been chosen. But that they were not may be explained by some of the reasons already mentioned as well as a number of other editorial judgments. Where these judgments may appear questionable, prejudice, blindness, or just plain old-fashioned human fallibility must be pleaded.

Given some of the major concerns and problems that have engaged Wolfe scholars and critics over the years, the present arrangement of the essays seemed logical. The first part deals with some of Wolfe's major themes. It begins with an early, somewhat general essay by Cargill on the gargantuan Wolfe, and as the essay proceeds it touches on important Wolfeian themes—loneliness, city versus country, introspection, and, finally, Wolfe's dawning social awareness. Holman analyzes Wolfe against a background of other Southern writers. In Wolfe's view, he says, the South was "maternal and subjective" as opposed to "the male citadels of the North." Reaver and

Strozier trace the death and corresponding isolation themes in Wolfe's work. Rubin and Church are both concerned with Thomas Wolfe and time. For Rubin, all of Wolfe's later novels are inferior to *Look Homeward, Angel;* in that novel "time and change . . . give direction and order to Altamont." Church points out that Wolfe is much influenced by Joyce and Proust. She also demonstrates that "the train and the river are for Thomas Wolfe two basic symbols in getting across to his readers his feelings about time. . . ." Finally, Slack's essay reviews what he calls the "first cycle" or search-for-a-father approach to Wolfe and then the "second cycle" or "social criticism" that he sees in *You Can't Go Home Again.*

The dating of the essays in this section could be somewhat misleading. Cargill's essay appeared in 1949; the others in the sixties. However, Church's essay in its earliest version was also vintage 1949. And the embryo of some of Rubin's ideas goes back ten years or so. Thus the essays of Part I could be said to represent critical interests which actually span the last half of the three decades of criticism concerned with in this volume. Essays from the thirties and forties appear in subsequent sections of this book.

In Part II it seemed appropriate to investigate the controversial topic of Wolfe's style. Here Wolfe himself speaks in one of his last pronouncements on this subject. The typescript from which this portion of Wolfe's essay is taken dates back to 1938, although it was not edited for publication until 1964. We also have statements by the two editors of Wolfe's works: Maxwell E. Perkins of Charles Scribner's Sons, who worked closely with Wolfe during his lifetime, and Edward C. Aswell, who edited Wolfe's major posthumous fiction for Harper and Brothers. Perkins discusses and defends the long and fruitful editing relationship he had with Wolfe. It was a mistake, he believes, for Wolfe to switch from the Gant to the Webber cycle. Aswell, in the excerpt used in this volume, defends the Webber cycle. For him it illustrates the objective Wolfe at work. In answer to those who belabor the spontaneous and undisciplined quality of Wolfe's writing, Aswell says that Wolfe had become a "tireless reviser and rewriter." The inclusion of the DeVoto essay, although it has been reprinted many times, is an obvious choice for this collection. In an essay written almost twenty-five years after DeVoto's, Maloney reflects a still fairly common view of Wolfe's style by reemphasizing some of DeVoto's charges. Maloney labels Wolfe's attempts to capture and record all of life the "Faustian Sickness." Wolfe, he believes, was "possessed" by his materials. Watkins and Walser provide more recent commentaries on Wolfe's style. Both see Wolfe as a poet. For Watkins, Wolfe is, in addition, a comic writer, and a "Southern rhetorician." Walser states that Wolfe used "an organic structure based not upon tradition but upon insight" to tell his story of America.

In Part III, two essays each were chosen to analyze *Look Homeward, Angel* and *Of Time and the River*. One essay each was given over to *The Web and the Rock, You Can't Go Home Again,* and *The Hills Beyond*. Of the many possible ways of viewing *Look Homeward, Angel,* the two approaches here involve Wolfe's humor and his ability to depict "growth." McElderry sees Wolfe as "one of the finest humorous writers in America since Mark Twain." And Kennedy says that Wolfe uses "a variety of styles" to achieve in *Look Homeward, Angel* "almost a classical example . . . of the *Bildungsroman*." On the other hand, Warren, in his 1935 review of *Of Time and the River,* castigates Wolfe for his stylistic faults. Warren feels that this book especially lacks "discipline, focus, and control." Wolfe, he claims, "sometimes wants it both ways: the structural irresponsibility of prose and the emotional intensity of poetry." In a brief explication almost twenty-five years later, Halperin tries to demonstrate that *Of Time and the River* does have form. He chooses the "train episode" in this novel as a touchstone to illustrate what he considers an "artistic whole," and one that "relates to the controlling idea of the novel."

In "Esther Jack as Muse," Reeves focuses on the Esther Jack-George Webber relationship in *The Web and the Rock*. He sees Esther as a dual-function muse to George: "She is both a source of inspiration and a fountainhead of information." Clements analyzes *You Can't Go Home Again* in terms of three groupings of "symbolic patterns": "Reminiscence, Progression, and Projection, reflecting stages in [George Webber's] search." And, finally, in this section, an examination of *The Hills Beyond* shows that Wolfe used various strains of folklore and was becoming much more objective as he attempted, late in the day, to create his fictional history of America.

The first two essays of Part IV deal with short stories taken from the collection in *The Hills Beyond;* the final essay is on a short story in *From Death to Morning.* Stegner calls "The Lost Boy" a "sub-surface story," one that "comes close to being pure necromancy." Hartley, in examining this same story as well as "God's Lonely Man," traces the themes of change, experience, and loneliness, but focuses on loneliness. In "Only the Dead Know Brooklyn," Bloom moves toward a meaning of the story through his exploration of Wolfe's techniques which evoke a certain mood and tone. It is regrettable that Part IV, an examination of Wolfe's short stories, is not larger. The truth of the matter is that very little work in depth has been done on Wolfe's short stories. As a supplement to the three essays here, one should look into Kennedy's treatments of the short stories in his *The Window of Memory* and into Holman's *The Short Novels of Thomas Wolfe.*

Unavoidably, the essays in one section occasionally overlap the concerns of essays in other sections. For example, an essay on a particular novel or a short story may deal with Wolfe's style or his general themes as well. However, one must agree that where this overarching enriches, it is welcome.

Clearly, despite a sampling of essays collected here and a number of others available elsewhere, the final word on Wolfe's work is far from being spoken. In a bibliographical study of Wolfe (*Texas Studies in Literature and Language,* I [Autumn, 1959], 427–45), C. Hugh Holman points out that "although Thomas Wolfe has called forth much scholarly and critical work since the publication of his first novel, too much of that work has been a part of a critical war and too little of it has been marked by judicious tolerance, good humor, critical acumen, and scholarly seriousness." He ends his excellent essay by saying that "the great need today is for a thorough-going critical examination of Wolfe in the light of the aesthetic assumption of the English Romantics. The challenge with which Wolfe's work confronts the serious critic is still largely unanswered." In the intervening years since Mr. Holman made these remarks, he himself has continued to shed light where darkness previously existed. Others have contributed a great deal also. But in great measure, his statements may still be applicable today.

V

A final word in partial answer to the questions that appear at the outset of this essay: If it seems that the questions are a ploy, it must be admitted that in a manner of speaking they are. If it also appears that the essay itself seems extremely defensive and acts as an apologia, again the present editor must plead guilty. If the number of lectures and articles which begin "the present writer needs no defense . . ." were bound and shelved, they would perhaps require more shelving than the many-volumed *Dictionary of National Biography*. In short, the lecturers and articles writers protest initially, but do, in fact, defend.

This introduction makes no such disclaimer. (However, it is hoped that some of the material in this collection which is openly hostile to Wolfe will act as a buffer to many remarks made here.) If ever there was a literary figure who needed defense, Thomas Wolfe is such a creature. One becomes somewhat weary of the fashionable remarks which dismiss Wolfe in one or another of the stereotyped ways: he wrote *only* autobiography; his writing is formless; he is a thoughtless juvenile; and so on. A notable exception often cited is Faulkner's evaluation of Wolfe, but even Faulkner's "rating" of contemporary novelists in a 1950 interview and his subsequent explanations of his views on Wolfe as a literary artist are frustratingly ambiguous.

At the Modern Language Association meeting held in Chicago in December, 1965, in a talk called "The Dynamic of American Literature," Norman Mailer pointed out that both Dreiser and Wolfe attempted "to capture the phenomenon . . . of something going on in American life which was either grand or horrible or both." He concluded that both Dreiser and Wolfe failed in the task—"Wolfe like the greatest five-year-old who ever lived. . . ." One can only praise the perceptiveness of Mailer's first statement on Wolfe; his subsequent remarks, however, point in a different direction. Moreover, when his talk appeared in *Commentary* magazine (March, 1966) as "Modes and Mutations: Quick Comments on the Modern American Novel," Mailer added this footnote concerning his last comments on Wolfe: "This remark brought laughter from the audience. Since I did not wish to insult the memory of Wolfe, it would have been happier and perhaps more accurate to have said: like the greatest fifteen-year-old alive."

One irony of this little episode is that Norman Mailer in much of his own fiction owes more to Thomas Wolfe than he would care to admit. If this be an indictment of Mr. Mailer, in one way or another it fits a large number of novelists, critics, and scholars everywhere.

Therefore, to the hundreds of Mailers everywhere, and to the hundreds of academicians in the MLA audience who laughed (or who would have laughed had they been present), this book is wistfully rededicated. May their laughter be tempered somewhat by a reading of the following essays. And if it becomes laughter of another sort as they rediscover the good as well as the bad in the writings of Thomas Wolfe, one can only say—Amen! If not, *quel dommage!*

L. A. F.
West Lafayette, Indiana
March, 1967

Contents

PART III   Specific Novels

PART IV   The Short Stories

PART I   *His Major Themes*

Oscar Cargill

1. Gargantua Fills His Skin

WHEN DEATH wrote *finis* to the turbulent artistic career of Thomas Wolfe in the Johns Hopkins Hospital on September 15, 1938, the cold magician capped a geyser of words none other could check, but he froze also a fountain which gushed sometimes the maddest eloquence. The youth—at thirty-seven he seemed still inexhaustibly young—was perhaps the only sure genius of the regional school of literature. Though part of his training was in the famous "47 Workshop" at Harvard and though perhaps he had spent as much time abroad as any writer of his years, Tom Wolfe was tightly corded to his birthplace, the "Altamont" and "Libya Hill" of his fiction. The life which seemed most significant to him was that which flowed through the streets leading from his mother's boarding house or those radiating out from the stonecutter's shop in Pack Square which belonged to his father. This, it is hard to comprehend, when one observes that passages of his prose are modeled on the writings of such cosmopolitans as Rabelais, Donne, Dostoevski, Burton, Sterne, Melville, Whitman, and Joyce. But Wolfe merely sucked these people through his teeth; he did not chew and digest them. His debt to Joyce was the greatest of all, yet what did he get from Joyce? A desire to be as lyrical as the Dublinite; a certain adolescent resistance to formal education, as in *The Portrait of the Artist as a Young Man;* the pattern of a mad plunge through life—not really the quest of Ulysses, as the "book" titles within *Of Time and the River* might lead us to suppose; and finally a kind of fierce localism, never balanced off, as in Joyce, by oblique glances through time and space, history and literature.

In part, this intense concentration on the locale of his birth was a product of an unusual absorption in himself, which lent a reflected glow, we may suppose, to the place of his origin. One episode in Tom Wolfe's life is telltale—his failure as a dramatist. He had the best instructors modern times have known in Frederick Koch of the Carolina Playmakers and George Pierce Baker of the Harvard Workshop. The latter, just dead, is brutally piloried in "Professor Hatcher" in *Of Time and the River* as a man of formulas who did not recognize true genius when it came to him. Why? Did he not acknowledge the budding boy from Asheville as genius? Possibly not, but in justice to Baker it should be pointed out that Wolfe supplied him with slim evidence, to judge from the sole surviving example of his dramaturgy, a one-acter entitled "The Return of Buck Gavin" found in one of the volumes of *Carolina Folk Plays*. Perusal of this sentimental melodrama convinces one that while the author might make a capital monologuist, dialogue and the interplay between characters were then beyond him: Baker might well have abandoned the incipient self-expositor in despair, for whatever Tom Wolfe's talent, it was not for the theatre. Detachment from his material, and this always meant detachment from himself, was, through most of his life, impossible for Wolfe. He was a kind of Cyclops whose one eye looked inward while he roamed about, batting his poor head against the stars.

II

Yet whoever accepts self-absorption as an explanation for Wolfe's concentrated localism must admit qualities in that self-absorption alien to mere egotism. Here is no simple Byronism. This has a terror to it, a horror, a stampeded fear, which suggests the mind of Poe rather than the wounded vanity of Byron—even though wounded vanity is not absent from it. Indeed, one cannot reflect upon the involuted terror of Tom Wolfe—his oft-repeated cry of loneliness—without conjecturing that a common explanation would suffice for some of the emotional extravagances of both Poe and Wolfe. "To live alone as I have lived, a man should have the confidence of God, the tranquil faith of a monastic saint, the stern impregnability of Gibraltar. Lacking these, there are times when anything, everything, all or nothing, the most trival incidents, the most casual words, can in an instant strip me of my armor, palsy my hand, constrict my heart with frozen horror, and fill my bowels with the gray substance of shuddering impotence," confessed Wolfe in one of those pieces of subjective analysis in *The Hills Beyond*—an analysis reminiscent of Poe's own. What had these two supersensitive Southern spirits in common beyond locale to infect their work with terror? Or is locale enough to account for them?

One common element in the careers of Edgar Poe and Thomas Wolfe was a familiarity with disease and abnormalcy. The nightmare of tuberculosis, of which his parents died and with which his brother Henry and later his wife were afflicted, stimulated Poe's interest in the victims of disease, an interest which created blue-veined, pallid sufferers of baffling maladies, lingering consumptives, opium addicts, psychotics, paranoiacs. With due allowance for the Gothic tradition in which Poe worked, one is yet able to attribute some of his terror to a fascination with unhealth. Though his reaction was different, Tom Wolfe, even as a youth, was more impressed by illness and death than by health, as anyone can testify who has read his repeated account of his brother Ben. Furthermore, the Asheville of his attachment was a health resort, with its accumulation of tuberculars, neurotics, hypochondriacs, and senile imbeciles, some extraordinary specimens of each being found among the lodgers in Mrs. Wolfe's boarding house. Tom's instinctive response—the response nature provided —was to assert loudly, positively, continuously his abundant well-being, his mighty physical powers, his gusto for eating and drinking, for sensing and experiencing. Reiteration, however, makes these assertions unnatural, indicators of a searching terror at the heart. Good health and virility made Wolfe lonely in Asheville in his young manhood, and the thinness of the sprinkling of literary genius in the South accentuated to that loneliness. Like Poe, he could look back upon the years of his becoming sentient and say, with some exaggeration,

> I dwelt alone
> In a world of moan
> And my soul was a stagnant
> tide . . .

It is this loneliness, fully as much as the Southern emphasis on Family, which prompts both writers to emphasize the "line" and heritage of their characters. How often the stories of Poe begin with an allusion to the hero's descent, as if that were the salient thing in evaluating or placing him. Though Wolfe never pretended to possess ancestors of social distinction, his creative work begins and ends with the problem of ancestry. The story of Eugene Gant, protagonist of *Look Homeward, Angel* (1929), begins with an Englishman named Gilbert Gaunt who arrived in Baltimore on a sailing vessel in 1837, and we are told that the publisher's editor cut out a large section of the book because it dealt with the forebears of the hero rather than with the hero. At the time of his death Tom Wolfe was working on a novel, *The Hills Beyond* (1941), once meant to describe his mother's ancestors, the Pentlands, as they are called in his earlier fiction, but now become the Joyners and elevated by having a home-spun governor in the family tree.

The security which both writers sought from association with imagined established forebears was no security at all, for it did not help them in the common severest test of their lives, adjustment to the alien cities where their work called them. Wolfe found the adjustment more difficult than Poe, for he had acquired none of the gracious manners of the Southland and his gawky awkwardness, his size, and his sensitivity made it harder for him to acquire friends. Whereas large men are customarily phlegmatic, Thomas Wolfe, "an oversized organism in a standard-sized world," was six-foot-six of raw and twitching ganglia—vibrant, all alive. No one could keep up with him—walk with him, talk with him, eat with him, drink with him. Consequently, on still another count, his mature years were lonely years: "From my fifteenth year—save for a single interval—I have lived as solitary a life as a modern man can have. I mean by this that the number of hours, days, months, and years that I have spent alone has been immense and extraordinary." The effect of this was to turn his mind backwards to the days before pituitary activity marked him off from his fellows, to the time when neither his person nor his appetites were Gargantuan, the years of his boyhood in Asheville, the years before his mother acquired the boarding house. Doubtless this accounts not merely for the vividness and detail of the total recall in *Look Homeward, Angel* but also for the tides of laughter and sunshine in the earlier part of that book. However indignant it may have made Ashevilleans, Asheville was a warm nest of memories for Thomas Wolfe.

Unspoken contrast (so far as that novel is concerned) helped to make it so. Tom Wolfe was living two lives—one in memory in Asheville, and one in torment in New York, while *Look Homeward, Angel* was being written. Ill prepared for the casualness of any metropolis, Wolfe, after desperate loneliness, had become infatuated with a wealthy Jewish stage-designer, a married woman nearly twice his years but apparently endowed with complete sympathy and understanding—his Mrs. Clemm. Yet from this woman, who may have provided him with "the single interval" of companionship to which he alludes, he got none of the solace due him. A chance remark that "Mrs. Jack" liked young men, a hint that he was just another in her life, became an insatiable worm at the core of his happiness and drove him into the jealous madness so faithfully and tediously recorded in the last three hundred pages of *The Web and the Rock* (1939). At the outset it had seemed to the boy that Mrs. Jack was the way through the wall of unfriendliness:

> It was not merely that he was in love with her. In addition to that, through his association with her it seemed to him that now at last he had begun to "know" the city. For, in some curious way, the woman had come to represent "the city" to him. To him she was the city he had longed to know. Hers was not the city of the homeless wanderer, the city of the wretched, futile people living in the rooms of little cheap hotels, the city of the lost boy and the stranger looking at a million lights, the terrible, lonely empty city of no doors, and of the homeless thronging ways. Hers was the city of the native, and now it seemed to him that he was "in."

"Mrs. Jack's" marital status, their racial differences, and Wolfe's own temperamental handicaps made this hope vain, but the thing that turned hope to vitriol was suspicion. The thought that he, a country greenhorn, a gawk, had been seduced by this woman for her amusement infuriated him; he saw her now as a leech, a vampire, an incubus, living upon his genius, destroying it. Worse yet, she became a symbol of all the evils of the city, its cynicism and treachery. She became one of "Them"—and "They" were the millions indifferent to genius and to Thomas Wolfe. Not unmixed with a sense of guilt, this foul emotion like flooding lye burned away the last desire of the novelist for connections with the city. No one could possibly have now been more alien to it. The New York of his acquaintance was "a world that seemed to have gone insane with its own excess, a world of criminal privilege that flouted itself with an inhuman arrogance in the face of a great city where half the population lived in filth and squalor, and where two-thirds were still so bitterly uncertain of their daily living that they had to thrust, to snarl, to curse, to cheat, contrive, and get the better of their fellows like a race of mongrel dogs." Thus Tom Wolfe, raging, was thrown back on Asheville.

III

What composition meant under these circumstances Wolfe has told in *The Story of a Novel* (1936), one of the most revealing books ever written by a man of genius who is yet short of maturity. Here is the confession again of utter loneliness—loneliness amidst crowds. Here is the intimation that his very hunger for home, when he was in Paris, London, and New York, made the re-creation of Altamont and Libya Hill more possible and valid. Here is the admission of his debt to Joyce who had made a persuasive fetish of memory. The record of Wolfe's efforts at total recall is at once astonishing yet thoroughly credible.

> . . . Now my memory was at work night and day, in a way that I could at first neither check nor control and that swarmed unbidden in a stream of blazing pageantry across my mind, with the million forms and substances of the life I had left . . . It seemed that I had inside me, swelling and gathering all the time, a huge black cloud, and that this cloud was loaded with electricity, pregnant, crested, with a kind of hurricane violence that could not be held in check much longer; that the moment was approaching fast when it must break. It broke that summer while I was in Switzerland. It came in torrents and it is not over yet.

It is this total recall that makes for grandeur and inanity in Wolfe; it is the source of his weakness and his power. Of course he is absurd when he pretends to recall perfectly orchestra records he heard played while he was still in the basket that served him for a cradle and the "strong smell, black and funky" of the young negress who cared for him when he was two. Only affection, however, could have registered as deeply all that Wolfe puts in his books about Asheville, but Asheville, appreciating only the sharpness of the etching and never the warmth that burned it in, reviled the novelist after *Look Homeward, Angel* was published, and *The Story of a Novel* tells how Wolfe was hurt and how his injury put confusion in his brain so that he floundered on for seven years unable to organize his work. How limited Wolfe still was by Asheville, how he still deferred to the judgment of that town though the world praised him, is the most significant admission of the book. "Eugene wanted two things all men want," Wolfe says of himself in *Look Homeward, Angel;* "he wanted to be loved and he wanted to be famous. His fame was chameleon, but its fruit and triumph lay at home, among the people of Altamont. The mountain town had for him enormous authority; with a child's egotism it was for him the centre of the earth, the small but dynamic core of all life." That is, fame without the approval of Asheville was no fame at all—he looked homeward for an affectionate response; he wanted to be the toast of the village. Now he was re-impaled "on the hook of that furious and insatiate desire that had absorbed my life for years." His development as an artist was arrested at the stage of raw, youthful endeavor for the praise of his native town.

The consequence of the reaction of Asheville to *Look Homeward, Angel*, by which Wolfe had set so much store, was the evocation of four huge novels instead of one on the conflict of the immature artist "with the world about him and with the element of confusion and chaos in his own spirit." In *Look Homeward, Angel* there is some sense of advance or adolescent growth, but in *Of Time and the River* (1935) and *The Web and the Rock* (1939) there is no further progress. And *You Can't Go Home Again* (1940) resumes the re-telling of what has been told and retold before, but now, at long last, as we shall see, release comes to Wolfe from his persistent infatuation with his local prestige. If Wilhelm Meister had proved himself incapable of education, if Goethe had impaled him on the prongs of his despair and disillusionment at the end of his acting career and had there violently rotated him through thrice the pages of the *Apprenticeship,* we should have something comparable to the published body of Wolfe's work. It is well known, however, that *Of Time and the River* was quarried by Perkins out of millions of words which

Wolfe wrote on the subject of Wolfe during his seven prostrate years, a fact which gave rise to Carl Van Doren's remark that "Thomas Wolfe is his own river and Maxwell Perkins his levee." Edward C. Aswell, Wolfe's second editor, has indicated that almost as much excision produced the later novels. Probably the mountainous manuscript from which Tom's books were drawn will never again be equalled as an exposition of adolescent sorrows. And certainly two of the books—*Of Time and the River* and *The Web and the Rock*— will not conceivably be matched by any subsequent attempt to reveal intentionally or unintentionally the chaos in the soul of the immature artist.

In *The Story of a Novel* Wolfe says that the central idea in *Of Time and the River* is a man's search to find a "father"—evidently a quest through limbo for him. Though this echoes a Joycean-Homeric theme, Wolfe seems to have been groping for something more intimate and personal. This "father" is "not merely the lost father of his youth, but the image of a strength and wisdom external to his need and superior to his hunger, to which the belief and power of his own life could be united." To be brief, Wolfe sought for some integration of his artistic personality after the dispersive shock of his Asheville reception. Artistic purpose—maturity—was the need he could not confess. Indication that he had some glimmering of his fatal lack is shown in this passage which identifies maturity with a father, yet the father whom he has drawn in his novels in the hell-roaring, poetry-spouting marble-cutter, W. O. Gant, was himself a huge adolescent, capable of demonstrating his manhood only by sprees and visits to cathouses. The fascination which this father had for Wolfe probably reveals a helpless, subconscious realization of his own inability to develop beyond a certain point. Wolfe drops this symbol of his quest in *The Web and the Rock,* but he can no more relinquish the theme than he can disguise the fact that the protagonist of his novel is himself, though he has banished Eugene Gant for the simian George Webber. No pattern can be seen in this book unless one assumes that the culmination of the quarrels of George Webber with Esther Jack is, in the author's mind at least, symbolic of a sort of maturity achieved when the hero is at last able to thrust the woman from him. But is not this maturity still maturity in the terms of W. O. Gant? The stonecutter would have thought his son a man to put a woman aside, and Webber's quarrels with Mrs. Jack have the same crude masculine violence of rhetoric that marked the stonecutter's connubial relationships, without the latter's poetry.

IV

Because the vision is immature, are *Look Homeward, Angel, Of Time and the River,* and *The Web and the Rock* to be wholly condemned? Are we to agree with the writer in the London *Spectator* who remarked in regard to Wolfe that there is "little reason to admire his fecundity except as an awful curiosity of the literature of our times"? Yes, and no. No, because, first of all, there is in these three books passage after passage of the grandest rhetoric and poetry. For example, Whitman in only a few choice pieces commands a more sweeping rhythm than that into which our author swings in describing the projectile-like flight of the Pullman train in *Of Time and the River.* But the word master is found also in things of smaller compass, as in "Gant grinned with a thin, false painting of mirth" and "Steve had a piece of tough suet where his heart should have been." No again, because if the author has not been able to comment critically on what he has seen, he has set it down so boldly that we may react to it as from situations in life. He is obtuse at times but rarely dull. The world of Altamont and even the university town of Pulpit Hill swim into our vision like a distant but clearly defined landscape under a pelucid sky. We view the death of the Pennock boys and the wild rampage of black Dick Prosser as if we were one of the citizens of Libya Hill, and we as a bidden guest see Elinor Wylie flounce away from a literary tea because Van Vechten had "insulted" her by remarking that "Eleanora Duse was the most beautiful woman he had ever seen." These things are too good to be dismissed as mere lush elegance.

Nor can Wolfe's characterizations even in his worst novels be passed over; he has drawn some unforgettable portraits: the bellowing stone-chipper who dominates *Look Homeward, Angel,* and whose death is the most moving episode in its sequel; Eliza Gant, Eugene's property-grasping mother; Ben and Luke and Steven, brothers all, but totally different in composition; Helen, the daughter who could quell Old Gant by slapping his face; and horsey Uncle Bascom with his rabbit wife, Louise. Of course, while conceding the durability of these family portraits, we must admit the sometimes monstrous failures Wolfe made in attempting to study people who were not kith and kin to him. There are no worse botches in good fiction than Wolfe's efforts to draw his sophisticated friends, Joel Pierce and Francis Starwick. And to whom is the portrait of Esther Jack convincing? Nevertheless comparative failure because of artistic immaturity does not justify hasty dismissal of such chaos-laden and fury-ridden books as *Of Time and the River* and *The Web and the Rock;* theirs is no ordinary chaos and fury, but that of laboring genius.

V

You Can't Go Home Again (1940) magically transforms Thomas Wolfe from a wallowing adolescent into a mature and tragic figure, but this magic works slowly in the book and the miracle is not completely accomplished before the last thirteen pages of this 713-page novel. The story of George Webber is resumed, but it is no longer the story of Webber the riotous sot, the bully, the lecher; it is the story of the serious artist bent on achieving lasting fame. Webber's first novel, *Home to Our Mountains,* instead of bringing him plaudits from his fellow townsmen in Libya Hill (too many of whom thought themselves portrayed), draws down upon him maledictions, curses, threats. Celebrity chasers and his Park Avenue friends interfere with his work, Mrs. Jack interferes; hence Webber resolves to break with his past. With grace wholly lacking in *The Web and the Rock,* he does this cleanly, without any emotional ripping and rending, without a quarrel, without recriminations. In the security of Brooklyn he toils prodigiously, always working with the advice of his publisher's great editor, Foxhall Edwards, whom he comes to venerate as much as he does the memory of his dead father.

After four years of obscure slavery George Webber decides to freshen his vision by a change of scene and he establishes himself in London to finish his book. He has but settled himself at his work when word comes from the United States that Lloyd McHarg, then basso profundo of our letters, has selected *him,* George Webber, for the subject of a eulogy when he responds to the conferment of great honor upon himself. Realizing that he is "made" by this generous notice, Webber waits upon his benefactor when the latter comes to London. Celebrity has been tapering off from the high pitch of excitement he had reached on the occasion of his great distinction and he honors Webber by doing some more tapering with him. After the episode is over, the younger man concludes that it was not a debauch for his idol but a way of drenching the nauseous aspects of fame. Webber realizes for the first time what stale provender is public applause, and after taking his completed manuscript back to New York, he has no disposition to await the effect it will produce. But in Germany, whither he goes for relaxation, fame overtakes him; the Germans have acclaimed his first book as an American epic and his new novel but adds to his prestige.

Germany, however, is not the Germany he had known on earlier visits: the Republic has fallen and the Nazis are in power. George himself sees neither brutality nor tyranny, but senses both. Repeatedly he is informed that *this* man is not the man to invite to a party, *that* man is not one to be seen with. He cannot endure "the dark messiah" with the comic opera moustache nor the latter's brown-shirted minions. He vows to express his feelings when he gets out of Germany, for he realizes suddenly that he wishes to get out of the land he has always loved. At the frontier on the Paris express he witnesses his only episode to prove the tyranny of Nazidom: the arrest of a little Jew who is trying to escape with a fortune in marks. The pasty, sweating face of the little Jew and the beefy, brutal swagger of his captors have a profound effect upon George Webber: the episode becomes a stone that starts an avalanche, for behind it has accumulated the memory of a thousand small acts of oppression everywhere that have worked into Webber's subconscious mind in the last few years: the "sacking" of his Libya Hill friend, Randy Shepperton, by the Federal Weight, Scales, and Computing Company because Randy, after years of faithful service, could not push the sales in his district to an impossible new quota; the suffocation of two elevator boys in Mrs. Jack's apartment house during a fire following an elaborate party at which he had been a guest; the attack of a meeching London apothecary on his half-starved errand boy; and other things of the same sort. On his arrival in America, he writes a letter breaking forever with the man who, for nine years, has been his guiding genius, Foxhall Edwards. This great and good friend, he declaims, is a fatalist, even as the preacher in Ecclesiastes was a fatalist; and though he and George agree that the end of man is tragic, they are really farther apart than the poles. For George Webber believes now that the salvation of "man-alive" is to deny this destiny, to "deny it all along the way." America (he admits) is lost, but America (he firmly believes) can be saved again. The enemy has a thousand faces, yet all wear a single mask—the mask of selfishness and compulsive greed. Venerating Foxhall Edwards as much as ever as an intellect, Webber cannot battle the enemy with his old counsellor at the head of his board of strategy. The austere and courageous way is alone.

Melodramatic and overdone perhaps, this grand renunciation is not merely the peak of George Webber's career: it is the high point of Thomas Wolfe's as well. A man predestined to make others suffer, Wolfe did not realize that this version of his break with his mentor would reflect upon that guide and friend, would make *him* responsible for whatever weaknesses there are in the preceding novels: he only saw the shining course for himself. In this, of course, he was as obtuse as a child. Yet we should endeavor to thrust out of our minds all notion of the book as an apologetic: Wolfe patently never thought of it as such; we should see *You Can't Go Home Again* as the prolegomenon to a series of novels which the author contemplated writing (even if we still have some suspicion that he could not have executed his grand plan) to stir up Americans to defeat "the enemy."

This novel as the preface to that contemplated work is a book of repudiations and rejections. Like Thoreau, Wolfe noisily signs off from many things he has never signed on to. The renunciation of Foxhall Edwards is the climax of the many renunciations of the novel. To be brief, Wolfe repudiates aestheticism, decadence, Marxism, naturalism, and pure intellectualism as objects, moods, methods, aims. He is particularly violent towards the people who make of "literosity" a profession, with whom he identifies most practising critics. Their concerns seem to him trivial in the extreme. Setting Foxhall Edwards above them, because his estimating eye at least gauges the worth of a man, Wolfe declares, "he was no little Pixy of the Aesthetes":

He had nothing to do with any of the doltish gibberings, obscene quackeries, phoney passions, and six-months-long religions of fools, joiners, and fashion-apes a trifle brighter and quicker on the uptake then the fools, joiners, and fashion-apes they prey upon. He was none of your little franky-panky, seldesey-weldesey, cowley-wowley, tatesy-watesy, hicksy-picksy, wilsony-pilsony, jolasy-wolasy, steiny-weiny, goldy-woldy, sneer-puss fellows. Neither, in more conventional guise, was he one of your groupy-croupy, clique-trique, meachy-teachy, devoto-bloato wire-pullers and back-scratchers of the world.

Granting a personal animus in this which cannot be ignored, one must nevertheless admit that, when its specific repudiations are cast up into one sum, they make a ponderable total. But Wolfe goes beyond and is categorical and specific. The rejection of decadence, for example, is symbolized by his majestic and thunderous broadside poured at close quarters into the hull of T. S. Eliot's creative work. Recalling Eliot's sneer that we are a nation of "hollow men" whose lives terminate "not with a bang but a whimper," Wolfe elaborates a small news item on "C. Green" who "fell or jumped" from the twelfth story window of the Hotel Admiral Francis Drake (as reported in the *Times,* that repository of the inconsequential doings of middle-class inconsequentials, so offensive to the nostrils of Pound, Eliot, and their clique) into a great prose poem, an elegy to those unobtrusive, inoffensive nonentities whose best efforts, having brought them to an impasse they did not foresee, choose to step into immeasurable space as the way to prolong the lives and comforts of those whom they have contracted to sustain, their act touching the very pith of other "hollow men" who do not regard their leaden obituaries in the *Times* as wearisome or revolting. "We are 'the hollow men, the hollow men'?" asks Wolfe. "Brave Admiral, do not be too sure." The rebuke is perhaps the most deserved in literature, but that it takes so impressive a form is tribute to the mistaken genius of the proud antagonist.

C. Green's requiem is sung in language fashioned by an earlier psalmist who celebrated the pain of man and the derision of the gods, Herman Melville, creator of mad Ahab and his luckless crew. Wolfe does not repudiate James Joyce specifically, though he admits that Webber was too much influenced by the Dubliner in his earlier books. Furthermore, *You Can't Go Home Again* is the least dependent of all Wolfe's books on Joyce for construction and development;

indeed, is not its whole thesis that the decadent nostalgias and re-treats of Joyce are a hopeless dissipation of the energies of "man-alive"? No, not quite, for there are other dissipations—one, in fact, more to be abhorred than decadence, and that is the coolly-arrived-at, irrefutable intellectual fatalism for which Foxhall Edwards stands. To Tom Wolfe, Edwards' cynicism is the most subtle virus of all, for seeping into the ganglia of good men, it enervates the will and corrupts the soul. It is steadfastly to be resisted, if not with syllogisms —for how can logic prevail against it?—with the flesh and spirit. The Artist must believe that the world can be better.

VI

It cannot be shown that Tom Wolfe had any premonition that he would escape scatheless from all his repudiations, renunciations, and denials. He had no foreknowledge that disease would afford him a swift release from the counterattacks of those upon whom he charged in his novel. He had counted the cost and was prepared to withstand the rage of those to whom he gave offense. There was no intentional ambiguity in his position. Before the Russo-German pact was even rumored he must have asserted the cousinship of the dictators of these states. In denouncing the Third Reich, in particular, Wolfe was well aware that he would be heavily penalized. As an author he was popular in Germany and his books had sold well there. His own loss, however, did not deter him from taking a position which he thought just. And it is to the everlasting honor of the man that he chose to make a miserable refugee Jew the instrument of Webber's conversion. Many of Wolfe's readers in the past must have been troubled by his pronounced anti-Semitism: it is good that he saw the illiberality of his position and recorded his sense of kinship with this persecuted race. The novelist emerges from *You Can't Go Home Again* a bigger person than we have known before. It is silly to object that he has no program: democracy is his program and whoever espouses that espouses the largest program of all. In this last book that he himself shaped, which was meant to be a first book (o fatal prolegomenon!), Thomas Wolfe stands poised, four-square against multiple enemies of a free way of life in the world. Going out of it with this volume, he went out, not with a whimper, Brave Admiral, but with a soundless salvo from the angels.

C. Hugh Holman

2. "The Dark, Ruined Helen of His Blood": Thomas Wolfe and the South

THOMAS WOLFE was born and grew to young manhood in Asheville, North Carolina. When he went North after his graduation from the University of North Carolina, he went as a Southerner, to write of Southern subjects in George Pierce Baker's "47 Workshop" at Harvard, and to compose his first novel out of the Southern scenes of his childhood with an autobiographical candor and an accuracy shocking to the residents of his native city. Yet Thomas Wolfe never returned for long to the South, once he had left it—indeed, he declared that "you can't go home again"—and the portrait that he drew of his native region in his first novel elicited from his former Chapel Hill classmate Jonathan Daniels the charge that "in *Look Homeward, Angel*, North Carolina and the South are spat upon." Some critics have believed, as Maxwell Geismar suggested, that Wolfe "was born in the South, but he shared with it little except the accident of birth" (*Writers In Crisis*, 1942, p. 196).

Upon his native region he heaped a Gargantuan scorn in his sprawling, loosely constructed tales and novels, condemning what in *Look Homeward, Angel* he called the Southerners' "hostile and murderous intrenchment against all new life . . . their cheap mythology, their legend of the charm of their manner, the aristocratic culture of their lives, the quaint sweetness of their drawl." In *The Web and the Rock* he expresses his anger at "the old, stricken, wounded 'Southness' of cruelty and lust," at men who "have a starved, stricken leanness in the loins," and at the lynchings that end with castrations, betraying his mingled disgust and sense of shame. The Southern intellectual fared little better in Wolfe's novels. He had contempt for the Agrarians whom he called in *The Web and the Rock* "the refined young gentlemen of the New Confederacy . . . [who] retired haughtily into the South, to the academic security of a teaching appointment at one of the universities, from which they could issue in quarterly installments very small and very precious magazines which celebrated the advantages of an agrarian society." And he wrote with feeling in the same novel of "the familiar rationalizing and self-defense of Southern fear and Southern failure: its fear of conflict and of competition in the greater world; its inability to meet or to adjust itself to the conditions, strifes, and ardors of a modern life; its old, sick, Appomattoxlike retreat into the shades of folly and delusion, of prejudice and bigotry, of florid legend and defensive casuistry . . ."

This South was feminine to him—what he called once "*the female principle*—the *earth* again . . . a home, fixity"—and in his thinking he opposed it to the father principle, which, in *The Story of a Novel,* he called "the image of a strength and wisdom external to his need and superior to his hunger, to which the belief and power of his own life could be united." From the maternal and subjective South, "the dark Helen of his blood," he turned to storm the male citadels of the North and to find in the "enfabled rock" of the Northern city a defense against the web of the South. Yet this South beat in his brain and pounded in his veins. "Every young man from the South," he said in *The Web and the Rock,* "has felt this precise and formal geography of the spirit," in which South and North are sharply dichotomized autonomies; and the qualities in young Southerners brought to the North:

> A warmth you lacked, a passion that God knows you needed, a belief and a devotion that was wanting in your life, an integrity of purpose that was rare in your own swarming hordes. They brought . . . some of the warmth, the depth, the richness of the secret and unfathomed South. They brought some of its depth and mystery. . . . They brought a warmth of earth, an exultant joy of youth, a burst of living laughter, a fullbodied warmth and living energy of humor.

Wolfe could proudly boast in a letter to James Boyd, "I'm a Long Hunter from Bear Creek, and a rootin', tootin', shootin' son-of-a-gun from North Carolina"; and he could write Maxwell Perkins that

"The people in North Carolina . . . are rich, juicy, deliberate, full of pungent and sardonic humor and honesty, conservative and cautious on top, but at bottom wild, savage, and full of the murderous innocence of the earth and the wilderness." What he said of his character George Webber is true of Wolfe himself: "He was a Southerner, and he knew that there was something wounded in the South. He knew that there was something twisted, dark, and full of pain which Southerners have known all their lives—something rooted in their souls beyond all contradiction." But all his knowledge of her darkness and damnation could not stifle his love for the lost and ruined and burning Helen in his blood.

That his vision of his native region was both obsessive and ambiguous was not surprising. Wolfe was born to a Northern father and a Southern mother, and the division of life into male and female, North and South, wanderer and homebound, was a simple extension of what he saw daily as a boy. He grew up in a Southern mountain town, but at a time when it was changing into a resort city, flourishing in the shadow of the baronial estate of the Vanderbilts, the pseudo-French château, "Biltmore," and literally mad for money. He went to college at Chapel Hill, a Southern state university, but at the time when that school was beginning the pattern of liberalism that made it the symbol of New South progressivism, completely opposite to the agrarianism of Vanderbilt University. Furthermore, at the feet of a locally famed teacher of philosophy, Horace Williams, he imbibed a form of Hegelian dialectic that made him see all life in terms of opposites and gave his work the fundamental structure of thesis and antithesis in sentence, paragraph, and scene as well as in its more obvious oppositions, such as South and North, female and male, Jew and gentile, mother and father, the web and the rock.

Ambiguous and contradictory though his views of his native region were, the South was a theme and a subject matter for much of Wolfe's work, and it existed for him in a sensuous, irrational emotional state of mutual attraction and repulsion. And this contradiction and ambiguity, this coexisting intense love and passionate hatred are characteristic not only of Wolfe's attitudes toward the South but also of his total work. His published writings consist of four novels (two of which appeared posthumously and were prepared for the printer by an editor), two volumes of short stories and sketches (one published posthumously), a play, and a few other items—plays and sketches in magazines—which are of minor importance. The six volumes of novels and short stories represent the significant corpus of his work, and they were carved out of a vast and complex outpouring of words.

The term most often applied to these works is "formless," for their structure is difficult, diffuse, uncertain. *Look Homeward, Angel* and *Of Time and the River* are the adventures of Eugene Gant in his growth from childhood to maturity, and Eugene Gant is an embarrassingly direct portrait of Wolfe himself. *The Web and the Rock* and *You Can't Go Home Again,* the posthumously published novels, trace the similar story of George Webber and carry it on through his love affair with Esther Jack and his success as a novelist. Webber is seemingly as autobiographical as Gant. The stories in *From Death to Morning* and *The Hills Beyond* were all—or almost all—written originally as episodes in the great "book," of which the four novels are parts. Here, in these millions of words, then, is the intensely felt experience of a single person, the author, presented almost entirely without benefit of formal plot or traditional structure. Subjectivity has seldom more totally dominated a major work, and it is difficult to read Wolfe without feeling the justice of Robert Penn Warren's wry comment: "It may be well to recollect that Shakespeare merely wrote *Hamlet;* he was *not* Hamlet" ("A Note on the Hamlet of Thomas Wolfe," *Selected Essays,* 1958, p. 183).*

But imprisoned within this vast body of words are hundreds of sharply realized scenes, dozens of characters who have an authentic existence—W. O. Gant, Eliza Gant, Bascom Pentland, Helen Gant, Francis Starwick, Esther Jack, Judge Rumford Bland, Nebraska Crane—and literally thousands of descriptive passages of such lyric intensity and sensuous directness that they impinge upon the senses of the reader and achieve for a moment in his consciousness a concrete reality.

Few American novelists have projected more ambitious programs or had more demanding plans for their novels. The task Wolfe set himself was, he once wrote in a letter, the representation of "the whole consciousness of his people and nation . . . every sight sound and memory of the people." In order to formulate this vast subject,

* See Chapter 16 in this book.

he sought encompassing themes. He concocted a three-part theory of time, which he found inherent in his materials: actual present time, past time, and "time immutable," and saw in their simultaneous projection in a work of fiction a "tremendous problem." He attempted to express the essential loneliness and isolation of all human existence. He borrowed Greek myths, sketching characters to fill the roles of Antaeus, Heracles, Poseidon, Kronos, Gaea, Helen, Jason—seeking to find in the patterns of their lives a controlling myth or metaphor for the meanings he wanted to convey. His letters are filled with the outlines of vast projects before whose scope Balzac seems limited and Faulkner cautious. As he himself once wrote in a letter, "The book on which I have been working for the last two or three years is not a volume but a library."

The motive force of his works seems to have been his desire to express the elements of a universal experience and this universal experience was for him closely tied up with the national, the American experience. To a remarkable degree Thomas Wolfe was using himself to describe and to define both this universal experience and his native land, to produce the American epic, to create the egalitarian and generic hero. In a letter to Perkins he once said, "My conviction is that a native has the whole consciousness of his people and nation in him; that he knows everything about it, every sight sound and memory of the people." Much of his career was a search for America, and he came to see fairly early that, as he expressed it in *The Story of a Novel,* "the way to find America was to find it in one's heart, one's memory, and one's spirit."

And thus he fell in with the powerful epic impulse that has motivated much American writing since the eighteenth century: the attempt to encompass in a fable or narrative the spirit and the nature of the land, to represent the soul of a people through a representative hero and archetypal actions. As Tocqueville suggested, over a century ago, in an egalitarian democracy the traditional heroes of the aristocratic plots and literary genres are forbidden to the artist, and somehow he must find in the common man the center of his patriotic art. Walt Whitman, feeling the demands of the epic impulse, attempted a solution by celebrating his own generic qualities.

> *One's-self I sing, a single separate person,*
> *Yet utter the word Democratic, the word En-Masse.*

This self of Whitman's became the spokesman of his nation by its ability to witness all things imaginatively and to participate vicariously in all actions.

For Wolfe the center of his art was in a similar view of the self, but the method was different. Like Whitman, he believed that the writer "ought to see in what has happened to him the universal experience." All the people, events, images, and visions that crossed his experience became a part of him, and were to be transmuted into a "final coherent union" in which America was to be embodied. For Whitman this embodiment was expressed in chants. The embodiment would be for Wolfe, as he said, "a story of the artist as a man who derived out of the common family of earth and who knows all the anguish, error, and frustration that any man alive can know." To find an adequate experience, an effective language, and a unifying structure for this man became for Wolfe the obsessive task of the American artist. He said in *The Story of a Novel:*

> . . . in the cultures of Europe and of the Orient the American artist can find no antecedent scheme, no structural plan, no body of tradition that can give his own work the validity and truth that it must have. It is not merely that he must make somehow a new tradition for himself, derived from his own life and from the enormous space and energy of American life, the structure of his own design; it is not merely that he is confronted by these problems; it is even more than this, that the labor of a complete and whole articulation, the discovery of an entire universe and of a complete language, is the task that lies before him.

In his efforts to accomplish that tremendous task, to realize the self as generic American and make his personal pilgrimage the national odyssey, Wolfe functioned with uneven effectiveness. He magnificently realized individual scenes and sections of his mammoth work, especially in the form of short novels, but he only imperfectly formed the faint outlines of the larger task. That the elements which made up his all-encompassing effort were woven from the filaments of his self and that that self was both woven and torn by his Southern heritage should be beyond dispute; but in the interest of illuminating a little of both Wolfe and the literature of his region it may be worth while to point to some of the Southern qualities in his work.

The urge to represent America, to embody it in a work of art, although by no means unique to the region, has been persistent in Southern literature. The Southerners of the antebellum period often raised their voices in support of a native literature and stood with the "Young America" group of critics in their intensely nationalistic demands for art in the 1840's and 1850's, despite the serious political differences between them and the New York critics. They distrusted the "internationalism" of New Englanders like Longfellow and of New Yorkers like the editors of the *Knickerbocker Magazine*. Yet these Southerners were aware that the nation could better be represented by drawing its particularities than by picturing the whole. In 1856, for example, William Gilmore Simms, of South Carolina, had written: ". . . to be *national* in literature, one must needs be *sectional*. No one mind can fully or fairly illustrate the characteristics of any great country; and he who shall depict *one section* faithfully, has made his proper and sufficient contribution to the great work of *national* literature" (*The Wigwam and the Cabin,* 1856, pp. 4–5). This view is not far from Wolfe's own, when he insists upon the representation of his unique self as the proper subject for a national art. Wolfe was like Thoreau, who said, "I should not talk so much about myself if there were anybody else whom I knew as well. Unfortunately, I am confined to this theme by the narrowness of my experience." However, for Wolfe, the observation of his fellow men was a basic part of that experience, as it was not for Thoreau.

It is also typical of the Southern writer that this epic portrayal of America should constitute a project of great magnitude and tremendous complexity. Wolfe's letters and *The Story of a Novel* carry the evidence of the vastness of scope and the complexity of design of the "work in progress" on which he expended his days and hours and which he left incomplete. It is startling to one who has accepted the standard view of Wolfe's work as the spontaneous and unpremeditated overflow of the author's powerful feeling, recollected in abnormal intensity, to find him writing to Maxwell E. Perkins, "I think you may be a little inclined to underestimate the importance of arrangement and presentation, and may feel that the stories can go in any way, and that the order doesn't matter much." In the light of his efforts to get on paper the theme, the argument, the structure of the large work as he labored on its parts, such a statement—although it does not redeem his novels from formlessness—makes poignant and telling Wolfe's protests against the publication of *Of Time and the River* in the form in which Perkins sent it to the press.

This large design would have traced the history of the Pentlands (or, later, the Joyners) from the Civil War to the present, emphasizing the Southern roots of the generic hero. It would have included thousands of characters and episodes—the whole, Wolfe said, to be "seen not by a *definite personality,* but haunted throughout by a consciousness of *personality,*" and that personality was to be the perceptive "self" through which the writer could know and express his America. Before a work of such magnitude as he projected, time became the great enemy. The scope of his ambitious plan—which was to be no less than the record of his nation and his people told through one representative man—merits in its magnitude comparison with the master projects of literary history, with Balzac and Zola and with Tolstoy. To embark upon such vast projects has also been typically, although by no means exclusively, Southern, perhaps because the Southerner tends to distrust abstraction and to doubt that one can see a "world in a grain of sand,/ And a heaven in a wild flower." Whatever the reason, twentieth-century Southern writers have tended to plan work of enormous scope, such as James Branch Cabell's many-volumed and incomplete record of Poictesme; Ellen Glasgow's fictional record in thirteen volumes of Virginia's social history from the Civil War to the 1940's (whether such a structure was her original intention or a design she imposed after a good portion of the fact); and William Faulkner's vast and growing record of Yoknapatawpha County. Wolfe, like these other Southerners, set himself a task that staggers the imagination and defies the reality of time. Little wonder that Faulkner considers him among the greatest of American writers because he dared the most!

Near the beginning of his first novel Wolfe wrote, "Each of us is all the sums he has not counted: subtract us into nakedness and night again, and you shall see begin in Crete four thousand years ago the love that ended yesterday in Texas. . . . Each moment is the fruit of forty thousand years." This concern with time grew more intense as his career developed. The artist's problem, he believed, is the resolution of a threefold consciousness of time into a single moment so that scenes can represent "characters as acting and as being acted upon by all the accumulated impact of man's experience so that each moment of their lives was conditioned not only by what they experienced in that moment, but by all that they had experienced up to that moment," and with these actions set somehow against a consciousness of "a kind of eternal and unchanging universe of time against which must be projected the transience of man's life, the bitter briefness of his day." Whether or not Wolfe is indebted to Proust and Bergson for these ideas, he certainly envisions his characters as set in a complex fabric of time, and their actions as having remote roots and immeasurable forward extensions. Louis D. Rubin, Jr., has noted elsewhere * that "The interplay of past and present, of the historical and the contemporaneous, causes all the modern Southern writers to be unusually sensitive to the nature and workings of time." This interplay is one of the basic materials of Wolfe's fiction.

Wolfe shares with many Southern writers his concerns with the reality of the past in the present and with the nature of time. One can find examples of the Southern writer's concern with time and his belief that it is, not only fact or sequence, but, more important, a key to the nature of human experience in Robert Penn Warren, particularly in *The Ballard of Billie Potts* and *World Enough and Time;* in Ellen Glasgow; in William Faulkner, with his elaborate dislocations of time sequence in many of his narratives; in Tate's *Ode to the Confederate Dead;* in William Styron's inverted structure in *Lie Down in Darkness;* and in many other places. It is not surprising that one of Wolfe's best-known short stories should be *Chickamauga* and that the novel fragment on which he was working at the time of his death, *The Hills Beyond,* deals with his Southern ancestors in the nineteenth century.† Among twentieth-century American novelists only the Southerners have with any frequency treated the past outside the pattern of romance and adventure. William Faulkner, Robert Penn Warren, Ellen Glasgow, and James Branch Cabell have written extensively with a historical orientation.

The mixture of styles in which Wolfe wrote is also not uncommon in Southern writing. On one level Wolfe illustrates with great effectiveness the concrete, the immediate, the sensuous. He accurately described himself when he wrote in *The Story of a Novel,* "The quality of my memory is characterized, I believe, in a more than

---

* *South: Modern Southern Literature in Its Cultural Setting* (1961).
† See Chapter 20 in this book.

ordinary degree by the intensity of its sense impressions, its power to evoke and bring back the odors, sounds, colors, shapes, and feel of things with concrete vividness." It is this quality in his work that gives many of his pages an intensity which almost approximates direct experience. This lyric aspect of his writing, in which the object is evoked with such power that it seems to be rubbed against the reader's exposed nerve ends, this ability to make "the world's body" vividly real, succeeds again and again in giving the reader new insights; in Wolfe's terms, in making "the utterly familiar, common thing . . . suddenly be revealed . . . with all the wonder with which we discover a thing which we have seen all our life and yet have never known before." A passage from *Of Time and the River* will illustrate the centrality of the concrete in Wolfe's writing. Eugene Gant is daydreaming and not worrying about where the money to fulfill his dreams is to come from.

> If he thought about it, it seemed to have no importance or reality whatever—he just dismissed it impatiently, or with a conviction that some old man would die and leave him a fortune, that he was going to pick up a purse containing hundreds of thousands of dollars while walking in the Fenway, and that the reward would be enough to keep him going, or that a beautiful and rich young widow, true-hearted, tender, loving, and voluptuous, who had carrot-colored hair, little freckles on her face, a snub nose and luminous gray-green eyes with something wicked yet loving and faithful in them, and one gold filling in her solid little teeth, was going to fall in love with him.

Here, where he is mocking Eugene's stereotype dreams, the rich young widow is made concrete and detailed; the lucky purse is found in a particular place. This use of the particular, this tendency to distrust the conceptual and abstract, is one of the most widely recognized characteristics of Southern writing. As Robert Penn Warren has pointed out, the Southerner lives in "the instinctive fear . . . that the massiveness of experience, the concreteness of life, will be violated . . . [in] the fear of abstraction" (*Segregation*, 1957, p. 15). Virginia Rock has noted that the Southern poet feels "not only a rage for order but also a rage for the concrete, a rage against the abstract" ("Agrarianism in Southern Literature: The Period Since 1925," *The Georgia Review*, XI [1957], 157). Even in criticism, Southerners have concentrated their attention on particular works of art and have not formulated abstract systems. As Allen Tate put it, "There was no Southern criticism; merely a few Southern critics" ("The New Provincialism," *On the Limits of Poetry* [1948], p. 290).

Closely associated with this concern for the concrete is Wolfe's delight in folk speech, dialect, and speech mannerisms. His works are full of accurate transcriptions of vivid speech. His characters seem sometimes to talk endlessly, but they always talk with vigor and with great distinctiveness of diction, syntax, and idiom.

Yet the same writer who displays these startlingly effective qualities of lyric concreteness and speech accuracy is also guilty of excesses in both quantity and quality of rhetoric perhaps unequaled by any other American novelist. With the power to evoke a particular object, scene, or character with remarkable clarity, he is unwilling to let these creations speak for themselves, but must try by the sheer force of rhetoric to give expression to the peculiar meanings that they suggest, to define ineffable feelings, to formulate the inchoate longings and the uncertain stirrings of spirit which he feels that all men share. These qualities are manifest in the following passage from *Of Time and the River,* where he is trying to define the "fury" that drives Gant toward the North and away from the South.

> It is to have the old unquiet mind, the famished heart, the restless soul; it is to lose hope, heart, and all joy utterly, and then to have them wake again, to have the old feeling return with overwhelming force that he is about to find the thing for which his life obscurely and desperately is groping—for which all men on this earth have sought—one face out of the million faces, a wall, a door, a place of certitude and peace and wandering no more. For what is it that we Americans are seeking always on this earth? Why is it we have crossed the stormy seas so many times alone, lain in a thousand alien rooms at night hearing the sounds of time, dark time, and thought until heart, brain, flesh, and spirit are sick and weary with the thought of it; "Where shall I go now? What shall I do?"

Set beside some of the apostrophes from *Look Homeward, Angel,* like the one to Laura James at the end of Chapter 30, this passage seems restrained, yet it represents pretty clearly that rhetorical groping toward understanding and expression which is a very large element in Wolfe's work. He is fascinated by language, enchanted by words, carried away by rhetorical devices. A kind of primitive logomania is in him: if the word can be found and uttered, vast forces are unleashed and great truths miraculously uncovered. The artist's search, Wolfe declared in *The Story of a Novel,* is the search for a language, for an articulation. "I believe with all my heart, also, that each man for himself and in his own way, each man who ever hopes to make a living thing out of the substances of his one life, must find that way, that language, and that door—must find it for himself as I have tried to do."

The drift toward rhetoric is the aspect of Wolfe's work most frequently called Southern. Alfred Kazin observed of Wolfe and Faulkner: "It is their rhetoric, a mountainous verbal splendor, that holds these writers together . . . the extravagant and ornamental tradition of Southern rhetoric" (*On Native Grounds* [1942], p. 468). Wilbur J. Cash believed that it was their use of the rhetorical tradition that tied Faulkner and Wolfe to earlier Southern literary traditions, and Joseph Warren Beach felt that "Wolfe's inclination to extravagant and ornamental writing" should be associated with "something in the tradition of Southern culture" (*American Fiction, 1920–1940* [1948], p. 211). As Floyd Watkins has asserted, "Wolfe must be viewed as a Southern rhetorician" ("Rhetoric in Southern Writing: Wolfe," *The Georgia Review,* XII [1958], 82).* Certainly the passion for the sound of the word, the primitive desire to give the name, the sense of the power present in the magic of incantation, show up with alarming frequency in Southern writing. The particular linguistic combination that Wolfe used—the combination of concrete detail, accurate speech, and incantatory rhetorical extravagance is also present to a marked degree in the works of Faulkner, particularly since 1932, and in the novels of Robert Penn Warren.

Wolfe likewise shares the Southerner's willingness to accept and find delight in paradox. At the heart of the riddle of the South is a union of opposites, a condition of instability, a paradox: a love of individualism combined with a defense of slavery and segregation, a delight in polished manners and at the same time a ready recourse to violence, the liberalism of Thomas Jefferson coexisting with the

* See Chapter 12 in this book.

conservatism of John C. Calhoun. Such paradoxes bother Southerners less than they would bother their Northern neighbors, for while they hunger for order and are moved by a rage for tradition, they can at the same time accept instability as a permanent aspect of human existence and the unresolved contradiction as a part of man's condition. Southern writers often value paradox as a primary element in art. Cleanth Brooks, for example, finds the meaning in poetry in the paradoxes that are to be found in word, image, and structure. The Fugitive poets, notably John Crowe Ransom, find the full meaning of an incident in the comprehension of its persistent ironies. Allen Tate sees the meaning of a poem in the "tension" created by the conflict between its intension and extension.

Wolfe saw his world and himself through an only semilogical application to life of the Hegelian dialectic. He seemed to need to define a thing's opposite before he could comprehend the thing, and to have a naïve faith that somehow the meaning was manifest if the opposites were stated. Hence, there is in his work on practically every level—sentence, paragraph, scene, theme, large project—a structure of paradox.

But all these attributes of Wolfe's work individually are essentially superficial qualities of his "Southernness." So strong a combination of these attributes as he displays does not often occur in America outside the South; yet these qualities suggest rather than define a distinctively Southern quality. In certain other respects, however, Wolfe seems definitively Southern. One of these is his attitude toward capitalistic industrialism; another is his sense of the tragic implications of experience; and a third is his deep-seated sense of human guilt.

That Wolfe had little patience with the group of Southern writers known as the Agrarians is obvious from what has already been quoted. He regarded their intellectualism as false, their devotion to the life of the soil as pretentious and unreal, and he heaped scorn on them more than once, calling them by the opprobrious name "New Confederates." Yet one has the feeling that much of his contempt rested on ignorance of what the Agrarians were advocating, and that he would have been pretty much of their party if he had known what the party really was. However, he belonged loosely to the New South school, which saw in industrial progress the key to a new and better life and believed that the South must emerge from its retreat into the reality of the modern world. In *The Web and the Rock* he wrote:

> There was an image in George Webber's mind that came to him in childhood and that resumed for him the whole dark picture of those decades of defeat and darkness. He saw an old house, set far back from the traveled highway, and many passed along that road, and the troops went by, the dust rose, and the war was over. And no one passed along that road again. He saw an old man go along the path, away from the road, into the house; and the path was overgrown with grass and weeds, with thorny tangle, and with underbrush until the path was lost. And no one ever used that path again. And the man who went into that house never came out of it again. And the house stayed on. It shone faintly through that tangled growth like its own ruined spectre, its doors and windows black as eyeless sockets. That was the South. That was the South for thirty years or more.
>
> That was the South, not of George Webber's life, nor of the lives of his contemporaries—that was the South they did not know but that all of them somehow remembered. It came to them from God knows where, upon the rustling of a leaf at night, in quiet voices on a Southern porch, in a screen door slam and sudden silence, a whistle wailing down the midnight valleys to the East and the enchanted cities of the North, and Aunt Maw's droning voice and the memory of unheard voices, in the memory of the dark, ruined Helen in their blood, in something stricken, lost, and far, and long ago. They did not see it, the people of George's age and time, but they remembered it.
>
> They had come out—another image now—into a kind of sunlight of another century. They had come out upon the road again. The road was being paved. More people came now. They cut a pathway to the door again. Some of the weeds were clear. Another house was built. They heard wheels coming and the world was *in,* yet they were not yet wholly of that world.

Yet Wolfe was also keenly aware that industrial progress and the things associated with it could have damaging effects on American and Southern culture. Writing to his mother, in May, 1923, he condemned "progress" and commerce in scathing terms:

> I will not hesitate to say what I think of those people who shout "Progress, Progress, Progress"—when what they mean is more

Ford automobiles, more Rotary Clubs, more Baptist Ladies Social unions. I will say that "Greater Asheville" does not necessarily mean "100,000 by 1930," that we are not necessarily 4 times as civilized as our grandfathers because we go four times as fast in automobiles, because our buildings are four times as tall. What I shall try to get into their dusty little pint-measure minds is that a full belly, a good automobile, paved streets, and so on, do not make them one whit better or finer,—that there is beauty in this world, —beauty even in this wilderness of ugliness and provincialism that is at present our country, beauty and spirit which will make us men instead of cheap Board of Trade Boosters, and blatant pamphleteers.

He defined the "essential tragedy of America" as "the magnificent, unrivaled, unequaled, unbeatable, unshrinkable, supercolossal, 99-and-44-one-hundredths-per-cent-pure, schoolgirl-complexion, covers-the-earth, I'd-walk-a-mile-for-it, four-out-of-five-have-it, his-master's-voice, ask-the-man-who-owns-one, blueplate-special home of advertising, salesmanship, and special pleading in all its many catchy and beguiling forms." Certainly for him, capitalistic industrial progress had as little appeal as it did for the Agrarians; for him, as for the Twelve Southerners who wrote *I'll Take My Stand,* the modern industrial world had become a perversion of the American dream. The Twelve Southerners declared, "If a community, or a section, or a race, or an age, is groaning under industrialism, and well aware that it is an evil dispensation, it must find the way to throw it off. To think that this cannot be done is pusillanimous. And if the whole community, section, race, or age thinks it cannot be done, then it has simply lost its political genius and doomed itself to impotence" ("Introduction," *I'll Take My Stand,* 1939, p. xx). George Webber shared these sentiments when he said, in *You Can't Go Home Again:*

"America went off the track somewhere—back around the time of the Civil War, or pretty soon afterwards. Instead of going ahead and developing along the line in which the country started out, it got shunted off in another direction—and now we look around and see we've gone places we didn't mean to go. Suddenly we realize that America has turned into someting ugly—and vicious— and corroded at the heart of its power with easy wealth and graft and special privilege. . . . And the worst of it is the intellectual dishonesty which all this corruption has bred. People are *afraid* to think straight—*afraid* to face themselves—*afraid* to look at things and see them as they are. We've become like a nation of advertising men, all hiding behind catch phrases like 'prosperity' and 'rugged individualism' and 'the American way.' And the real things like freedom, and equal opportunity, and the integrity and worth of the individual—things that have belonged to the American dream since the beginning—they have become just words too. The substance has gone out of them—they're not real any more."

Admittedly, this sounds more like Sidney Lanier's condemnation of "trade" than Donald Davidson's advocacy of the agrarian way, yet the enemy that all three faced was an enemy well known to the South and commonly confronted by Southerners.

Wolfe looked upon himself as a radical, even, as he once called himself, a "Revolutionary," and he angrily expressed his hatred of the gross injustice and inhumanity that the depression produced. But to him the solution was never material; indeed, the substitution of the material for the spiritual was the cause for his belief "that we are lost here in America," and only his confidence that ultimately America would put aside the material for the spiritual made it possible for him to add, "but I believe we shall be found."

Wolfe is peculiarly Southern, too, in the degree to which he sees the darkness, pain, and evil in life, and yet does not succumb to the naturalistic answer of despair. "The enemy," he tells us in *You Can't Go Home Again,*

> is old as Time, and evil as Hell, and he has been here with us from the beginning. I think he stole our earth from us, destroyed our wealth, and ravaged and despoiled our land. I think he took our people and enslaved them, that he polluted the fountains of our life, took unto himself the rarest treasures of our own possession, took our bread and left us with a crust.

Wolfe seemed to feel, as George Webber did, "the huge and nameless death that waits around the corner for all men, to break their backs and shatter instantly the blind and pitiful illusions of their hope." He was supremely the novelist of death in American literature, for the ending of life was an obsessive theme with him. All his characters come to face the fact of death; as he expressed it, "They knew that they would die and that the earth would last forever. And with that feeling of joy, wonder, and sorrow in their hearts, they knew that another day had gone, another day had come, and they knew how brief and lonely are man's days." And the end, at least in its physical sense, was ugly. In *Of Time and the River* he described it this way:

> This was the sickening and abominable end of flesh, which infected time and all man's living memory of morning, youth, and magic with the death-putrescence of its cancerous taint, and made us doubt that we had ever lived, or had a father, known joy: this was the end, and the end was horrible in ugliness. At the end it was not well.

In *The Story of a Novel*, Wolfe is explicit about this darkness and evil in life. "Everywhere around me . . . I saw the evidence of an incalculable ruin and suffering," he said, and enumerated the "suffering, violence, oppression, hunger, cold, and filth and poverty" he saw, so that through "the suffering and labor of [his] own life" he shared the experiences of people around him.

This sense of evil and suffering is more typical of Southern writers than of other Americans, for a variety of reasons: the South's distrust of progress, its refusal to believe in perfectibility, its experience of compromise and paradox—all culminated in the defeat in the Civil War and its long and bitter aftermath. As C. Vann Woodward has cogently argued, the South is the only American region where the principles of progress and the concept of perfectibility are demonstrably false. "Nothing," he asserts, "about [its] history is conducive to the theory that the South was the darling of divine providence" ("The Irony of Southern History," *Southern Renascence*, ed. Louis D. Rubin, Jr., and Robert D. Jacobs [1953], p. 65). This sense of defeat could lead Ellen Glasgow to say that she could never recall a time when "the pattern of society as well as the scheme of things in general, had not seemed to [her] false and even malignant" (*The Woman Within* [1954], p. 42), and the same feeling found expression in the dark damnation of Faulkner's world and the ambiguous calamities of Robert Penn Warren's.

When, however, the nation as a whole began to experience the cataclysms of the twentieth century and to react to scientific and philosophic views of man that were less optimistic, the American artist outside the South tended to turn to programs of Utopian reform, or satiric correction, or naturalistic despair. The Southern writer on the other hand, older in the experience of calamity and defeat, saw the tragic grandeur of man, the magnificence of his will in the face of disaster, and the glory with which he maintained the integrity of his spirit in a world of material defeat. Southern writers have often used their history to make a tragic fable of man's lot in a hostile world, and to celebrate the triumph of the human spirit when challenged by an idea or a responsibility. As Ellen Glasgow asserts, "One may learn to live, one may even learn to live gallantly, without delight." And as Ike McCaslin says in Faulkner's *Delta Autumn,* "There are good men everywhere, at all times. Most men are. Some are just unlucky, because most men are a little better than their circumstances give them a chance to be." This view of man changes defeat into tragic grandeur and touches the spectacle of suffering with the transforming sense of human dignity.

Thomas Wolfe's view of man and life had this tragic sense. In *The Story of a Novel* he expressed it very directly. "And from it all, there has come as the final deposit, a burning memory, a certain evidence of the fortitude of man, his ability to suffer and somehow to survive." At the conclusion of Chapter 27 of *You Can't Go Home Again,* in what is a too-obvious extension of a speech by Hamlet, Wolfe attempts to answer the question, "What is man?" and in his answer states as clearly as he ever did the extent to which his vision of experience had tragic magnitude. Man to him is "a foul, wretched, abominable creature . . . and it is impossible to say the worst of him . . . this moth of time, this dupe of brevity and numbered hours, this travesty of waste and sterile breath." Yet Wolfe stands in awe of man's accomplishments. "For there is one belief, one faith, that is man's glory, his triumph, his immortality—and that is his belief in life. . . . So this is man—the worst and best of him—this frail and petty thing who lives his days and dies like all the other animals and is forgotten. And yet, he is immortal, too, for both the good and evil that he does live after him."

The Southern writer is often obsessed with a sense of guilt and the need for expiation. Robert Penn Warren calls this feeling by its theological name in his poem *Original Sin,* and sees it as the inevitable result of our lost innocence; in Allen Tate's *The Wolves* it is a threatening evil to be faced always in the next room; in William Faulkner it may be symbolized by the vicariously shared guilt which Quentin Compson must assume and die to pay for in *The Sound and the Fury,* or the inheritance of the father's which Ike McCaslin vainly tries to repudiate in *The Bear.* This sense of guilt may be the product of the pervasive Calvinism of the region; it may be the product of the poverty and suffering that the region has known; it is certainly in part the result of the guilt associated with slavery in the nineteenth century and the Negro's second-class citizenship in the twentieth— a guilt most thoughtful Southerners have felt. In any case, it appears to be a hallmark of the serious twentieth-century Southern writer. And it is a hallmark that Thomas Wolfe's work certainly bears.

He states his own sense of guilt explicitly in *The Story of a Novel:*

And through the traffic of those thronging crowds—whose faces, whose whole united and divided life was now instantly and without an effort of the will, my *own*—there rose forever the sad unceasing murmurs of the body of this life, the vast recessive fadings of the shadow of man's death that breathes forever with its dirgelike sigh around the huge shores of the world.

And *beyond, beyond*—forever *above, around, behind* the vast and tranquil consciousness of my spirit that now held the earth and all her elements in the huge clasp of its effortless subjection— there dwelt forever the fatal knowledge of my own inexpiable *guilt.*

In *You Can't Go Home Again* he explicitly links this sense of guilt with the South, and in turn sees the South as a symbol and in a sense a scapegoat for the national hurt.

Perhaps it came from their old war, and from the ruin of their great defeat and its degraded aftermath. Perhaps it came from causes yet more ancient—from the evil of man's slavery, and the hurt and shame of human conscience in its struggle with the fierce desire to own. It came, too, perhaps, from the lusts of the hot South, tormented and repressed below the harsh and outward patterns of a bigot and intolerant theology. . . . And most of all, perhaps, it came out of the very weather of their lives. . . .

But it was not only in the South that America was hurt. There was another deeper, darker, and more nameless wound throughout the land. . . .

We must look at the heart of guilt that beats in each of us, for there the cause lies. We must look, and with our own eyes see, the central core of defeat and shame and failure. . . .

Thomas Wolfe did not live to complete his representation of his America through the portrait of himself as generic man, and out of the novels, short stories, and letters we piece out the pattern he was trying to follow and we guess at meanings and intentions. One thing seems clear: Wolfe was a Southerner, torn by the tensions and issues that thoughtful Southerners feel, oppressed as they tend to be with the tragic nature of life, and feeling as they often do a sense of guilt that demands some kind of expiating action. The work he completed had demonstrable Southern qualities; the total work, had he lived to complete it, would probably have had these qualities too. The South did, indeed, burn in his blood and on his pages like a "ruined Helen"—beautiful, passionate, and dark with violence and guilt.

J. Russell Reaver
and Robert I. Strozier

3. Thomas Wolfe and Death

STUDENTS of Thomas Wolfe's fiction fully realize its autobiographical basis, but his former critics have overlooked the intimate connection between his protagonists' evolving attitudes toward death and the corresponding maturity of Wolfe. The effusive Eugene Gant of *Look Homeward, Angel* forms a striking contrast to the more restrained George Webber of *The Web and the Rock* and *You Can't Go Home Again*. A major aspect of this difference in Wolfe's heroes lies in the significance they place on death. This study traces Wolfe's achievement of emotional maturity and shows the corresponding effect that his development had on his stylistic methods.

Wolfe's first novel *Look Homeward, Angel: A Story of the Buried Life* derives its title from Milton's "Lycidas," a poem of isolation and the growth of self-awareness. The title is noteworthy because it combines the two central kinds of isolation that troubled Wolfe throughout his life: the inevitable separation of physical death and the agonizing isolation of creative defeat.[1] Wolfe thought of isolation as a kind of death, yet it held a tantalizing promise.

In *Look Homeward, Angel* Eugene Gant's existence becomes an emotional combat against death and the pressures denying him psychological freedom. Eugene's unceasing struggle, from the moment of Grover's death to the awful dying of Ben, makes us aware that isolation and death amount to the same thing for him.

Ironically, his family attachments, which he keenly feels, prevent him from a solitude that might help him realize his creative power. Wolfe could say he cherished as well as feared death because from facing the inevitable he could gain strength. Death must be faced and

feared, said Wolfe, claiming those who said they did not fear it were
". . . liars, and fools, and hypocrites" (TWLM, p. 79). In this early
fictional version of his youth, Wolfe presents Eugene as deeply involved with a paradox. Separation is to be feared but also to be
cherished. Facing death matures Eugene in a very special way. Each
death he endures makes him more capable of coping with his next
experience with it. But each event also redeems him; it allows him to
begin to understand that death can be seen as something more than
a personal experience with the end of a physical process. Gradually
from seeing the deaths of loved ones he constructs an analogy that
permits him to discern his own life's struggle as a peculiarly personal
attempt to conquer death, and at the same time to work his ". . . way
toward an essential isolation; a creative solitude; a secret life . . .
toward freedom; in a way toward bondage . . . one is as beautiful as
the other" (LTW, p. 111). By the time of Ben's death he can look
on dying as a redemptive, not a destructive process. "Eugene thought
of death now, with love, with joy. Death was like a lovely and tender
woman, Ben's friend and lover, who had come to free him, to heal
him, to save him from the torture of life" (LHA, p. 560).

But this cherishing of death occurs in Eugene only at the end of
Look Homeward, Angel, and he arrives at this view slowly. Like his
father, Eugene fears physical pain and annihilation. Young Eugene's
feelings at Grover's death reflect Oliver Gant's earlier response to the
death of his first wife, Cynthia, and closely resemble the father's
behavior in the presence of other deaths.

Wolfe shows the childish self-pity of Oliver's reactions to all his
personal problems, but the father's immaturity appears most obvious
in his reactions to the deaths of his first wife and of his sons Grover
and Ben. The imminence of Ben's death stimulates him to depths of
mawkish self-pity. In tones of ludicrous pathos he wails that Ben's
death has come to torture not Ben, but him. Only shortly before his
own death can the father face up to his end, as Wolfe shows in *Of
Time and the River:* ". . . he knew that he was done for and he no
longer cared" (OTAR, p. 256). But Gant's acceptance of death is an
act of precipitate desperation, coming only when he senses ever-
nearing Necessity hovering like the Furies about his bed (pp. 258–
68).

No so with Eugene. Since Ben's death he has tried to combat his fear of death by disciplining himself to face it. The degree of maturity he has reached becomes apparent when he decides to break away from home. In his letters Wolfe significantly describes this experience:

> It is like death. I know that people do not die once, but many times, and that life of which they were once a part, and which they thought they could never lose, dies too, becomes a ghost, is lost forever. . . . If, then, I am dead to people who once knew me and cared for me, there is nothing more to say or do—I must go on into a new world and a new life. . . . (LTW, pp. 216-17)

Unlike his father, Eugene matures with experience, each incident building toward his final achievement. Gant's psychic stagnation contrasts with Eugene's growth. Eugene learns to realize how callous and introverted his father's feelings are. The infantile quality of the father's grief over his first wife parallels the shock and grief of the four-year-old Eugene's response to Grover's death. Neither can get beyond the fear and pain of physical loss. And just as the father is saved from an earlier madness by Eliza, who becomes his second wife, so, ironically, the father, though still suffering himself, can save his son from the darkness weighting down his young mind by the cheerful warmth of the family fire and hearty food (LHA, p. 61).

Later when Ben dies, Oliver still shows a pathetic self-centeredness contrasting with Eugene's efforts to gain control of himself. In spite of his fear, Eugene can accept Ben's dying. Alone among the assembly Eugene does not boil over with hate toward others responsible for Ben's death. Only he can quiet his mother whose grief is heightened by Ben's refusal to have her near him. Following their father's example, the others are too concerned with themselves. Although Eugene's "soul plunged downward, drowning in that pit" (p. 548) at his first horror of knowing Ben will die, he controls himself to maintain a selfless awareness of those around him, and from this perception he gains strength. He can finally think of death as a tender, lovely, power to be cherished. After this solution Eugene knows the saving grace of humor: he draws the family out of their morbidity soon after Ben's death by reminding them that at least Ben "won't have to drink mama's coffee any more" (p. 559). And he can joke at the artistry of the undertaker who reddens Ben's cheeks with a rouge stick. Wolfe concludes about Eugene in *Look Homeward, Angel:* "Thus, through the death of his brother, and the sickness that was rooted in his own flesh, Eugene came to know a deeper and darker wisdom than he had ever known before" (p. 587).

This release from his youthful fear of death causes Eugene to think of himself as something unique. He believes that the conquering of his great grief at its very height has made him a new person—a genius, he thinks. From reciting the names of literary greats, military leaders, political emancipators, religious martyrs, he tries to classify himself. The fear of physical death can no longer hold him immobile. After his desperate fantasies conceived to escape from self, he faces the future: "Over that final hedge, he thought, not death, as I once believed—but new life—and new lands" (p. 593).

At this point Eugene benefits further from his father's example. His father had lived a kind of death-in-life since he was unable to escape from the family trap. Eugene must escape this kind of spiritual death that continues to threaten him, for he feels that this death-in-life builds a wall separating him from the new lands. He will not allow himself to sink into the buried life. He must step out of the psychic grave his family lives in (pp. 599–626).

This new life he finds when his mother agrees to send him to Harvard. He dies to one life hoping to be born again. But this escape paradoxically resembles another death, for it leads to another isolation. Yet he now feels willing to face his destiny alone. If this struggle to survive proves fruitless, he will, if necessary, endure spiritual death.

At the end of the novel Ben's ghost advises Eugene to make the voyage to a new life. From facing isolation he may learn that it will bring life to him. Grasping this hopeful vision, Eugene answers:

> I have lost the blood that fed me; I have died the hundred deaths that lead to life. By the slow thunder of drums, the flare of dying cities, I have come to the dark place. . . . And now prepare, my soul, for the beginning hunt. I will plumb seas stranger than those haunted by the Albatross (p. 625).

The buried life is over, and the angel can look homeward.

In addition to the direct narrative, the gradual maturing of Eugene is revealed by two stylistic devices culminating at the death of Ben, the point of Eugene's greatest maturity.

The first device is the persistent references to various kinds of death in preparation for a death scene. It is used in a pattern of association often enough to seem typical of Wolfe's earlier response to the experience. Prior to a death scene, such associations appear abundantly. Then there is a lull in which these references sharply decline. After this lull the scene of dying is narrated. This stylistic pattern occurs for all the death scenes in *Look Homeward, Angel* except the final one, the death of Ben. This break in method suggests the shift in Eugene's point of view.

Three instances of Wolfe's strict adherence to his pattern should suffice: Grover's death, the death of the young prostitute Lily, and the revelation that Oliver Gant is dying of cancer. The prototype is the preparation for Grover's death. From incessant references to death, the subject becomes a leitmotif in the poetic themes of the novel. It is mentioned twenty-three times in the first thirty-five pages, including four euphemisms for death like "the gaunt spectre" (pp. 4–35 *passim*). Then occurs the lull of twenty-two pages. The associations with death are allowed to seethe in Oliver Gant's mind. He howls when he learns Eliza plans to leave him since it reminds him of his isolation after his first wife's death. He fears another isolation. Then Grover's death occurs. Although the word "death" is used twice during the four pages narrating Grover's death, it always occurs outside of Eugene's thoughts.

The same pattern leads up to the description of the prostitute's death (LHA, pp. 265–69). Since the pattern of Grover's death is developed in a span of fifty-seven pages, the same number is considered in examining this second pattern. In this group of pages, the first thirty-five refer to death fourteen times. The next twenty-two pages have only one mention of death. Again the lull is conspicious. It is also significant that during this lull the horror of isolation is once more emphasized by Gant's knowing that his children are growing up and leaving him. Immediately following this lull, Gant is told of the death of Lily Reed, a young prostitute he knows. Dreading his own impotence and his sure death, Gant sells his cherished Carrara angel to be used for marking her grave.

The familiar pattern appears prior to the pronouncement that Gant is dying of cancer: references to death are often repeated (pp. 316–58 *passim*) followed by the characteristic lull that prepares for the revelation of death. The pattern here is only slightly modified, the lull with a single mention of death being only twelve pages long (pp. 358–70). The climax arrives when the surgeon tells his assistant to close the wound because Gant is dying of cancer. No details of a death scene are given. The impact of the doctor's announcement is sufficient. Eugene has sensed his father was dying. Further allusions to it would be artistically and psychologically superfluous.

A secondary device that reveals Wolfe's involvement with the theme of death is his use of poetic allusions to the extent that they become refrains. This method of allusion appears later in the novel than the "death" pattern and is used after it. Primarily it serves only to underscore Eugene's experiences with death, which the first pattern has shown.

In the early chapters the references to literary works mainly record the desultory reading habits of Eugene or his father: popular songs and hymns, Stoddard's lectures, *The Iliad,* and *The Odyssey.* After Eugene's fourteenth year, however, the allusions are no longer only records of reading habits and tastes. They begin to appear in a stream-of-consciousness style as Eugene's thoughts and speech suggest the death theme or the life-in-death motif dominating his growth toward maturity (pp. 324–411 *passim*).

This device appears most effectively in Chapters XXIV through XXVII. Here Eugene's reading begins to work its way into his conversation and into his subconscious thoughts. Eugene has read heavily in the Romantics (Coleridge, Keats, Wordsworth, Burns, Scott), the Elizabethans (Shakespeare, Jonson, Dekker), and the Metaphysical and Cavalier poets (Donne, Herrick, Carew, Suckling) (pp. 309–15 *passim*). Constant allusions to these poets and their poems show not only how thoroughly he has absorbed his reading but also his preoccupation with death. The allusions forebode the death of Ben Gant, pointing to the climactic scene in the novel with artistic power. The most recurrent allusions in this section are to Ben Jonson and to Robert Herrick's "Ode to Ben Jonson" (pp. 310–44 *passim*). The other poets alluded to more than once are Keats ("Ode to a Nightingale") and Coleridge ("The Rime of the Ancient Mariner"). Both of these references are of course particularly appropriate to the death, death-in-life themes. Poetic allusions appear singularly effective when they occur in the chapter immediately following Ben's death. The references become especially frequent to Keats's "La Belle Dame Sans Merci" and Shelley's "Ode to the West Wind" (pp. 561, 562). These literary echoes serve to intensify the life-in-death, death-in-life thoughts occupying Eugene's mind at the time. Phrasings from these poems course through his mind as Ben's death dominates the scene. These echoes from the emotions of Keats and Shelley richly convey the turbulence and insecurity of the other Gants. Although they have no literary sophistication, they are probed by Eugene's stream-of-consciousness refrain. Wolfe suggests through Eugene the aura hovering over the Gants, the aura of death that will direct their future.

The two devices of using the pattern involving references to death and repeating poetic passages concerning death generally serve to suggest the vestiges of immaturity and the approaching maturity in Eugene's thinking. Overlapping the poetic allusions is the "death" pattern. But the older Eugene becomes, the less occupied he appears to be with the fear of an approaching death. Following the doctor's announcement of Oliver Gant's fatal illness, there is a conspicuous absence of any reference to death. In effect this section of one hundred and five pages is another lull. Following it, the language of the novel becomes filled with "death." The story returns to Gant's pain and his ominous death. Also Ben's existence becomes a virulent sickness; his dark angel hovers above him ceaselessly.

In the meantime, Eugene has gained some maturity. He has gone off to school, has loved both physically and spiritually, carefully and carelessly, has become acutely aware of the lost years, the lost faces. "And there was sorrow in his heart for what would come no more" (p. 474). This maturing process, giving Eugene some of the perspective suggested by the evidence of his intellectual sophistication in his literary responses, occurs during this one-hundred-five-page lull preceding the depiction of Gant's pain, itself a prelude to Ben's death. Only after these experiences is Eugene more able to face life's problems. The psychological involvement with death becomes less evident, and the "death" pattern is not used significantly when Bob Sterling, Eugene's roommate, dies. Eugene is affected by Sterling's death but he does not ponder it. It is almost irrelevant artistically except as a signal of Ben's death.

Although Eugene's feelings about death appear repeatedly through the pages preparing for Ben's death, which Eugene is not sure he can face, Wolfe has revealed Eugene's increasing strength of character. For in the summer before Ben's death Eugene has had experiences that helped him mature even more than his loves and college life have. Alone in Norfolk and Richmond, he has lived through a self-imposed isolation and survived. He has thoughts of his own death during this survival and it has toughened him (LHA, pp. 521–22).

He can face Ben's death not just to fit Wolfe's stylistic scheme of varying intensities in feeling but to discover for himself the real strength he has gained. His response to Ben's death is a final test of character. Wolfe shows the shift in Eugene both narratively and stylistically. Eugene is no longer the child who mourned the loss of physical things and shuddered at ". . . the high horror of death and oblivion, the decomposition of life" (p. 101). He leaves his childhood in which he had mourned that men left nothing behind them to keep their memories alive—something physical, imperishable, like a tombstone. Now he knows that his father's tombstones are perishable. He also outgrows the craning of his neck and the spastic jerks of his foot lifted suddenly in moments of anguish. The spirit is stirred but not the body. He can look on his early thoughts of death as stupid fantasties (p. 331). Wolfe points to this developing maturity through the episodes of his novel and two overlapping stylistic devices. As Eugene increases in maturity, the complex patterns of emotional outbursts lessen in number and intensity. After the final death scene Eugene is ready to face life because he has faced death. He has risen from the life that buried him and only appeared to be his real home. He must now search for another father, another brother, another life. This search Wolfe never completed, for it continues as a recurring theme throughout his novels. Eugene in *Of Time and the River* and George Webber in *The Web and the Rock* and *You Can't Go Home Again* discover it is spiritual death that is to be feared more than physical death. In *Of Time and the River* Eugene is seen as struggling to realize spiritual, creative life. Buffeted about for a long time, he finally begins to understand what creativity really is. Then instead of being controlled, he controls. As the record of *Look Homeward, Angel* closes, Wolfe's hero begins this new struggle in utter isolation. He has only the will to survive.

II

Of Time and the River picks up the story of Eugene where *Look Homeward, Angel* left it, but it is more than a sequel. In it the idea of an American saga developing in Wolfe's mind begins to unfold. Much that he wrote during the time of his working on the material that became *Of Time and the River* does not appear in that novel but was published as his last two novels. With a saga in mind, Wolfe wrote various sections of *The Web and the Rock* and *You Can't Go Home Again* months or years apart. The gaps in chronology were so obvious, however, that editing the manuscripts was no problem. Edward Aswell compiled the completed sequences not used for *Of Time and the River* to make two novels.[2] The body of material comprising the last three novels should be considered as a single piece of work. Although the stylistic patterns that emphasize the psychological maturing of Eugene in *Look Homeward, Angel* are absent in Wolfe's later work, the same themes persist through his last three books: the concern with death or isolation, the struggle for maturity, and the search for self-awareness and creativity. Wolfe's later writing expands with thoroughness and depth the problems dealt with on a smaller scale in his first novel.

Since only vestiges of his early stylistic devices exist in his later work, it is futile to attempt any close study of such details as literary refrains developing the theme of death, but enough key phrases do run throughout his last novels to suggest the psychological condition of the protagonist. When Wolfe began writing this material, he said he was haunted by the ". . . Idea of the river—of Time and Change" (LTW, p. 282). *Of Time and the River* is filled with the evolution of Eugene. Epiphany-like outbursts mark each climax in Eugene's progress toward maturity, accompanied by a refrain appearing only at these moments: "flows by us, by us, by us to the sea" (OTAR, pp. 333, 510, 860), or a variation of it, "earth is flowing by us in the darkness" (p. 34), or "the dark and secret river, full of strange time, is forever flowing by us to the sea" (p. 156).

The protagonist's escape from death to life becomes enhanced in *The Web and the Rock* and *You Can't Go Home Again* with the use of the word "fury." After *Look Homeward, Angel* Eugene (or

George) consciously struggles with his problem so that he seems less a victim of circumstances. His search for meaning begins to have some direction. He feels an inner fury to realize his full creative life. This fury replaces the wind-driven ghost of *Look Homeward, Angel,* where it haunted and stifled Eugene. Through his fury to free himself from all that stands in the way of his creative development, the protagonist becomes conscious of a vitality that inspires. This fervid intensity in Wolfe appears in such phrases as "the fury of creation" or "tormented tenement of fury" (YCGHA, pp. 20, 571).

Such lyric underlining of the hero's moods becomes less frequent in the later Wolfe. He uses other means to point to emotional crises. As his protagonists become more capable of controlling their emotions, the lyrical patterns are less evident. This movement toward emotional maturity develops from the elaborate repetitions of key words and phrases in *Look Homeward, Angel,* through the refrains marking climaxes in *Of Time and the River* to the peripheral lyricism of phrasing in the last two novels, where Wolfe relies more on dramatic episode and character in action than on highly charged phraseology to gain sympathy for his hero.

In the later novels the highpoints of the hero's growth as indicated by his reactions to death, physical or psychological, occur in the deaths of his father and Aunt Maw and in the breaking up of friendships that mark his continual emergence into a life of creative independence, whose source finally becomes mankind, not man.

Eugene (or George) discovers his real identity from the values he learns through his friendships with Francis Starwick (*Of Time and the River*), Esther Jack (*The Web and the Rock* and *You Can't Go Home Again*) and Foxhall Edwards (*You Can't Go Home Again*).

In *Of Time and the River* Eugene arrives at Harvard anxious to do something creative. Most frightening is the memory of the admonition Ben's ghost gave him to escape from a death-in-life. Shortly before meeting Starwick, Eugene visits his father at a Baltimore hospital, where he shows his lack of emotion when saying good-bye to the old man. His father is already dead and is to be avoided. His presence is disgusting. The pity he feels at the moment is but the garbage of emotion. It offends him. No good can come from it. Eugene wants to escape the memory of Death and Pity, which follow him like two swift horsemen. At all costs he must drive out the death so deeply imbedded in his life. At this moment comes Starwick, who can free him from death.

The new life Starwick offers seems to be able to satisfy Eugene's hunger because his friend appears to have the creative power that Eugene admires. Eugene even begins to exchange his crude, explosive words for Starwick's studied phrases. The adventure with Starwick contrasts with the futility Eugene felt when his family had derided his intellectual efforts. He believes he has found someone to help him as he embarks like another Faust on a search for knowledge.

The stimulus of the friendship causes Eugene to get out of himself. He notices kinds of people he had never noticed before. He meditates on the deathlessness of men. For the first time he begins to see himself in perspective by trying to understand others. This escape from self helps him see "a life more happy, fortunate, golden, and complete than any life before had ever been" (OTAR, p. 152).

When his father dies, Eugene finds that Starwick's influence has given him new strength. Starwick's presence has helped him escape from the death-in-life of Gant. But Eugene's relief also derives from his empathy with Gant when his release comes. He feels the lonesomeness and brevity of man's life. The father has left to the son the memory of his stonecutter's hands, his means of creativity. Eugene believes that if his father's creations are not remembered, perhaps his creating force will be. Gant will stay alive as long as Eugene remembers him. The son no longer fears physical death as much as total death: death of all creative, spiritual power. His father's death reinforces Eugene's determination to create. To Eugene his father's stifled creative urge has turned into the cancer that consumed him. The son must escape from duplicating his father's failure.

Eugene returns to Starwick believing that their friendship will bring the great creative moment. The friends seem to grow together in mind and spirit. For a time Eugene loses his sympathy with the people of the city. The control exercised in coping with his father's death has exhausted his ability to develop the social awareness that Starwick's friendship first stimulated. The people now become but "mongrel faces" (p. 595). Their ugliness is a kind of death; it is disgusting and evil. He knows it exists but he feels it holds no promise for him. Only Starwick's friendship promises new life. Inspiration is more likely to come, Eugene believes, from Starwick's easy tones than from the City-Voice.

When Starwick leaves him, he feels a weariness of the flesh. His literature classes and casual friends leave him feeling sterile and defeated (pp. 477–78). When he goes to Europe to find Starwick, the million-footed man-swarm begins to overwhelm him again. At first he hopes for rejuvenation when he discovers Starwick, but the signs of creative death appear in Eugene's apathy and inertia. He seems to be unable to break the evil spell: psychological death threatens him. The signs appear only too similar to Ben's agonizing death from pneumonia and Gant's ever-gnawing cancer not to be recognized. But Eugene feels helpless. He does not want to break the bond that holds him to Starwick although Starwick stifles his creative enthusiasm. Eugene can exert himself to destroy the bond only when their relationship becomes physical. The ugliness of it reminds him so much of the ugliness of the physical deaths he has known that he is no longer immobilized by ignorance and fear. He has withstood Ben's death and Oliver's death. When the psychological death resulting from the collapsing friendship with Starwick becomes associated with the physically repugnant, he withstands it too. Eugene calls Starwick his enemy: the enemy of creativity. Starwick has duped him, for Starwick is not really creative. He is a dilettante, a hyper-aesthete who talks about creativity. Eugene associates his disgust for Starwick's homosexuality with his offense from his literary fraud. In every way, Starwick is a destructive force. Seeing Starwick as uncreative, Eugene can face this separation after his violence against Starwick has calmed down. Eugene is developing a stoicism in the face of death. He indulges in no lyrical outbursts or literary refrains. Controlled dialogue expresses the break in place of the narrative rhapsody accompanying Ben's death. Eugene does not even need to philosophize as he did over his father's death. The break with Starwick leads to his first real progress toward creative expression. Now he leaves Paris and goes south to Tours, where he writes driven by a burning fury of mind and heart. Starwick ironically has released him from weariness and apathy. Death, as always in Wolfe's novels, has brought life again.

The pattern of eager acceptance, admiration amounting to worship, and disillusioned rejection established in the relationship with Starwick becomes the model for the later major friendships of Wolfe's hero. The world of Esther Jack is a completely new world for George Webber. It offers him both artistic creativity and mature love. But as usual the young man does not distinguish between the promise of his imagination and the reality of his experience. Only later can he admit the difference between the imagined worth of Esther's world and its actual value. Eugene had first met her in *Of Time and the River,* but it is George who continues the affair in *The Web and the Rock* and *You Can't Go Home Again.* From the moment he sees her, he idolizes her. He feels that she will become all things to him: peace, love, hope, life. As he had done with Starwick, he sees incorrectly or exaggerates what he sees. He has indeed entered a lotusland. Yet at times the orderliness of Esther's life leads him to carry out plans he had forgotten to fulfill in the heat of composition at Tours, for she believes in honest work well done. Although George sees other Starwicks in the shams of Esther's world, her being able to create in spite of their phoniness gives George courage. Above all, Esther has abilities that George desires: the sensitivity to notice worth in the simplest things, and the insight to see the worthlessness of most complex appearances. George's more mature response to Esther appears through dramatic dialogue contrasting to the still immature lyric enthusiasm Eugene had used when he first saw her (pp. 908–11). Together with this restraint goes the playing down of the protagonist. Wolfe frequently presents Esther in her own right without giving George's responses to her. His abandoning poetic rhapsody for dramatic objectivity reaches a climax in Book II of *You Can't Go Home Again*: in "The World that Jack Built" George speaks only three or four lines and is seldom referred to. He is attending a party at Esther's to discover for certain what the other people of her world are. Here he remains offstage. On stage are Esther's friends who show themselves as the death of the creative spirit. The reader comes to know them directly and can approve George's judgment.

At the peak of his need for love and understanding, George is driven to curse, revile, and mistreat Esther. Her world is too peopled with uncreative frauds for him to dare linger in it. Her love is not enough for him. His need for creative isolation kills their love. But from the start there have been premonitions of danger in Wolfe's protagonists. Wolfe has shown that Eugene sensed his father's death, and early in the Starwick relationship he had a flash of intuition suggesting something wrong between them. Yet characteristically Wolfe's young hero is too anxious to explore every new experience to listen to any warning. Early in his affair with Esther, George senses danger ahead: "And yet, with all his love for her, he had felt for one brief moment the cold and chilling shadow of that ring around his heart" (TWAR, p. 467).

The cold ring of uncreativity, of death-in-life, he feared vaguely from the beginning. Eager to love, he forges ahead. Even while she helps him write, he feels death hovering over his partly finished book: "These evidences of the unfinished book were like epitaphs of dissolution, tombstones to ruin and distintegration" (p. 457). He gradually begins to understand that Esther is not spiritually akin to him. Esther's sure successes as a painter cannot teach him how to re-discover and re-exploit his genius. Without this life-giving power to grow, the imaginative writer will die. The genius of the poet, George feels, "can bring death to men as surely as it brings them life" (p. 463). Unless he can learn to use it, it will "rend him like a tiger" (p. 463).

The irony is now clear. Esther is life but potentially death. As she fulfills him, she is creativity. As she threatens death, she must be rejected. But the dilemma Wolfe had faced through Eugene in the Starwick episode has a new aspect now: Esther is not physically repulsive as Starwick finally became. George fights the idea that her attractiveness is death for him. His confusion appears in his violence toward her, and he uses substitute words for death when he curses her as a Jew and an adulteress. He fears the break that will bring death to their love. Until he can reconcile himself to creative isolation, he cannot bring himself to break with Esther. He must learn how life can be regained.

George tries to reduce his love for Esther to physical ugliness, for he feels her way of life performs a monstrous "castration of the spirit" (p. 539). When his quarrels with her only show him how inept he is at facing the most painful death of spirit he has known, he realizes that he cannot transfer his dissatisfaction to her. His un-rest within himself must be faced. If he wants peace he must try to break away: he must "tear and strip her very memory from his blood, his brain, his heart" (p. 614).

He believes he will discover a spiritual renewal if he goes to Germany. His trip there becomes a search for a resurrection of the creative impulses he has lost. In Germany, "a kind of second home-land of his spirit" (p. 622), he may save himself by understanding the furies within himself. Perhaps this new land and its people will satisfy his cravings for emotional fulfillment that single friendships had failed to provide. George now develops a more mature social awareness than Eugene had felt in *Of Time and the River*. But he still idealizes mankind as "the whole family of the earth, all men living [who] seem friendly and familiar to him" (p. 631). George needs a painful self-awakening before he can build a concept of mankind that will stand where personal friendships fall. His free-dom from an oversensitive self comes as the result of a fight he gets into at the *Oktoberfest*. When George wakes up in a hospital with his face and head battered, the shock of physical violence jars him into the deeper discovery of self that he had been seeking. While looking into a mirror, George finds that Body and Spirit take turns discussing his new knowledge. Again, physical repulsion is associated with spiritual rebirth in Wolfe's hero. George has learned from his rough treatment in the fight that he had been protecting himself from the abuses of the world because he had thought his artistic soul too fine for it. He sees how callow he has been. Only "by losing self in something larger than itself" (TWAR, p. 692) can he find a place in a man's world. George recognizes the maturity of his vision: it seems to him that most men have known the wisdom of loving life and their fellow men and have hated the death-in-life (p. 693). Like Antaeus, he has become invincible by touching earth and being revived.

From a last meeting with Esther he learns that her world offers only the death-in-life he feared. He cannot live among her friends. Even his love for her will not conquer the sterility her world threatens. He believes that a "hollow pyramid of a false social structure had been erected and sustained upon a base of common mankind's blood and sweat and agony" (YCGHA, pp. 320–21). His break with Esther becomes possible since he is thoroughly repelled by this society symbolized in Piggy Logan's dummy circus. He can break the personal bond with Esther when it becomes associated with a false, sterile, brutal society. Too much of her world is peopled with the physically repulsive: homosexuals, nymphomaniacs, pederasts, charlatans in general. These frauds are his deadly enemies.

Although this episode at Esther's presents her friends with dramatic objectivity, Wolfe allows George a moment of meditation on this death-in-life: he cannot belong to two worlds. The world of the artist and the world of fashion do not mix. He must forsake one to gain the other (pp. 261–62). He changes this counterfeit coin for honest gain.

George's introspection reveals his pain at parting. This new maturity in George is reflected in Wolfe's attention to the distress of Esther. The break causes suffering described in the poetic terms of Ben's death in *Look Homeward, Angel*. Esther feels that her world is filled with a roaring wind, drowning out all sanity and life. She too feels a death of the spirit. Yet her separation from George appears only another of the inexorable events through which Wolfe shows the gradual maturing of the artist.

The last crucial friendship for George is with Foxhall Edwards. This relation, Wolfe shows, is in some respects the most spiritual one for George: Fox's spirit is George's. Or so it seems at the outset when Wolfe's hero starts a new probing of the self. The pattern of quick acceptance, exaggeration of value, and ultimate rejection is repeated. The elation in the beginning is intense. As Germany is George's spiritual fatherland, so Fox is his spiritual father. Fox seems to understand him as a friend and helps give him the fame he wants as an artist. When he begins to associate with Fox, his intuition tells him the relation is right, for each man without quite knowing it had "performed an act of spiritual adoption" (p. 437). Through his heroes Wolfe has always sought this identity of spirit. Here the giving of the self to another appears more rational since it is done with a greater awareness of the individual's need and of his relationship to society.

Wolfe significantly describes the intellectual perceptions in his hero as a prelude to the full development of the friendship between George and Fox. George philosophizes about mankind. Although man can be base, obscene, cruel, and treacherous, he remains noble through his love of life. This power binds men together. It creates man's religions, which, George believes, are the sources of faith in the eternal life of the spirit (p. 436). Now that he has recognized it, he is trying to find a way to keep his spirit alive. The fury that drove him from Esther was not a false personal concept. George rationalizes that this drive is common to all men. Man's spirit wills to live in spite of everything. Seldom do men deliberately ally themselves with death. The fear of death, he thinks, often leads to the development of philosophies and religions that try to establish theories regarding the essences of life. Those whose fury does not direct them to such an aegis find that the fury uncontrolled will drive them mad unless it finds some identity that fulfills it. Spirit must meet spirit.

Having avoided the usual shields for his spirit, George seeks his own. In Foxhall Edwards he believes he has found it. Similar to the twofold decision George made at the Munich hospital before his break with Esther, his solution now involves both seeing mankind's worth and identifying himself with it as well as concluding that ideally his spirit can be fully realized only through another congenial spirit. But George cannot yet entirely identify himself with mankind, for he continues to see this step as an idea, a device, a means to an end. Only after the failure of his friendship with Fox is he ready to let himself accept mankind as the source of creative power and realization. From his disappointment with individuals, he gradually develops this intuitive insight similar to the resolution of Goethe's philosophy. It is just the reverse of Jonathan Swift's philosophy: the rationalist hates mankind but loves the individual. The intuitive poet decries the individual and admires mankind.

When George turns to Fox he hopes he may be able to understand himself fully. Through this friendship he may escape the loneliness that has seemed to be his fate. In Fox he finds release from solitude. The scene concerning the newspaper report of a Mr. Green who has killed himself by jumping from the Admiral Francis Drake Hotel shows that Fox, like Eugene and the younger George, is capable of expansive ramblings on the subject of death. Fox reveals himself through a display of feeling in a stream-of-consciousness filled with catalogs of American hotels and cities: "It didn't happen in the Penn-Pitt at Pittsburgh, nor the Phil-Penn at Philadelphia, nor the York-Albany at Albany, nor the Hudson-Troy at Troy, nor the Libya-Ritz at Libya Hill. . . ." (p. 462) Fox reveals his inner self to George: he ponders deeply on the symbolic meaning of death. The death of this Mr. Green makes Fox feel that any man's death symbolizes all men's deaths. What had Mr. Green thought, felt, acted, expressed? Did he fulfill himself? Was his death a final settlement?

In a lengthy monologue Fox meditates on man. He feels that death is the only way people can gain life, status, fame, or whatever they are seeking. To him Mr. Green's suicide is an act of vitality: through death he has become a man. As one death symbolizes all deaths, so the life after this death symbolizes his conviction that any death becomes also a potential life-giver. Mr. Green has been able "to identify a single spot of all our general Nothingness with the unique passion, the awful terror and the dignity of Death" (pp. 481–82).

The two outstanding aspects of Fox's personality, then, are his understanding that death gives life and so must be faced philosophically, and his knowledge that nondescript humanity, like a Mr. C. Green, has an inherent dignity. Fox also sees through the dilettantes, the liars, the aesthetes, the despised critics, the pseudo-artists. George admires Fox's "burning crystal of the brain" (p. 484) that allows him to have intuitive insight into people. Fox sees, feels, senses as George does. Of the three outstanding friends, only Fox understands the ambivalence of death, the value of the common man, the blinding flash of intuitive conviction. George believes that Fox sees life in full perspective, keeping a proper balance between the physical and the spiritual. Having the wisdom of Ecclesiastes, Fox knows man's birth is his misfortune, but Fox will not fold his hands or consume his flesh. While the end of all is vanity, he still says, "Get work done" (p. 493). Fox does not hate life, yet he does not hug it like a lover. Death would not tear life from him, for Fox has no desperate clinging to mortality. He realizes the vexed, grieved, unfathomed adventure and knows death as a friend.

But George's friendship with Fox, like the rest, is doomed to fail. The break comes over George's altering his ideas about the worth of American culture. Fox remains disappointed with the progress of America: he thinks America is intellectually dishonest, too proud, too lacking in self respect. America holds little promise for Fox. In contrast, George's allegiance is given more and more to the American way of life because it furnishes him worthwhile subjects to write about. George's faith in America cannot long abide Fox's cynicism. George has evolved to a point where he has something to say about humanity that Fox does not accept. The differences in their values make their friendship impossible on an ideological basis. Yet George does not want to break off the friendship entirely. Although he could disparage Starwick and Esther, he does not disparage Fox. He still hopes to continue the friendship at a distance even though he no longer wants Fox as editor or fellow thinker. George has been able to think his way through the dichotomies of this friendship and resolve them in a new unity: his release of Fox is the final dramatic freedom from the strong bonds individuals have held for him, and he replaces individuals with a practical faith that will not let him down. His rejection of Fox is only partial, however, for George still needs personal friendship, but it must remain subordinate to his new ideal.

As the conflict between the men becomes apparent, George decides to go to Germany because he believes such a trip would be particularly valuable to him now. Maybe he can recapture the old magic. But he knows this trip may be his last: he knows that Germany's creative potential has turned into destructive reality. George's painfully growing ideas about the spiritual worth of mankind were first given direction in Germany, so he feels he must go. Perhaps even now, in a land infected with the cancer of Naziism, some of the spirit of Goethe may remain. If the Germany he knew has died, he must witness its death. He needs to test his maturity by facing reality.

In Germany he discovers sickness underlying the pageantry of the Olympic games. Germany has the collective might that George wants to understand, for he feels it derives from an inner strength, but he fears its power to destroy. He recognizes that he can admire the strength of this society but must shun its ultimate goal, for he sees the psychic wound of a great people. His feelings of tragedy cut deep when he reflects that in Goethe a world spirit was made articulate: it knew no boundary lines of nation, politics, race, or religion (YCGHA, p. 631).

George's talk with his friend Franz Heilig reveals the depth of Germany's spiritual corruption. In his confused mind, Heilig wants the Nazis destroyed, for they may destroy him like the Communists, the Chamber of Commerce, and American capitalism, but he wants to destroy the Jews. The quick, tension-charged language dramatically portrays the emotional confusion of Heilig. He can think of Germany only as the destroyer. George must leave, for Germany is no place for the creator.

So George transfers the promise that was Germany to the promise of America. Germany is death, America life. The only spirit that George can now identify himself with in any full sense is the creative future of America. The identity with Fox is weakened because Fox can see no worth in a world spirit. George resolves that he must move beyond Fox as he has left Germany and Esther, as Eugene left Starwick, Oliver Gant, his home and family. He has lost brother and father; he cannot go home again. George has become mature enough to break off his intimacy with Fox before violence occurs, for George has equated Fox's lack of faith in mankind with conditions in Germany. Although Fox's attitude is never likely to manifest itself in premeditated destruction of mankind, it contains the seeds of destruction and death. From Fox's rejection of humanity can come no revival of spirit. George must reject this sort of death for it allows no fuller expression of spirit, no resurrection of creative impulse. George's conviction, coming from the depths of his mature experience, gains for him the creative isolation he has been seeking. As artist George realizes he must depend only on himself.

George's rejection of his closeness to Fox comes at last. This step is the climax of the artist's increasing restraint in style, growth in dramatic skill, and a concern with people not as individuals but as part of the great flow of humanity. George can finally be true to the creative fury in him, for it is this power that inspires mankind: the way to find America is to find it in his own heart, which he believes is now the common heart of humanity.

His mature vision even has the strength to encompass the death of the lost lives in America. The life that America fashioned will lead to destruction, Wolfe believes, because self-interest has damaged democrarcy. But to Wolfe the people of America are "deathless, undiscovered, and immortal, and must live" (YCGHA, p. 741). Thomas Wolfe through Eugene and George has shown the great discovery for mankind and for himself as artist: "To lose the earth you know, for greater knowing; to lose the life you have, for greater life; to leave the friends you loved, for greater loving; to find a land more kind than home, more large than earth" (p. 743).

The struggle of Wolfe's protagonists against death ends in victory. The unreasonable world becomes reasonable, hope replaces despair, direction replaces drifting, drama replaces lyricism, psychological objectivity replaces hyper-emotional subjectivity; egoism is supplanted by social consciousness. The sheer counting of life's quantity and number appears trivial. The details of the fascinating flux are no longer endless isolated phenomena but continuous symbols leading man to an understanding of the essence of the flux. To discover his essence, man must move with nature on the everflowing river of time. The artist lives only when he is constantly discovering and rediscovering himself.

Through his protagonists Thomas Wolfe reveals his own maturity after progressing through several stages of feeling toward the attainment of a social ideal. Each step in his emotional development resulted from his becoming less temperamental in responding to environment and friendship. By cleaving instinctively to the American scene, he overcame the disillusionment that plagued his relationships with individuals. Wolfe's responses to his experiences show an achievement of maturity that rejects disillusionment and despair. His concept of death places his fiction outside the stream of contemporary naturalistic fiction, which often, as in Hemingway, cannot rise above the idea of death as nothing but an unreasonable wound, the culmination of an irrational existence.[3] Wolfe has faith even in death since his experience has taught him that it offers a release from an outworn phase of life to a new height of spiritual promise.

Notes

1. See W. P. Albrecht, "The Titles of *Look Homeward, Angel: A Story of the Buried Life*," *Modern Language Quarterly*, XI (1950), 50–57.
For references in the text to the titles of Wolfe's writings, the following abbreviations will be used:

LHA: *Look Homeward, Angel* (New York: Charles Scribner's Sons, 1929).
OTAR: *Of Time and the River* (New York: Charles Scribner's Sons, 1935).

TWR: *The Web and the Rock* (New York: Harper and Brothers, 1939).

YCGHA: *You Can't Go Home Again* (New York: Harper and Brothers, 1940).

TWLM: *Thomas Wolfe's Letters to His Mother, Julia Elizabeth Wolfe*, ed. John Skally Terry (New York: Charles Scribner's Sons, 1951).

LTW: *The Letters of Thomas Wolfe*, ed. Elizabeth Nowell (New York: Charles Scribner's Sons, 1956).

2. Edward C. Aswell, "A Note on Thomas Wolfe," in *Thomas Wolfe, The Hills Beyond* (New York: Harper and Brothers, 1941), pp. 370–76.

3. See Frederick J. Hoffman, "No Beginning and No End: Hemingway and Death," *Essays in Criticism*, III (1953), 73–84.

Louis D. Rubin, Jr.

4. Thomas Wolfe: Time and the South

THOMAS WOLFE was born in Asheville, North Carolina in 1900. His origins and upbringing were squarely lower middle class. All the other writers of the modern South came from families that were among the cultural leaders of the community, the Southern squire-archy, with its antebellum roots. Not so Wolfe; his father was a stonemason from Pennsylvania, a man who worked with his hands and was proud of it—though, as his son several times reminds us, he always wore a starched collar and tie on the job, with an apron pulled up over his good clothes to protect them from the dust. His mother's people, the Westalls, were a numerous mountain family; many of its members had come down to the town at about the time of the Civil War. They were "new people," and had no strong ties with the prewar Southern aristocracy. Some of them grew quite wealthy during the late nineteenth and early twentieth centuries. Thomas Wolfe was the first member of his immediate family to go to college; he wanted to go to the University of Virginia or to Vander-bilt—it is interesting to speculate on what might have happened had he been sent to the latter school—but his father insisted that he attend the state university in Chapel Hill.

When we look at Eugene Gant's childhood as pictured in *Look Homeward, Angel,* what is most striking about it is its cultural impoverishment. There were a few books in the house—of poems, the obvious ones, for his father liked to declaim sentimental verse—but of literary and artistic interest there was almost none, save perhaps his sister's ambition to be a successful popular singer. A scene in *Look Homeward, Angel* describes how Eugene Gant, inspired by the tercentenary of the death of William Shakespeare, affixes a portrait of the poet to the wall, scrawling under it Ben Jonson's words, "My Shakespeare, rise!" He is tortured about it thereafter by the family: "Will My Shakespeare pass the biscuits?" and so forth. Despite the humor, however, an element of pathos is apparent in the episode. It shows us something of the kind of understanding a young man of Wolfe's temperament and interests must have received from his family.

Mrs. Wolfe ran a boardinghouse, a sprawling, cheaply constructed affair with bare, calcimined walls and poorly lighted halls. Jonathan Daniels describes how Wolfe's body lay in state in the boardinghouse after his death in 1938. The coffin, he writes,

> filled half the front room, which was hall also, of the old boarding-house. Above it there were long cracks in the yellow plaster ceiling. He was home.
>
> "Those melancholy cracks in the yellow plaster looking down at him!" the woman who was his friend said. "I know he fled from those cracks, and there he lay helpless while they triumphed over him."

The observation was an apt one; Wolfe's childhood was a time of much ugliness, and sometimes the depiction of Altamont that we read in *Look Homeward, Angel* is as bleak, as barren, as unlovely as any description in the work of the Midwestern naturalistic novelists such as Dreiser and Anderson. Eugene Gant's career, no less than Thomas Wolfe's, was a search for loveliness, for aesthetic joy. He dreamed of the shining city beyond the mountains, where all would be radiant and beautiful. In 1923 he wrote from Harvard to his mother, about the plays he was going to write:

> What I shall try to get into [people's] dusty, little pint-measure minds is that a full belly, a good automobile, paved streets, and so on, do not make them one whit better or finer,—that there is beauty in this world,—beauty even in this wilderness of ugliness and provincialism that is at present our country, beauty and spirit which will make us men instead of cheap Board of Trade Boosters, and blatant pamphleteers. . . .

The life that Eugene Gant knows as he grows up, from his childhood to the moment when he prepares to leave Altamont for the golden city, involves drunkenness, violence, drabness, pain, penury, death. His recoil from the ugliness of so much of his environment is into himself; by his twelfth year, we are told, he has learned to "project mechanically, before the world, an acceptable counterfeit of himself which would protect him from intrusion." He is sent out early to earn money, first by selling magazines, then by delivering newspapers in the early morning on the Niggertown route. His mother is preoccupied with real estate; his father, grown old and sick, engages in periodic violent drinking bouts from which he staggers home, reeling and cursing.

Sent to a private school, Eugene comes under the protection of the wife of the principal, who mothers him and reads poetry to him. It is an oasis of beauty in a wilderness of drabness and pain: "Against the bleak horror of [the boardinghouse], against the dark road of pain and death down which the great limbs of Gant had already begun to slope, against all the loneliness and imprisonment of his own life which had gnawed him like hunger, these years at Leonard's bloomed like golden apples." At school he reads Wordsworth, Burns, Shakespeare, Jonson; meanwhile his father is dying, his brother Ben growing more aloof and bitter each year, his sister Helen off singing in theaters somewhere.

Yet set against the cultural impoverishment of family life and the town, the barrenness of the boardinghouse, is the outdoor world, the mountains that ringed Altamont, nature, the seasons. This aspect, largely missing in the novels of the Midwestern naturalists, is abundantly present in Wolfe. Frequent episodes are given over to the description of natural beauty, the coming and going of the seasons in the Carolina mountains: "Spring lay abroad through all the garden of this world. Beyond the hills the land bayed out to other hills, to golden cities, to rich meadows, to deep forests, to the sea. Forever and ever." In nature, and through his imagination, Eugene escaped from "the dim fly-specked lights, the wretched progress about the house in search of warmth, Eliza untidily wrapped in an old sweater, a dirty muffler, a cast-off man's coat." In the twenty-fourth chapter of *Look Homeward, Angel*, Eugene walks downtown. It is a humorous chapter, quite unlike the bleak naturalistic depictions of wretched prairie towns by Dreiser, Anderson, and Lewis. The portrait is done not in harshness and viciousness, but in affection and joy for the people and places seen and known. We must not forget this when we discuss Wolfe's attitude toward the community in which he grew up: there is attraction and revulsion, pleasure and pain, and their often contradictory mixture is essential to an understanding of Wolfe.

Look Homeward, Angel is a chronicle novel, describing the first twenty years of Eugene Gant's life. It is dominated by the passing of time. Old Gant is dying; the family is falling apart; Eugene is growing up. Everywhere is the massive fact of change. The Gants are always in a state of turmoil. Eliza sets up a separate establishment at the boardinghouse, busies herself with real estate. Early in the novel Grover dies; much later on Ben too dies. Helen marries and leaves. Eugene goes off to college. Of stability and certainty there are almost none. The only fixed element is Eugene's own consciousness, and that too changes and expands as he becomes an adolescent and discovers sex, desire, art. Even as a child he had stared at a baby picture of himself, and "turned away sick with fear and the effort to touch, retain, grasp himself for only a moment." The novel is a series of episodes strung out in time: almost every chapter of *Look Homeward, Angel* contains in its first paragraph a reference to the flight of time and the coming and going of the seasons.

Occasionally the characters observe themselves caught in time, and can only look with awe and fear at what they see. Old Gant sells the stone angel of his youth to adorn a prostitute's grave, then steps out onto the porch of his monument shop. For an instant all life in the town square below seems suspended, "and Gant felt himself alone move deathward in a world of seemings. . . ." At the very close of the novel, when Ben has died and Eugene has completed college and is preparing to depart for the North, he stands on the porch of the shop exactly as Old Gant had done, and converses with the ghostly shade of Ben. The fountain in the square is suddenly motionless, frozen in time. The stone animals of the monuments get up and walk. All that he has seen and known parades before Eugene's unbelieving eyes. Then, in the climactic moment of the novel, he sees, coming along past the fountain carrying his load of newspapers, "himself—his son, his body, his lost and virgin flesh." His own childhood self passes by, the self lost in time, vanished down the years. Eugene calls to him. "His voice strangled in his throat; the boy had gone, leaving the memory of his bewitched and listening face turned to the hidden world. O lost!" So swiftly has it all happened, almost without his knowing it; he has grown to manhood, and whatever he once was is lost and unrecapturable. Time, chronology, change; these are the only reality he knows. Then the fountain begins splashing again, and the novel is concluded.

There are two narrative progressions in *Look Homeward, Angel*. Eugene, as we have noted, is born within the community, grows up, and prepares to leave. His father comes to the community from the outer world, becomes increasingly trapped within it, struggles vainly to escape, grows old and sick, will soon die there. This dual movement, into and away from Altamont, constitutes the structure of the novel. W. O. Gant is the frustrated mortal, the lonely American never acquiescent in his lot, who wanders from childhood onward, drifting to Altamont by chance, taking up residence there, marrying a woman he does not love deeply, fathering children, growing old and sick, and finally waiting to die. As a boy he had learned stonecutting; he wanted to carve an angel, but his skill was sufficient only for lettering monuments. He keeps a stone angel on the porch of his shop, curses it, reviles it; it is a reminder of what he wanted to do and be. Finally he sells it to adorn the grave of a prostitute. *Look Homeward, Angel* is subtitled "A story of the buried life," and Old Gant's life is buried, hidden under the debris of the years. "Where now? Where after? Where then?" Wolfe asks after Gant sells the statue and watches the town square grow still.

Important though W. O. Gant's journey is, *Look Homeward, Angel* is his son Eugene's book. It is seen through his consciousness. We do not need the foreword "To the Reader" to tell us that the point of view is that of Eugene looking backward. The meaning and unity of all the events in the novel lie in their impact on Eugene, not only the Eugene who grows up in the book, but the Eugene who is remembering it all. Eugene is the youngest son of W. O. and Eliza; as his father grows old, he grows to manhood. His early years are filled with conflict—between his father and mother; between the claims of the Woodson Street home his father owns and the boardinghouse his mother buys and operates; between Altamont's small-town ways and its ambitions to become a metropolis; between the conservative instincts of the society and the boomtown atmosphere of everyday life; between his own artistic leanings and the thoroughly middle-class attitudes toward such interests held by his family and the townsfolk.

As the novel develops, so does Eugene's gradual estrangement from family and community. The death of Ben culminates the process of Eugene's alienation from the family. His developing aesthetic and intellectual interests, his revulsion from trade and business, his growing ambition separate him from his fellow townsmen. Hatred of the ugliness and pettiness of small-town life causes him to withdraw into his own consciousness; after Ben is gone his isolation is almost complete. The Eugene who looks not townward but toward the distant hills at the conclusion of the novel is done with life in Altamont; his gaze is on the shining city, the promise of artistic achievement. He will avoid the entombment within the town that his father suffered, the emotional suffocation that was Ben's lot, for unlike them he will be saved by his genius, by the miracle of his art. (That his best art would be the recreation of life in the same town is an interesting irony, and not unimportant to what the town meant for Wolfe.)

The midway point in the process of alienation, it seems to me, is the part of the twenty-fourth chapter, mentioned previously, that describes Eugene as he leaves Leonard's school with his friend George Graves and walks into the city. Laughing and bantering as he goes, Eugene sees the people, places, and events of Altamont life as in a moment of stasis, before his own vision has become so subjective that it will permit him to see things only as they affect his private identity. It is a matchless portrayal of a small city's downtown area, one neither distorted by adult prejudgments nor overly simplified by a child's naïveté. Afterward Eugene will discover sex, and love, and death, and art, and never again will he be able to look at Altamont with so much objectivity as he does on that day. It is the halfway mark; before it comes, Eugene is a small child, still largely unseeing; afterward he is a preoccupied, self-centered adolescent, caught up in his moods and desires. Just once, in this chapter, Altamont is seen whole. Thereafter Eugene is growing away from it too rapidly to look at it for what it is.

At the close of *Look Homeward, Angel,* Wolfe's autobiographical protagonist is about to leave for the city; not for New York—his rendezvous with the greatest of American metropolises is to come later—but for Boston, and graduate study at Harvard University. Wolfe's stay there is recounted in the opening chapters of *Of Time and the River.* His ambition is to become a great playwright, and not surprisingly he soon finds the drama workshop of Professor James Graves Hatcher (George Pierce Baker) an insubstantial, artificial affair. When the New York producers who have been considering his play reject it, he stages an epic alcoholic bout while back home with his family, then departs for New York, the "enfabled rock."

New York is where Art is to be found, promise made good, love, romance, discovered, fame attained. All that has been desired supposedly will come true in the city, which in Wolfe's work takes on the mystical vision of an impossibly rich and glorious land of fulfillment. In one of his many gastronomic metaphors, Wolfe has Eugene address himself to the city and declare his desire "to devour you, golden fruit of power and love and happiness; to consume you to your sources, river and spire and rock, down to your iron roots; to entomb within our flesh forever the huge substance of your billion-footed pavements, the intolerable web and memory of dark million-visaged time." With growing excitement he races northward on the train, plunges into the streets of the metropolis, begins his life there.

Soon, however, as Wolfe is quick to point out, the golden city loses its sheen, the fabulous towers become cold and menacing, and Eugene and his creator grow to hate their minute, impoverished, laborious existence as one of the city's many millions. "What have we taken from you, protean and phantasmal shape of time?" Wolfe asks the metropolis on Eugene's behalf; "What have we remembered of your million images, of your billion weavings out of accident and number, of the mindless fury of your dateless days, the brutal stupefaction of your thousand streets and pavements? What have we seen and known that is ours forever?" He answers the query himself:

Gigantic city, we have taken nothing—not even a handful of your trampled dust—we have made no image on your iron breast and left not even the print of a heel upon your stony-hearted pavements.

The possession of all things, even the air we breathed, was held from us, and the river of life and time flowed through the grasp of our hands forever, and we held nothing for our hunger and desire except the proud and trembling moments, one by one.

Eugene rejects the metropolis; in the process he has become George Webber, a somewhat more sullen and socially conscious protagonist who nevertheless is almost as autobiographical as his predecessor. He—George-Eugene-Thomas—has experienced loneliness, love, fame, success, and finds them all barren, as forsaken and as untenable as he had once found Altamont (and its successor, Libya Hill). What the Wolfean protagonist finally attains, however, is not the social conscience that is supposedly George Webber's by the end of *You Can't Go Home Again,* so much as the entire isolation of the self. All that remains to him is the immediate response to various aspects of his experience as they impinge upon the consciousness of the protagonist, but these aspects possess no meaning except in the way they register upon the protagonist's own identity. By this I mean that for the mature George Webber the world is entirely subjective, and not only that, but entirely solipsistic. In other words, it exists only as it affects him. This is not what Wolfe *says* about George and the world; he says precisely the opposite. But dramatically, fictionally, it is what we as readers *see.* The scenes, episodes, events described by Wolfe in his fiction after *Look Homeward, Angel* are given unity and meaning only in that they occur to the same person; of themselves they contain little or no structure or form. Nor do they, in truth, change the Wolfean protagonist very much. He is much the same person at the end of *You Can't Go Home Again* as he is when he leaves for the city after *Look Homeward, Angel*—a little more sober and heavy-handed, perhaps, a little less fervent, but not really very changed. Whatever meaning finally emerges in Eugene-George-Thomas's life is no more (or less) than the knowledge that he exists, that life changes, that eventually he too will die. The rejected order of Altamont has been succeeded by no greater order, no more genial, more golden community; once Altamont has been put aside, as it has been by the time of Ben's death, only the private self remains.

Wolfe is a writer, after *Look Homeward, Angel,* of fragments. Some are glittering, some are sensuous, some are sordid, but they are are not joined in any order. The only unity is vague and for the most part rhetorical; again and again Wolfe resorts to the device of simply saying that they are "all" part of "something," but he does not know what the "something" is that they "all" constitute. "*All* the vision of the magic earth," he says, and "*all* the grime and sweat and violence of the city," just as it is "the *whole* wrought fabric of life in the city," and "*all* that we know is that having everything we yet hold nothing," and "*all* these memories of his father's life" and "*all* the noises, rhythms, sounds and variations of the train" and "*all* man's living memory of morning, youth and magic"—there are long catalogs, and more often great, adjectival outbursts of agony and ecstasy, especially throughout *Of Time and the River* (from which the preceding phrases were selected at random), but there is no more organization, no more meaning or unity than that of simple accumulation. *Of Time and the River* is fragmentary, becoming increasingly so as it goes on, and eventually we realize that nothing is going to "happen," that as we read we receive only so many episodes, adding up to no more than their cumulative accretion. And even *The Web and the Rock,* the love story that constitutes the closest approximation to a plot provided by Wolfe after the first novel, leaves George Webber essentially unchanged, unaffected by what has happened to him.

The extent to which Wolfe's work, after *Look Homeward, Angel,* is composed of such fragments is hardly recognized, I think, by most of his readers. The fact is that he did not give direction or unity to any of his books after the first. He toiled over the various parts of *Of Time and the River* for years, until suddenly his editor, Maxwell Perkins, sent it to the printer while Wolfe was out of town. Had it not been for Perkins' insistence that *Look Homeward, Angel* be followed by another big book, the episodes in *Of Time and the River* might have appeared in more fragmentary form—and perhaps to their advantage. Wolfe's last two novels, published after his death, were even less the product of a single imagined pattern; indeed, they were given their status as novels primarily by Edward Aswell, Wolfe's second editor, who joined them together, provided transitional passages, and titled them. The contents of the last two volumes were by no means composed as portions of a unified narrative; many of the better episodes were first published separately, and are read best that way. It is no more than accurate to say that Wolfe completed only one long novel, *Look Homeward, Angel;* and a host of short novels, novelle, stories, and sketches. Their published appearance in the form of long novels was not his doing—which is not to say that he would not have acquiesced in their presentation in that form, as he did with *Of Time and the River.* But he did not compose in that fashion; he had in mind only a vague plan into which everything was supposed to fit. Whether he would ever have worked it out coherently cannot be determined. Perkins decided that Wolfe would never do it, and he gathered together the material that constitutes *Of Time and the River* and sent it to the printer, after changing the entire narrative from the first to the third person! The extent to which Wolfe's later decision to leave Perkins and Scribner's was due to his secret knowledge (despite his and Perkins' public disclaimers) that it was not *his* book is hard to say. At the suggestion of Professor C. Hugh Holman I have read over the published correspondence of the period of the famous break, and it seems to me that no other explanation is really credible.

If Wolfe had insufficient control over the publication of *Of Time and the River, The Web and the Rock* and *You Can't Go Home Again* were even less the books he intended them to be. In February of 1938 Wolfe wrote a long synopsis of "the book" to his new editor, Edward Aswell. That summer he went westward on a trip. He left Aswell an enormous quantity of manuscript with which Aswell was to familiarize himself while Wolfe was away. Wolfe fully expected that the rewriting and organizing would require at least another full year. But he was never to have the chance. In Seattle he came down with the illness that caused his death in September of 1938. After Wolfe's death, Aswell went to work, grouping and collecting. To guide him he had only a long but sketchy outline which Wolfe had left with him. He drew not only upon the manuscript, but on Wolfe's letters, notes, and other materials. Some of the manuscript dated back to the days of *Look Homeward, Angel;* some had been written just before Wolfe's last trip. For one sequence Aswell actually used part of the synopsis in the letter of February 14, which had never been posted and was discovered only after Wolfe's death.

There is no doubt that Aswell labored devotedly and tirelessly to edit all the material into coherent form. But the fact remains that it was *not* the form that Wolfe gave it, and there is no telling what might have evolved had he been around to spend the year of rewriting he planned. And it seems to me that it is, finally, something of a disservice to Wolfe to have brought out his posthumous work in the way that it was done. He is presented as the author of four full-length novels, when in fact he wrote only two novels by himself (if one counts *Of Time and the River*) and a great mass of shorter materials that he intended to fashion into novel form, but did not live to accomplish. To publish material as if it were a novel arouses certain expectations on the reader's part which, when not fulfilled, result in a disappointment that interferes with his appreciation of what actually was written. Wolfe's reputation, it seems to me, would have been far better served had the manuscripts he left been edited and published as a group of short novels. It is quite true that Wolfe intended for them to be part of a longer work, but since he did not live to do the rewriting and editing this would have entailed, it was not the task of an editor do it for him, no matter how close his friendship with Wolfe.

What I am saying, in effect, is that I should much rather have read three or four short novels, for their own sake, than the same material as combined and edited into *You Can't Go Home Again*. It seems to me that a considerable task remains for Wolfe scholars to do: a close textual study of the manuscript left by Wolfe when he died, including all that placed by Wolfe's editor into novel form, leading to the preparation of a definitive published text. I should like to know, for example, the dates of composition for each episode. I should also like to know the extent to which Wolfe's editor cut and edited his material. Was any of the Eugene Gant material edited to read "George Webber" by Mr. Aswell? Did Aswell himself actually write many of the transition passages between episodes? If so, which ones?

I am perhaps being unfair to Aswell; certainly his labors on behalf of his dead friend were selfless and devoted. It is true, too, that had Wolfe been offered the choice, he might well have approved of Aswell's doing what he did. Yet I question, not Aswell's intentions, which were of the best, but his judgment. The fact cannot be gainsaid that the two final novels were presented as if Wolfe wrote them that way, when he did not do any such thing, and that he left only the most sketchy of plans for his book. It will not do to maintain, as Aswell did in his account of the editing of the post-humous material, that Wolfe "did not know whether in the end it would make one book or a dozen, and he didn't much care. That seemed to him the publisher's problem, and he was right about it. What went into each volume was largely a matter of convenience and practicability." What Wolfe and his editor, acting in concert, might have done with finished material is one thing; but this was unfinished material, written over the course of almost a decade, in-volving at least three different protagonists. ". . . My very strong hunch at present," Wolfe wrote to Aswell shortly before leaving for the West, "is that it may be best to allow me to proceed with my work without any great assistance until I have brought it to a further stage of development and completion." To present such material as Wolfe's finished work, and in a form purported to be the one that Wolfe intended for it, is to give a very misleading im-pression of Wolfe's literary work after *Of Time and the River*.

If I have labored this matter of texts and editions, it is because I feel that there is an almost universal misunderstanding about the nature of those last two novels, and thus about Wolfe's work as a whole. Most readers of Wolfe's fiction with whose views I am ac-quainted believe that Thomas Wolfe wrote two novels and left behind the manuscripts of two others, which his editor subsequently tied up and published. *He did no such thing.* All that he left behind were *fragments*. After *Of Time and the River* he never wrote another novel. And this important to realize for what it means about Wolfe's imagination. The act of creating and forming a novel involves giving a meaning to the material, seeing it as a whole unified action. The truth is that once Wolfe left Altamont and the community of his childhood he was, as an artist, unable to give any meaning to his experience except that it had happened. *Of Time and the River* starts off as if headed for somewhere, but it never gets there. Wolfe's art was essentially one of recall, and in such a process only the life of his childhood fell into orderly place and direction. Atlamont he saw whole, as a place with real people living in it who belonged there, in which he, as a child, had his role into which for a time at least he fitted, and in which his father, his mother, his family each had their positions. Looking back at his childhood, he saw it as a growing away from the town, a mounting alienation from a community that became, so far as his judgment was involved, increasingly less orderly and meaningful; so that at the end Eugene Gant stands on the porch of the marble shop, and is awed by the way that what he has known and understood has vanished in time. Then he turns away toward the city.

Significantly, I think, Wolfe is the only one of the major Southern novelists whose fiction, after his first book, is no longer set primarily or even importantly in the community of his origins. The forces that propelled him away from Asheville were so intense, so relentless, that once he had described the process of alienation he could not return there artistically. He never came home again, physically or spiritually, save for short visits. The only meaning he could discover for Asheville was, finally, that of change. It is time and change that give direction and order to Altamont; and since time is inevitably a process of loss, there remained at last only death and memory. No wonder Wolfe is the most eloquent writer about death of his generation! It was the only surety he could deduce from what he had known—life briefly is, and then it ends.

He was caught up in the process of time, fascinated by it; like his friend Scott Fitzgerald he saw himself as a creature of time and change, but unlike Fitzgerald he was never detached about it, never able as an artist to see himself as a limited and finite participant in the spectacle. As an artist he was, as it were, the very eye of time itself, recording and experiencing it. He was bound utterly to it, unable, for purposes of fiction, to separate himself from the actual force and direction of the experience that he underwent as boy and man. Fitzgerald had the same vision of himself in time, but between Fitzgerald the artist and Fitzgerald the man in time there was a great—and for the man a tragic—difference. In Wolfe no such division existed; the art suffered accordingly, for only when the conditions of the experience itself, and not the implied meaning of the experience, possessed a discoverable unity and direction was Wolfe able to give wholeness to his fiction. *Look Homeward, Angel* is the story of Wolfe's growth from birth to young manhood; it has the cohesion of the novel of growth, the developing self-consciousness of the individual. Eugene comes to realize his isolation, his separation from his family and community; this is the progression of *Look Homeward, Angel*. He did not have to discover that meaning; it is manifestly and physically there.

A Yoknapatawpha County, a continuing community such as Faulkner created, was impossible for Wolfe, because he could not separate himself from his experience and use it. The milieu of Faulkner's childhood furnishes the texture for a number of novels, each possessing the form of individual works of art. Faulkner could select from what he knew and use it for his own purposes as a novelist. Wolfe could not pick and choose from his experience, for it was not real enough, when viewed apart from its personal impact on him, to permit him to convert and manipulate it. Altamont exists as part of Wolfe's consciousness, and since his experience of Altamont had been one of change, progressive alienation, death, that was all that Altamont could mean for him. Apart from that process he could not take the mileu with sufficient seriousness to give it a meaning of its own in other novels.

Wolfe's reputation as a novelist, it seems to me, will rest primarily on *Look Homeward, Angel,* and, to a considerably lesser extent, *Of Time and the River.* Nothing Wolfe wrote afterward has anything like the appeal of the Eugene Gant material. Eugene is romantic, extravagant, self-indulgent, histrionic—and he is one of the great characters of modern American fiction. So, for that matter, are the other Gants; taken together they are a remarkable fictional family. The intensity that Wolfe brought to Eugene and his family goes along with the dramatization of fully realized characters functioning in a vivid, believable social situation. Eugene is autobiographical and ardent; in *Look Homeward, Angel* Wolfe dramatized himself and his milieu with consummate skill.

As he grew older, Wolfe came to realize Eugene Gant's limitations. In the winter before his death he wrote to Edward Aswell that "the value of the Eugene Gant type of character is his personal and romantic uniqueness, causing conflict with the world around him; in this sense, the Eugene Gant type of character becomes a kind of romantic self-justification, and the greatest weakness of the Eugene Gant type of character lies in this fact." He went on to say that in his new novel there must be "no trace of Eugene Gant-i-ness in the character of the protagonist; and since there is no longer a trace of Eugene Gant-i-ness in the mind and spirit of the creator, the problem should be a technical one rather than a spiritual or emotional one."

When one reads a statement such as this, the only thing to do is to look at the writing Wolfe was doing in his last years, to see whether what he says is true. We do not know for sure which portions of the posthumously published material were written at which periods in his life, though it is obvious that much of the middle portion of *The Web and the Rock* is, in content and attitude, a direct continuation of *Of Time and the River,* with only the names changed. By contrast, the early portions of *The Web and the Rock,* and perhaps the closing chapters too, obviously were composed much later. The same is manifestly true of much of *You Can't Go Home Again;* in most instances we can tell from dates of periodical publication and from references in Wolfe's published correspondence. Was Wolfe, then, correct in his claim that in the later material "there is no longer a trace of Eugene Gant-i-ness in the mind and spirit of the creator"?

The answer is, No. There is little evidence, insofar as Wolfe's fictional imagination was concerned, that he ever managed to get far outside of the sense of "personal and romantic uniqueness," of "romantic self-justification," that he rightly associates with Eugene Gant. He *says* that such associations were not true of him any longer; obviously he did make a militant attempt to leave romantic subjectivity and write socially conscious, politically conscious fiction. But as a novelist he continued to see his experience with the same kind of personal absorption, the self-justification, the thoroughly egocentric valuation of the world that characterized the earlier novels. There is, to be sure, somewhat less romantic rapture; his protagonist no longer goes about uttering wild "goat cries"; but Monk Webber's view of the "real world" is just as egocentric as Eugene Gant's ever was, and he takes himself just as seriously as Eugene ever did. Wolfe could not write fiction otherwise than in terms of himself. Unlike Fitzgerald, he could never look at his "real-life" self with sufficient irony to create a consciously romantic, innocent character. He views his adult experience precisely the way he viewed childhood and adolescent experience, and as fiction it works not nearly so well—as indeed one might expect.

Eugene Gant is first a child, then a youth, and finally a very young man. In *Look Homeward, Angel* the romantic intensity of his self-justification and self-importance is more attractive than not. But by the time we get halfway through *Of Time and the River* it has long since begun to wear thin. A good rule of thumb in the Wolfe novels is that the closer in age the protagonist is to Thomas Wolfe, the less believable he is as a created, fictional character. The only perspective Wolfe ever seems to have gained on his material as a novelist is that of temporal distance. That is to say, as long as he is reasonably older than his protagonist, he is able to distinguish between the protagonist's values as a fictional character and his own as a novelist. But once this autobiographical distance is gone, he has no perspective from which to evaluate the character's motivations and actions except those of the character himself. For the character is always himself.

He could never write otherwise. Toward the end of his life he turned back to the country of his origins. In his long novel there was to be a first section, a prologue, that was to be about his mother's people and their place in the mountain country. Nine chapters of the prologue, published posthumously as *The Hills Beyond,* were completed at the time of his death, and we can read them and watch the same process happening as before. What begins as an objective chronicle of mountain forebears soon comes to center more and more in the consciousness of young Edward Joyner, in spite of the fact that Edward is supposed to be only an ancestor of the true protagonist. Wolfe's father appears on the scene, in a fictional guise only slightly different from that of W. O. Gant in *Look Homeward, Angel,* and soon the "prison walls of self" close around young Edward, until the last chapter Wolfe wrote is very close to the same kind of subjective, private meditation that we associate with Eugene Gant. It may be that had Wolfe lived he could have forced the narrative focus back outside of Edward's mind and gone on to finish the prologue, but it is impossible to say. When the fragment closes, Wolfe seems close to the point where he began and ended in all his other fiction—himself.

In this respect Wolfe's fiction is importantly different from that of almost all his fellow Southern authors. With all the others, the fictional is usually third-dimensional, external; there is little or no authorial intrusion into the independence of the characters. We almost never have the feeling, when reading the fiction of Faulkner, Warren, Welty, and the others, that the author is dramatizing not only the character, but himself as well. There is an achieved anonymity about most novels by the contemporary Southern writers, and for that matter about their poems as well; we never sense that the authors are imposing their personal, "real-life" values upon the fiction, artificially and from without. They seem as artists to be able to step away from the book, to give it an objective representation, an independence, whereby the meaning is inherent in the fiction. Faulkner, for example, is never limited to his own personal preoccupations; he can give his novel whatever meaning the developing fictional situation requires. Not so Wolfe; the emotions of the central character, the evaluation of the experience being described, are always the author's "real-life" feelings about a "real-life" situation. Wolfe never knew the meaning of artistic anonymity, so far as his own work was concerned. He is always *subjective;* he can never go out beyond himself to create life independent of its impact on the autobiographical protagonist.

In *Look Homeward, Angel,* that kind of approach to the central character, Eugene Gant, was highly appropriate to the demands of the characterization, for Eugene *is* an egocentric child. We expect him to consider himself a unique person, to view the world entirely through his own responses. "Romantic self-justification" on the part of the author works, so far as Eugene is concerned; and the intensity of Wolfe's sense of isolation from the world gave Eugene Gant a believable intenseness about everything he did and thought. Besides, Wolfe the adult author was removed from Eugene the adolescent character by the physical fact of age; an adult is writing about a boy, and is thus able to perceive some of the limitations of the character's view of his experience. And not only that; there is also the fact that the members of his family, whom he used as models, are not merely reflections of Wolfe's personal needs, as almost all the characters drawn from his adult life are. He saw the Gants as individuals and could write about them in their own right, not as they affected him alone.

When, however, Wolfe wrote about Eugene the man, and George Webber the man, that perspective was missing. An adult author is writing about an adult character; and, because he is Wolfe, he cannot perceive any difference between the character's attitude toward his experience and the meaning of the experience itself. All he knows is what the character feels, and all the character feels is what Wolfe felt. We have to accept completely and without reservation the character's subjective version of "real life," or else the character appears ridiculous; and to do this we have to identify ourselves with the character. And the character's view of himself and his life is *very* romantic. If, then, the reader cannot take just as romantic, as egocentric a view toward the character's experience as the character himself takes, the author's fictional imitation of "real life" will not be very convincing.

This is what is wrong with most of the fiction after *Look Homeward, Angel.* In *The Web and the Rock* he writes as follows:

What is it that a young man wants? What is the central source of that wild fury that boils up in him, that goads and drives and lashes him, that explodes his energies and strews his purpose to the wind of a thousand instant and chaotic impulses? The older and more assured people of the world, who have learned to work without waste and error, think they know the reason for the chaos and confusion of a young man's life. They have learned the thing at hand, and learned to follow their single way through all the million shifting hues and tones and cadences of living, to thread neatly with unperturbed heart their single thread through that huge labyrinth of shifting forms and intersecting energies that make up life—and they say, therefore, that the reason for a young man's confusion, lack of purpose, and erratic living is because he has not "found himself."

In this, the older and more certain people may be right by their own standard of appraisal, but, in this judgment on the life of youth, they have really pronounced a sterner and more cruel judgment on themselves. For when they say that some young man has not yet "found himself," they are really saying that he has not lost himself as they. For men will often say that they have "found themselves" when they have really been worn down into a groove by the brutal and compulsive force of circumstance. They speak of their life's salvation when all that they have done is blindly follow through an accidental way. They have forgotten their life's purpose, and all the faith, hope, and immortal confidence of a boy. They have forgotten that below all the apparent waste, loss, chaos, and disorder of a young man's life there is really a central purpose and a single faith which they themselves have lost.

There, it seems to me, is the real issue. For Wolfe is asserting in this passage what I think he passionately believed all his days, for all his disclaimers of continued "Gant-i-ness": that the youthful romantic view of the world is the *true* view. The world is a place of boundless possibilities, endless opportunities; and the proper response to the world is one involving just such wild, romantic fury and ecstasy. Note that he speaks of the "*apparent* waste, loss, chaos, and disorder"; he does not really concede that the romantic attitude is in the least chaotic and disorderly. Persons who "follow their single way," who seek to "work without waste and error," who have "learned the thing at hand," are those who have lost their life's purpose and faith, whom experience has "worn down into a groove." It is not, in other words, the work, but the "feeling" about it that counts. This is an entirely subjective attitude toward experience; reality exists not in the experience of life itself, but in the way one feels about it. Life is "that huge labyrinth of shifting forms and intersecting energies," and to attempt to come to grips with life by setting out along any particular approach or "thread" is to lose oneself. For life is best understood by abandoning oneself to its "chaos and confusion," not by searching for order and purpose. Indeed, the only way to achieve order and purpose is through an ardent embracing of disorder without trying to understand it. In that case, therefore, any order must consist of the individual's perception of disorder. Thus order and meaning are entirely personal and subjective.

That Wolfe believed this as an artist, whatever he may have said as a man, is very clear. The "real world" is only what it meant to Eugene Gant or George Webber. And what it meant to them is the way they *felt* about it. The intensity of feeling, not the truth of the thing felt, is what matters. This is why, I think, Wolfe is the writer for so many younger readers. Not only does Wolfe glory in the ecstasy of his feelings; he tells his readers that nothing matters except feeling. The ability to channel, to direct one's emotions, to set them in motion toward action and accomplishment, is not important.

The evaluation Wolfe attaches to the adult Eugene Gant's and

Monk Webber's attitude toward the world and to their place in it is precisely that of many of Wolfe's most enthusiastic admirers. For them, as for Wolfe, it is a Brave New World. The reader who cannot, however, judge things as he did when, like Monk Webber, he was twenty-three years old, is too often likely to find the adult Eugene and Monk more than a little silly. The younger reader prefers *Of Time and the River*. The older reader will probably prefer *Look Homeward, Angel*. There is no reconciling the two viewpoints. Of the two viewpoints, one might say that one of them is more mature than the other. If one happens to be twenty-three years old, however, he will doubtless admit no such thing.

But Wolfe was *not* twenty-three years old when he wrote his novels. How can we account, therefore, for the tenacity with which he held on to such a perspective, for the intense self-justification, the colossal subjectivity that characterize him as man and writer? What caused him to see his experience so completely in terms of himself, to remain imprisoned within his own feelings, so to speak, so that, try as he might, he could never break away from what he termed his "Eugene Gant-i-ness"?

It would be foolhardy indeed to hope to single out an explanation. The creator of Eugene Gant was a very complex person, and, just as with Faulkner, one must finally halt before the phenomenon of genius. And whatever else we may think of him, Wolfe possessed a large supply of the quality we call "genius."

All the same, I want to speculate a little about Wolfe and his relationship to his culture. I have already noted that almost alone of the Southern writers of his generation, Wolfe came not from the gentry, but out of a solid lower-middle-class background. And I have noted, too, that there was a singular barrenness, an absence of cultural and aesthetic richness, about his childhood; the ugliness of much of his early experience, the aesthetic and cultural impoverishment, is strikingly evident in his description of life in the Gant household. Now if we compare Wolfe's childhood with that of other Southern writers of his generation, we will see that every one of the others came from families in which intellectual and cultural interests were far more likely to be part of the customary events of their daily lives. In *The Story of a Novel* Wolfe declares that for his kind of people, the idea of being an author was something strange and exotic, in no way part of their experience. This was hardly true for any of the others. Faulkner's great-grandfather, for example, was a novelist, and Faulkner grew up in a university community in which his father was a college official. John Crowe Ransom's father was a distinguished linguist and theologian. Donald Davidson's father was a schoolteacher, his mother a musician. Robert Penn Warren's father was a banker, his mother a schoolteacher. Allen Tate's family was of distinguished, well-educated stock; his grandfather was a Latin teacher, and his great-grandfather a newspaper editor. Eudora Welty's father was president of an insurance company. And so on. The point is that in the upper-class South, from which all these authors came, there was always a literary and aesthetic tradition. Young men and women growing up in such circumstances would not ordinarily find that intellectual and aesthetic inclinations on their part automatically set them rigidly apart from their neighbors, isolated them from family and community.

With Wolfe it was very different; there was almost nothing in Wolfe's background and surroundings that would enable him to share whatever intellectual and artistic impulses he may have had as a small child. He could look for no real sympathy, no genuine understanding for any such inclinations. Whatever embryonic literary interests the young Wolfe must have possessed would have been kept solitary and secret. "My Shakespeare, rise!"

I do not want to make too much of this, but I think it no more than true to say that everything about Wolfe's childhood conspired to turn his deepest sensibilities inward, to cause him to erect a barrier between himself and the world around him, to give him a tremendous defensiveness about his literary and intellectual interests. Wolfe speaks of Eugene's "secret world, so fearfully guarded," and when he has Eugene write a composition in school describing a girl listening to a lark, it contains these words: "The girl has had a hard life. Her people do not understand her. If they saw her listening to the lark, they would poke fun at her." (My own guess is that this is probably an actual composition that Wolfe himself wrote.)

The picture Wolfe gives of Eugene Gant's boyhood is far from that of a happy, normal child in harmony with his environment. One continually encounters such sentences as these: "The agony and humiliation it caused him was horrible, but she was unable or unwilling to understand it . . ."; "The herd, merciless in its banded instinct, knew at once that a stranger had been thrust into it, and it was merciless at the hunt . . ."; "shame gathered in him in tangled clots, aching in his throat . . ."; "Once, deathly sick, but locked in silence and dumb nausea, he had vomited finally upon his cupped hands . . ."; "Eugene was startled and confused, feeling that his secret world, so fearfully guarded, had been revealed to ridicule . . ."; "He writhed with shame and humiliation . . ."; "his shame, his distaste for his employment was obvious, although he tried to conceal it . . ."; "He felt now the petty cruelty of village caste . . ."; "He rushed at the wall like an insane little goat, battered his head screaming again and again, wished desperately that his constricted and overloaded heart would burst, that something in him would break, that somehow, bloodily, he might escape the stifling prisonhouse of his life. . . ." It was not a pretty childhood.

Is it, then, entirely without explanation that this particular North Carolina youth, whose childhood was filled with wretchedness, pain, and bewilderment, whose innermost thoughts and feelings set him far apart from the attitudes of his family and community, whose deepest instincts and values were in continual conflict with those of his environment, should have developed into an adult who was preoccupied with himself, who considered himself "God's lonely man," who poured out an intense fictional assertion of his own uniqueness and of the justification for it? "He believed himself thus at the centre of life," Wolfe says of Eugene Gant as a youth. And at seventeen Wolfe wrote to his mother from Chapel Hill that "I am changing so rapidly that I find myself an evergrowing source of interest. Sounds egotistical, doesn't it?" I suggest that both remarks are literally true.

If in the instance of the other Southern writers of Wolfe's generation the breakdown of the patterns of the old community life produced a growing alienation from the values of the community, then it is hardly surprising that in Wolfe the sense of alienation should have been especially intense, manifesting itself in a violent, intensely lyrical assertion of separation and loneliness. The others at least grew up in a society that possessed a tradition of intellectual and cultural activity that, mannered and genteel though it was, permitted a measure of expression for the developing aesthetic sensibilities. With Wolfe there was no such outlet. I do not mean that his family did not recognize his talent; but it was something foreign and strange to them. There was no convention for him to follow, no accepted pattern, however inadequate, of formal, objective utterance; the Wolfe family's lower-middle-class situation had no place for aesthetic expression. Anyone who displayed intense artistic inclinations would have been considered a freak, a misfit. And when the qualities of mind that made Thomas Wolfe into a novelist instead of a stonemason or a real-estate salesman did come fully to light, there was not surprisingly an explosive force to their emergence, a furious emotional subjectivity that could be disciplined only with great difficulty and always imperfectly.

As a child growing up in a North Carolina community, Wolfe knew the social milieu of the Southern town for his own and experienced its breakdown in the new century, but his view was greatly modified and distorted because of his personal circumstance and that of his family. In H. M. McLuhan's words, "Wolfe has all the passion without any of the formal means of constraint and communication which make it tolerable. He was a Southerner by attitude but not by tradition." Small wonder that before he turned to the novel, Wolfe failed as a dramatist; the very nature of the theater, precluding as it does any save the most external modes of expression, was uncongenial to one whose aesthetic was overwhelmingly autobiographical, subjective, lyrical. It it said that *Look Homeward, Angel* was originally composed in the first person, and that Wolfe at one point went through it substituting "he" for "I." *Of Time and the River* actually was a first-person narrative at one point, with David Hawke as the narrator, and the change to Eugene Gant and the third person was done in the publisher's office by John Hall Wheelock. If anything, the change only intensifies the "romantic self-justification," because the apparent objectivity enabled Wolfe to pretend all the more that he was writing about someone other than himself, and so he was not restrained either by modesty or reserve. He told everything, omitted nothing.

The circumstances of his childhood never lost their hold on Wolfe's imagination. He spent his life trying to understand and find an order for his experience. And the longer he lived, the more experience there was to understand. The violence with which he was both drawn toward and repelled by his past was such that he could never step away from the immediate circumstance of his personal experience and judge how it might best be employed for fiction. The personal experience *was* the fiction; he was unable to modify it or change it in any essential respect. In *Look Homeward, Angel* Eugene Gant quotes Catullus: "Odi et amo; quare id faciam." It is an apt reckoning of Wolfe's attitude toward his origins; he castigates the South, his family, his childhood, rages at his youthful circumstance; yet so strongly is he drawn toward all of it, so obsessed is he with its memory, that he cannot look at it with the objectivity needed to master it in fiction.

In the later fiction the narrowness of Wolfe's viewpoint, the subjectivity with which he viewed his experience, was a crippling disability, for he could not describe a man living among other men in a convincing fashion. There are only fragments, moments of illumination. But *Look Homeward, Angel* is bathed in color and light from beginning to end. The child's world he saw whole, and although Eugene Gant is in conflict with it almost from the outset, this did not prevent Wolfe from describing that world with great fervor and vividness. The fabric of a small city's life is unrolled before us. We see its workings, its hold on its inhabitants, especially on the Gants who live there. We see a Southern community in the toils of transition, growing from a small mountain town into a busy tourist city; we see the inhabitants adjusting to accommodate themselves to the change. The members of the Gant family embody the process. Eliza Gant, the canny, conservative, slow-moving mountain woman, becomes the real-estate speculator, the woman of property, who participates zestfully in the commercial mania. Luke Gant takes to the business world with great success. Ben Gant yearns for a home, love, certainty, and dies without them. W. O. Gant, a violent, tumultuous person, comes from the outside, settles down, but finds no peace for his mind. Eugene, born into the community as it is changing, is caught up in the process, cannot find a place for himself, and leaves to pursue his art in the shining city.

It is the process of the change that is foremost, and means most to Eugene and to Wolfe. From childhood Eugene is conscious of time and change. Finally these become the only reality, the only logic and order he can find for what he has known and been. Thus Wolfe wrote his novel of change and alienation. A boy grows up in a Southern town and goes off into modern America, leaving behind him death, taking with him only the memory of the past. So terribly and so indelibly had the process of alienation marked him that the art he went away to pursue became one of recapture, of searching the memories of the past for whatever reality there might be in life.

He was a thoroughgoing Romantic; his writing has the intensity of fiction written by an artist who is seeking furiously, through his literary craft, to impose on his recalcitrant experience his own highly personal valuations. This is the way it was! he insists, and in order to convince us of the justice of his contention, he marshals the force and excitement of a tremendous rhetorical talent. It is his chief concern in *Look Homeward, Angel,* his self-appointed mission: to recreate the circumstances of his childhood, to give to his chaotic experience the order and the importance of a work of art. He wrote a beautiful tale of growth and alienation, in which he, who had experienced it and known both, was the chief character. He recaptured the past, recreated his family, his community, himself, the love and the pain he had felt there, and the loss he knew as he saw it vanish in time.

So far as any American fiction endures, Altamont endures, in motionless vision, timeless chronology. In one great novel Thomas Wolfe fixed the transient world he knew so well into changeless art.

Margaret Church

5. Thomas Wolfe: Dark Time

And time still passing . . . passing life a leaf . . . time passing, fading like a flower . . . time passing like a river flowing . . . time passing . . . and remembered suddenly, like the forgotten hoof and wheel. . . .[1]

THE TRAIN and the river are for Thomas Wolfe two basic symbols in getting across to his readers his feelings about time—time at whose mystery Wolfe never failed to marvel. The river with its ceaseless flow, its continually new combination of particles, its irrevocableness, contained for Wolfe in its essence the sadness, the loneliness, and the loss that time passing brings. The river represented, although Wolfe would not have named it in this way, a sense of Heraclitean flux. Against the river, acting as its foil, stands the train. For the train, although carrying with it a sense of sadness and loneliness as its whistle sounds in the Virginia night, is not irrevocable. There are always tracks leading in the opposite direction and trains traveling on them, and roundhouses where trains may be reversed. Thus although Louis Rubin [2] suggests that the train was comforting to Wolfe because on it he "kept up" with time, it would seem that on the train Wolfe was able also to counteract time. It is in this sense that James Joyce uses trains, trams, and ships as imagery in his Viconian system of return. It is evident too that the river as well as the train represents a kind of immobility, for as Wolfe himself points out the river is "eternal in its flow" and thus immutable as well as transient.

These two ideas are represented again in the often interpreted symbols, the stone, the leaf, and the door. The leaf like the river is transient; it is continually changing until it disappears into the earth as the river merges with the sea. In the stone as in the train there is a kind of immobility although it is a different kind from the circular recurrence represented by the train. It is the immobility of the earth which Wolfe never tired of comparing with man's transient existence. With the stone and the leaf stands the door which acts as a catalyst and represents the possibility of merging that which changes and that which is immutable. It was in the hope of discovering this door which stood between permanence and change that Wolfe wrote the novels of his tetralogy.

Critics have written of Wolfe's relation to philosophers and systems of philosophy, but Wolfe's only attempt * to formulate his theories of art came in a short volume, *The Story of a Novel*. In the following summary of critical theories on Wolfe's work, it is necessary to keep in mind that Wolfe himself was a novelist and not a metaphysician. It is, nevertheless, helpful to see where Wolfe stands on the question of time in relation to his contemporaries.

A great deal has been written about the time concepts of Wolfe, and distinctions have been made between his idea of time and the ideas of Proust and of Joyce on time. Wolfe apparently read Proust in the original in 1925.[3] In a letter from Wolfe to Henry T. Volkening in August, 1929, we find that Wolfe still read Proust. Later letters speak of his admiration for Proust, and in two letters Wolfe admits the Proustian character of "The Party at Jack's." [4] Wolfe has several times expressed his debt to James Joyce—in *The Story of a Novel*, in *Of Time and the River*, and in letters. Wolfe speaks of *Look Homeward, Angel* as his "*Ulysses* book," [5] of Joyce's great talents, of *Ulysses* as containing the best writing in English.[6]

It was inevitable that Wolfe's concept of time should be influenced by the concepts of these two writers, but Wolfe took from Proust and from Joyce only that which was already congenial to him. Thus Herbert J. Muller points out that while both Proust and Wolfe depended upon sensory impressions to recall the past, Wolfe lacked the keen subjective analysis of Proust and stayed closer to the actual experience that produced his memories. Wolfe's interest was in fixity and change as they are in real life, whereas Proust "aspired to

* See Chapter 7 in this book.

the realm of Essence or Being, where change is mere appearance." [7] Muller sees that Wolfe was less subjective than Proust, that he had a firmer grasp of "the elemental emotions." Other critics who point out a relation between Wolfe and Proust are Daniel Delakas, who discovers many ties between them.[8] Karin Pfister, who attempts to relate both Bergson and Proust to Wolfe,[9] and Marcel Brion, who sees that Proust is more precise than Wolfe although the mechanism of memory is similar for them.[10]

Joyce's influence on Wolfe is discussed by Herbert Muller, who sees the influence chiefly in terms of techniques, by Karin Pfister, who writes that both are concerned with the drama of the single fate and the epic of time, by P. E. Kilburn who devotes an entire thesis to Joyce's influence on Wolfe.[11] Marcel Brion writes that Wolfe's word choice, his belief that time remakes itself, his *monologue intérieur* are like Joyce's but unlike Joyce's, Wolfe's picture of the past was not an ordered one.[12] Nathan Rothman says that both Joyce and Wolfe ranged far back into the personal and the racial past.[13]

In addition to those who seek to establish the influence of Proust and of Joyce, there are critics who find in Wolfe something of the transcendental or the essential. B. R. McElderry, Jr., sees that Wolfe's and Emerson's concepts of "flow" are alike.[14] And Louis Rubin (in *Thomas Wolfe: The Weather of His Youth*) writes a chapter on "intimations of immortality."

Probably the best discussions of the time theme in Wolfe are those of W. P. Albrecht, Karin Pfister, and Louis Rubin, Jr. Albrecht sees that Wolfe reconciled permanence and flux first through the act of literary creation and later through a cyclical concept of time.[15] According to Karin Pfister, Wolfe never really solved the problem of change and of mutability, for his heroes are constantly competing with time,[16] but Rubin thinks that Wolfe solved this dilemma through a kind of "semi-mysticism in which he was influenced by Wordsworth and by Coleridge." [17]

It is apparent that some further examination of Wolfe's sense of time is in order since views on it vary to such an extent. First, it is necessary to point out that Wolfe never consciously worked out a philosophy of time which he then employed in his novels. His references to time are haphazard and often mere clichés that he uses again and again because of his partially subconscious obsession with the time idea.

Only once, in *The Story of a Novel,* did Wolfe attempt a formulation of his literary creed. Early in the book Wolfe states his debt to James Joyce's *Ulysses.* "I was strongly under the influence of writers I admired—one of the chief writers I admired was Mr. James Joyce with his *Ulysses.* . . . The book I was writing was much influenced by his own book." [18] What is often overlooked is that Joyce's *Portrait* must also have exercised a strong influence on Wolfe. In fact, in a letter to Robert Raynolds, Wolfe thinks of calling *Of Time and the River* "The Image of Fury in the Artist's Youth." [19] What Wolfe seemed to have gotten from Joyce was Joyce's ability as Wolfe says in a letter to Julian Meade "to make live again a moment in lost time," as well as Joyce's ability to make his scenes radiate both backwards and forwards. Wolfe feels that perhaps Joyce did succeed in "penetrating reality" in "creating what is almost another dimension of reality." [20] Wolfe's ability to re-create the past is often attributed to his interest in Proust; thus it is important to realize that it was Joyce as well who possessed this talent for Wolfe.

Another aspect of Wolfe's interest in Joyce lay in Joyce's use of myth, which we find Wolfe also using. In a letter to Maxwell Perkins (December, 1930) Wolfe describes the argument of *Of Time and the River* in terms of the legend of Antaeus, who seeks for his father, Poseidon, but is overcome by Heracles. As in *Ulysses,* the mythical background is implicit not explicit in the book and the story is only "given shape by the legend." "The idea of time, the lost and forgotten moments of people's lives, the strange brown light of old time . . . is over all the book." [21]

In *The Story of a Novel* Wolfe goes on to mention the quality of his memory which could "bring back the odors, sounds, colors, shapes, and feel of things with concrete vividness." [22] For instance, he would be sitting in the Avenue de l'Opéra and watching the people move past when suddenly he would remember the railing at Atlantic City. "I could see it instantly just the way it was, the heavy iron pipe; its raw, galvanized look; the way the joints were fitted together." [23] The exact dimensions, an entire scene would thus return to Wolfe through seeing a certain street, hearing a train whistle, or viewing muddy banks or a particular bridge. Wolfe, like Joyce, wanted to find words for this experience with memory, to write so vividly that the past would be reanimated for the reader. Proust's influence must also be seen in this passage from *The Story of a Novel,* although Wolfe never generalizes as Proust does on the metaphysics of the return of the past and although the "raw, galvanized look" of the pipe seems to contain more the flavor of Joyce than of Proust. In a letter written in August, 1930, Wolfe "owns up" to the fact that some of the "flavour" of Joyce "has crept into his book." [24]

In a later passage in *The Story of a Novel,* Wolfe says that in the embryonic form of his book there was a section entitled "Where now?" in which he recorded all the lost moments of the past, "the flicks and darts and haunting lights that flash across the mind of man." These flashes of the memory concerned more than man's immediate past, for they went back into "the farthest adyt of his childhood before conscious memory had begun." [25] Often, Wolfe continues, these flashes seem of no consequence, but they live with us longer than apparently more important events. This kind of memory brings unity to life and human experience.

This passage has in it more of Joyce than of Proust and more of Jung's theory of the collective unconscious than of Bergson. Wolfe had written in a letter to Maxwell Perkins: "My conviction is that a native has the whole consciousness of his people and nation in him; that he knows everything about it, every sound and memory of the people." [26] Wolfe's sense of a collective memory is more than a national memory as can be seen in the legendary background he planned for *Of Time and the River.* Wolfe felt at times that in him all experience existed.

A third passage of importance in *The Story of a Novel* is Wolfe's explanation of the time elements in *Of Time and the River.* There were three elements: present time; past time, which showed people "as acting and as being acted upon by all the accumulated impact of man's experience"; and time immutable, "the time of rivers, mountains, oceans, and the earth; a kind of eternal and unchanging universe of time against which would be projected the transience of man's life, the bitter briefness of his day." [27] In Wolfe's definition of the past we find again a suggestion of Joyce. Wolfe's time immutable is in one of his letters applied only to the earth whereas the river and the ocean represent movement and wandering.[28]

In *The Story of a Novel* Wolfe formulates, then, three aspects of his interest in time: the power of involuntary memory to re-create the past, a sense of the collective unconscious which contains events from our national and racial past, and a sense of time immutable. The time concepts of Proust, of Joyce, and even perhaps of Wordsworth are evident in these formulations, but beyond them lies Wolfe's own fascination simply with the word *time* so that he could write: "I am haunted by a sense of time and a memory of things past, and, of course, I know I have got to try somehow to get a harness on it." [29]

The themes that have been enunciated in *The Story of a Novel* are clearly evident in *Look Homeward, Angel*. Early in the book Wolfe mentions his urge to return to the past through actual, not secondhand, experience with it. He speaks of his acute realization of the past which exists in each one of us and which needs only night or nakedness to reveal it. Each of us, he says, is the sum of many things we have not known or counted. Look behind the screen of the present, return to the darkness of the womb, to night, "and you shall see begin in Crete four thousand years ago the love that ended yesterday in Texas." [30] This passage is more nearly related to Joyce's sense of return and to his interest in recurrence than to Bergson's *durée*. For Bergson time was like a snowball; therefore, for him two love affairs exist simultaneously but they are still *two* love affairs. Wolfe is emphasizing, on the other hand, the collective aspect of experience, the fact that perhaps the individual is less important than the whole of which he is a part. Wolfe erected this defense against his fear of the fleetingness of time at the very beginning of his work although it receives more complete expression in *Of Time and the River*.

In *Look Homeward, Angel* Eugene's experience with the train is one that gives him further ballast against the time experience, even though the train symbol is an ambiguous one for Eugene. The train for Eugene, from boyhood on, denoted freedom from mountain fastness. On the train alone he felt the security that fixity never gave him, because, for one thing, on the train there is always the possibility of return whereas time sells no round-trip tickets. And yet the whistle of the train sounding in the reaches of the night filled him with longing and with terror. "And it was this that awed him—the weird combination of fixity and change" (p. 192). The train enabled him to flee and yet it brought him back to Altamont; on it he competed with time and in a sense became temporarily the winner. Scenes in Virginia sped by him and yet he was able to transfix certain scenes. As he passed a town, a slattern standing in a doorway, both seemed suspended or frozen in time. They stood "without the essential structure of time. Fixed in no-time, the slattern vanished, fixed, without a moment of transition" (p. 192). To the viewer on the train the landscape speeds by like a moving film and yet certain scenes from this film are immutably fixed in the mind of the viewer. On the train Eugene achieved thus a detachment from time, a God-like view of the universe, the ability to choose what he wished to retain from experience. It gave to Eugene a sense of being beyond change and at the same time it gave him the security of knowing that "he *could* go home again." Yet its whistle heard in the night represented the very fleetingness that he escaped when he was on board. Eugene's insecurities in regard to time arise from this sense of not being "on board" in life; a recognition of his role in life would later give him the sense of detachment which he achieves through the substitute of the train at this point.

His need to transfix time in a suspended instant is illustrated elsewhere in the book. Two scenes are described in the square of Altamont when time is suddenly suspended. W. O. Gant, standing on his porch, is the God-like viewer in the first scene. Fagg Sluder, a policeman, the fireman, a farmer, Yancey stop simultaneously their activities. The fountain, which plays in the center of the square, is suspended. And Gant feels as if he were looking at a photograph of himself taken years earlier and as if he alone were moving toward death in this world of shadows of reality. He feels like a man who recognizes himself in a photograph—perhaps on "his elbow near Ulysses Grant before the march" (p. 269). This scene is for Gant a a kind of effort to stem the tide of time, and it is also a prelude to the final scene in the book when Eugene meets the ghost of Ben in the square.

In both scenes the square lay in moonlight, but whereas for Gant the square had been full of people, for Eugene it is empty. Gant's search for meaning depends on others; Eugene must seek within himself for the meaning of his role. In the final chapter of *Look Homeward, Angel* Wolfe imitates perhaps unconsciously the consecration scene of Stephen in *A Portrait*. "Do you know why you are going, or are you just taking a ride on the train?" (p. 619) Ben asks. This question makes clear Eugene's substitution of the train experience for the real experience of life. Ben knows that Eugene is *not* coming back; that this is not just a ride on the train. Like Stephen Dedalus, Eugene goes forth "to forge in the smithy of my soul the uncreated conscience of my race," [31] and there is no more turning back home. "He was like a man who stands upon a hill above the town he has left, yet does not say 'The town is near,' but turns his eyes upon the distant soaring ranges" (p. 626). Thus Eugene finds the sense of detachment which he has sought.

Furthermore, in the square Eugene discovers, as Stephen had in his vision of the Danes, his relation to all experience. He sees fabulous cities, Thebes, the temples of Daulian, and Phocian lands. He sees all the life and death of all time. In the square this night "all the minutes of lost time collected and stood still" (p. 623), lost shapes, lost events, lost meetings. But whereas for Gant the fountain had stood still, for Eugene it pulses "with a steady breezeless jet," and whereas for Gant, the life of Altamont had been suspended, for Eugene the square contains all of life, from Thebes to the demons of the South, standing transfixed before him. Eugene's vision is one that foretells not death, as Gant's had, but a new life, a new point of view, for the stone angel raises its arm, and in the shop the heavy tread of angels may be heard, angels that through his art Eugene will bring to life. Against the vision of the passage of millions to their death stands the rhythm of the seasons, the continual return of spring granting a surer security than the rail-bound return of the train.

In his need to reanimate the past, his need to achieve a sense of the identity of all experience, his need to transfix the moment, his need to achieve artistic detachment, Wolfe (in *Look Homeward, Angel*) is very close to Joyce. He has deduced the very essence of Joyce's experience and translated it into terms of "the artist as a young man" in the United States. Proust's moments of recall and a Wordsworthian sense of preexistence lie perhaps in the background, but the temper of the book is more akin to Joyce's than to the reflective temperaments of Proust and of Wordsworth. Wolfe himself called *Look Homeward, Angel* "my *Ulysses* book." [32]

In *Of Time and the River* the influence of Proust is much more evident although what Wolfe learned from Joyce has not been forgotten. Wolfe's concepts of time are analyzed more fully here than in his first book. *Of Time and the River* is, as the title indicates, a kind of time epic. Wolfe's preoccupation with time still concerns, of course, its fleetingness, its grandeur, its pathos, "the immense and murmurous" [33] sound of time which rises over great railroad sheds or over huge cities. But here he is sometimes concerned with the nature of time and its properties. Passages that inquire into its nature are more frequent in this second novel than in the others.

At the opening of the book Wolfe thinks, for instance, of the relative qualities of space and time on his trip between Asheville and New York. The distance, he says, is more than seven hundred miles. "But so relative are the qualities of space and time, . . . that in the brief passage of this journey one may live a life" (p. 25).

Again in the train the present fades and, as he fingers the watch that Ben had given him, the image of Ben appears and the scene changes to his twelfth birthday when he had received the watch from his brother. He wonders what time is. The watch is to keep time with. "What is this dream of time, this strange and bitter miracle of living?" (p. 52) This scene with the watch is, of course, reminiscent of Proust. Here the watch instead of the *madeleine* recalls the past into the present and fuses them into one timeless instant.

And once again on the train present and past time fuse when he thinks of his life with his father. Suddenly the thousand images of his father become as "one terrific image." But here in contrast to the preceding scene with the watch, there is no key, no magic word with which to unlock the past. Only in his memory does time become a unit; he does not re-experience the past as he does with the watch.

It must not be forgotten that Eugene Gant and, consequently, Wolfe were persistently searching for a key that would admit them into the past. Proust's *madeleine* was only one of the keys that Wolfe tried. Through the memories and tales of his mother Eugene comes closer to the actual past than he is able to come by other means.

When he meets Bascom Pentland in Boston, he thinks that his uncle will reanimate for him all the scenes and faces of old about which he wanted to know. But Bascom can not do this; he has somehow lost the key and is unable to give Eugene a feeling of the reality of his past life. This intense desire on Wolfe's part to reanimate things lost and dead is probably closely connected with his search for a father or an antecedent. And it is ironical that it is his mother who most nearly fulfills his desire with her stories of the Pentland tribe. Yet his seekings into past time almost exclusively concern men, Ben, his father, the Joyner brothers, "The Four Lost Men," Garfield, Arthur, Harrison, Hayes. "Who had heard the casual and familiar tones of Chester Arthur?" [34] This familiar and exact quality of the living was what Wolfe sought to capture in much the same way that Proust desired to, but Proust more nearly succeeded, for Wolfe never ceased to feel that the past was irrevocably lost. Change was but appearance to Proust, whereas to Wolfe, despite rationalizations, it was a bitter fact of existence, separating him from all life.

Loneliness was another condition that often made Eugene see time in unusual perspective. At Harvard and later in Tours, there were periods when he would spend days or weeks by himself without seeing a face he knew. These days were like dreams and during them weeks seemed like a single day, and then he would awake and find time once more in normal perspective.

His childhood recurred frequently during these years. "A voice half-heard, a word far-spoken, a leaf, a light that came and passed and came again. But always when that lost world would come back, it came at once, like a sword thrust through the entrails, in all its panoply of past time, living, whole, and magic as it has always been" (p. 200). This description of the return of the past reminds one of Proust's description of recalling bygone days. It also contains perhaps some of the longing that Wordsworth felt for lost childhood. Although Wolfe did not aspire to the "realm of Essence," he incorporated into this book some of the aspects of time that he held in common with Proust.

That he had become curious about the metaphysics of time is apparent in the excerpt from his notebook, which he included near the end of the novel. He believes that his query about the nature of time has been finally answered after a visit to the American Library in

Paris where he reads the *Americana* and William James. In fact, William James, rather than Bergson, is probably Wolfe's source for his ideas on duration.

Here he discovers that "the time-units of both time and space are neither points nor moments, but moments in the history of a point" (pp. 670–71). The significance of the title, *Of Time and the River,* becomes clearer if we examine this statement in the light of certain passages. He speaks, for instance, of "the moving tide of time as it flows down the river" (p. 510). Again and again the river and time are connected, especially in the scenes in which he travels up the Hudson to meet Joel. Time, for Wolfe, is an unchangeable, unalterable thing, like a river, but paradoxically it always changes. "Moments in the history of a point" would apply to either time or the river. Time-units and the waves of the river are only the surface of a larger reality. James and other theorists on the metaphysics of time put the emphasis on the larger unit while the rest of us swimming or sinking in the river and time worry about the waves. Wolfe at least implies then that his book is to deal with time in both its aspects, fixity and change. The fixity of change constantly impresses Eugene, the stillness of the macrocosm and the disturbing fluctuation of the microcosm. Life, he says, is "like a river, and as fixed, unutterable in unceasing movement and in changeless change as the great river is, and time itself" (p. 245). The earth, sweeping past a train on which he rides, has this same quality of "unchanging changefulness," but time is "as fixed and everlasting as eternity" (p. 245). And for Abe's mother seven thousand years, "yesterday, tomorrow, and forever [are but] a moment at the heart of love and memory" (p. 492).

The idea of song as a means of invoking the past is part of Wolfe's heritage from Proust. For Wolfe often "trashy" songs like "K-K-K-Katy," he says in a letter, "are able to make me live again some night in summer twenty or twenty-five years ago and hear the people talk on their porches." [35] In Book VII, "Kronos and Rhea: The Dream of Time," Wolfe invokes the past by means of music as Swann does in Proust. "Play us a tune on an unbroken spinet" (p. 853) is Wolfe's thematic sentence. And through this tune of the spinet he recalls Athens as it actually was, people in the Middle Ages, their casual words, the trains in Baltimore in 1853. The difference between Wolfe and Proust here is that Wolfe wishes to reproduce all time, for a recurrent dream while he is in France would take Eugene back to the days of Homer, while Proust was interested only in his own segment of it.

As the sexton rings the church bell in Dijon, sounds of another bell come to Eugene. He is once more ringing the college bell "and now the memory of that old bell, with all its host of long-forgotten things, swarmed back with living and intolerable pungency" (p. 896). This is like an illustration of Proust's assertion that the past is hidden in some material object. If there is a difference it is that Proust would say the college bell was still there, that he had unconsciously been carrying its sound with him, for time only served to obscure the true perspective in which things stand, whereas Wolfe meant that one bell reminded him of another although his actual experience may not have been unlike Proust's.

For as he watches the scene in Dijon the lonely sounds of his native Catawba awaken in him, and there in the square in the French village he sees the square of his own town, Altamont, hears his father slam their iron gate, feels "the magic of full June," smells turnip greens, and hears the slamming of screen doors. The life of twenty years past is thus recalled to him, but for Wolfe it tends to be *recalled* and not *recaptured*. Proust was surer of his ability to stem the flow of the river, and it is because of his uncertainty that Wolfe is continually faced with the mystery of time, "the mystery of strange, million-visaged time that haunts us with the briefness of our days" (p. 899).

Although the influence of Proust has been stressed in discussing *Of Time and the River,* the mythical implications of the headings of the books are obviously inspired by *Ulysses.* However, the parallel between the present situation and its mythical counterpart is much less carefully worked out by Wolfe than by Joyce. Thus, for instance, the book entitled "Telemachus" describes Eugene's trip with three rich young men to Blackstone and his being jailed there with the others and his release paid for by his brother, Luke. Only in a most general way can this incident be understood as Telemachus' search for the father. Close similarities between the myth and the present are impossible to find. However, the headings do indicate that Wolfe was conscious of the recurrent nature of reality and of its function in his work. *Finnegans Wake* (*Work in Progress*) was being published in *Transition* during the time that Wolfe was writing *Of Time and the River*. Joyce had remarked to Eugene Jolas: "Time and the river and the mountain are the real heroes of my book." [36] Joyce's influence on this second book of Wolfe's should not, therefore, be overlooked. The relationship between the river and the mountain, transience and immobility, is one that stands at the very core of the work of both men.

In *The Web and the Rock* and *You Can't Go Home Again,* Wolfe treats the subject of time much less fully than in his second novel. Nevertheless, several passages, which are worth mentioning here, further develop Wolfe's thoughts on time. Aunt Maw in *The Web and the Rock* is, of course, substituted for Eliza in the earlier books, and it is through her that George hears "lost voices in the mountains long ago." [37] But George laments Aunt Maw's callousness, for he says she cannot know "the eternity of living in a moment" (p. 24) or the swift flash of change. The old problems of fixity and change and the desire to recall lost voices continue to haunt Wolfe. Aunt Maw's words bring to George the voices of his Joyner ancestors, the smell of a pine blaze, but, somehow, like Uncle Bascom's words, they fail actually to re-create the past.

During his trip to Richmond to see a football game, Monk takes part in events that happened during the Civil War. He hears Grant and his soldiers fighting their way into Richmond, he knows Lee is digging in at Petersburg, that Lincoln is waiting to hear the news, that Jubal Early "was swinging in his saddle at the suburbs of Washington" (p. 153). Monk and his friends did more than just imagine these events, for "they felt, they knew, they had their living hands and hearts upon the living presence of these things" (p. 183). Thus Richmond reanimates for Wolfe a past era; he sees no ghostly procession of historical events, but rather the living images of them. Like the memories of his childhood, these memories become "living, whole and magic." [38] But in Wolfe no matter how live memories become they still tend to be memories and images, not actual events. One main difference between Proust and Wolfe is that Wolfe sees that the whole past, not only the individual's past, is recoverable. In this he is close to Joyce.

However, Wolfe, like both Proust and Joyce, recognized the

immobility of time, its immeasurableness, its relativity. For he describes an estuary of the sea as "motionless as time"; the fight between Firpo and Dempsey lasts a three minutes that seem like hours; men measure immeasurable time by arbitrary symbols; they even measure the timeless sea; and "every man on earth held in the little tenement of his flesh and spirit the whole ocean of human life and time" (p. 262). Then suddenly a sound, an odor, a city square brings to him the "streets of noon some dozen years ago" (p. 276), the shuffle of leather on the pavements, the shouts of children, the smell of turnip greens, the slamming of screen doors. Constantly he cries out that he may find lost eras, knowing his wish impossible of accomplishment, for man is but "that little, glittering candle-end of dateless time who tries to give a purpose to eternity" (p. 299).

Even Esther fits into his schemes of recovering the past, for in his manhood it is Esther, and not Eliza or Aunt Maw, who regales him with tales of bygone days. It is Esther who gives him "a blazing vision of lost time" (p. 367), Esther who makes "ghosts of forgotten hours" (p. 367) move about her. As she talks all life reawakens for Monk, all the lost and secret recesses of the past are opened, and she brings her living warmth and presentness to reanimate lost faces, her father's world of the theater, her first party. "She was like time," Monk says, for she could give the feeling of distance and memory to events that had occurred only an hour before. But sometimes during her descriptions of her childhood days he would think that there was no way actually to bring back even a few seconds of lost eras. Always he is haunted by past moments, by a devouring curiosity, which makes him go to any lengths to secure a peephole through which he can view the past. For the time of each man is different; there is the time of great bells in a tower, the time of a tiny wrist watch, the time of each human being. And the "dark rich river [is] full of strange time, dark time, strange tragic time" (p. 427).

That spring in New York with Esther and the new novel he is writing, he feels that both mistress and novel make "the past as real as the present" (p. 541). He is living "the events of twenty years ago with as much intensity and as great a sense of actuality as if they had just occurred" (p. 541). There is no *now* and no *then,* for George feels a unity with the larger purposes of time and destiny. And as he looks at the green tree that stands outside his window, he feels as if it had the magic qualities that had unlocked the past. Like the *madeleine* for Proust, the green tree is the key that admits Wolfe into lost days. Wolfe comes very close to Proust here, for in this passage change is mere appearance to Wolfe; and the green tree, like the *madeleine,* unlocks memories that the author is to record in a book. But still this process of recall is not the central theme of Wolfe's tetralogy, though an important coulisse of the central theme, the recovery of past. For Wolfe never tires of repeating that each man has his own time, that there is the time of clocks, of mountains, of rivers, for time has ten thousand faces and yet is a fable, a mystery.

In the last section of *The Web and the Rock,* the hero flees to Paris. By the end of Wolfe's third book one knows that Eugene and George have become Eugene-George. For example, in Paris George feels "that he has been here before" (p. 631), and he immerses himself in the "fixed and living eternity of the earth" (p. 631). Eugene-George came to stand in Wolfe's mind as a symbol, the kind of symbol that Thomas Mann's Joseph was. Mann uses Joseph as a figure who represents many, who is not sure even of his own identity, and Wolfe eventually sees his hero as representing the summation of all young men's experience and especially of the experience of the creative artist of the 1920's. For the episode in the French town of *Of Time and the River* is repeated in *The Web and the Rock.* Instead of the bell, here the laughter of a woman recalls to him a scene from his childhood in Old Catawba, the sound of a distant train, the sleeping streets, and the start of a motor. Mortal time is clock time George knows, as he lies in a German hospital and listens to a clock strike "with a solemn and final sweetness" (p. 674).

From *You Can't Go Home Again* the party at Jack's reminds one of Proust's description of the party given by the Guermantes, while George, like Proust's hero, stands broodingly in the background observing and commenting. In two letters Wolfe has mentioned that this scene is "somewhat Proustian." He writes: "its life depends upon the most thorough and comprehensive investigation of character," [39] and yet he feels that despite its "unintentional" Proustian characteristics, it does contain a good deal of action. Wolfe here points out quite clearly a central difference between his writing and Proust's.

Proust did achieve a stasis of a kind through his minute character analysis. Wolfe, on the other hand, worked to re-create the flow of his characters in action.

As George looks at a portrait of Mrs. Jack as a young girl the mystery of time passes over him. It seems to him that 1901, when the portrait was painted, was centuries ago. "Yes, he had lived and died through so many births and deaths . . . that . . . the sense of time had been wiped out." [40] These years had become a "timeless dream." For had they not been Thracian captives together? Had she not launched the ship? And had she not "come to charm remission from the lord of Macedon?" (p. 253) And now she had stepped out of these former selves and stood before him. The portrait here is the means of momentarily freeing George from the present. He travels far, into the days of Thrace and Macedon, and all time is for him vivid and immediate.

Thus the four novels of Wolfe's tetralogy echo the voice of time. Like the great railroad sheds, they harbor its sound. For Wolfe was secure only when he was in motion and never so sure of himself as when he was on a moving train. His books came from the huge railroad stations of his mind where "the voice of time remained aloof and imperturbed, a drowsy and eternal murmur," [41] and where the train whistle evoked for him a million images: "old songs, old faces and forgotten memories." [42]

It is not surprising that in Wolfe's last piece, "A Western Journey," he should have resurrected past days. For as he journeyed through western plains, he saw the thundering Sioux in storm-herds, and he knew that long ago some man had stood and, looking over those same rolling plains, had envisaged the future with its thundering trains. And in Arizona he watches from a mountain a distant train, "advanceless moveless-moving through timeless time." [43]

In fact, it is fitting that Wolfe's last words concerning his "dark time" should also concern trains. For the train, like the square in Altamont, was changeless in its change. There is a danger in attempting to formulate in terms of philosophy Wolfe's theories of time, for in such an attempt the critic tends to move far away from the works themselves and from Wolfe himself. For Wolfe it was the experience with time which counted, and although this experience was often not unlike that of Joyce, of Proust, of Wordsworth, or Coleridge, Wolfe never became involved in metaphysics. Such an involvement would have perhaps brought him closer to the solution to the problem of change and transience which haunted him all his days. The title *You Can't Go Home Again* indicates not only that Wolfe was now oriented toward the future but that he had never solved the mystery of the past as Joyce, who had influenced *Look Homeward, Angel,* had found it in eternal recurrence, as Proust, whose influence is everywhere in *Of Time and the River,* had found it in involuntary memory, and as Wordsworth, whose "intimations of immortality" appear now and then in Wolfe's work had found it in a semi-mystical connection between man and nature. One sees Wolfe reaching out toward a cyclical concept of time in his last books, but it is never a driving force for him. In the last chapter of *You Can't Go Home Again,* he feels that the circle has "come full swing" (p. 741). But in the next sentence he talks of the future as if there were a linear progression in time. What offers hope for Wolfe is not a sense of cycles in *You Can't Go Home Again* but a faith in the future of America and a blind faith at the very end in "another world" beyond this one. Cyclical recurrence and involuntary memory were facets of his bulwark against time passing, but they never completely eased for him the ache of separation when "the doors are closed, and the ship is given to the darkness and the sea." [44] The last words of *You Can't Go Home Again* concern the flowing of rivers.

Notes

1. Thomas Wolfe, *The Hills Beyond* (New York, 1941), p. 348.

2. Louis D. Rubin, Jr., *Thomas Wolfe: The Weather of His Youth* (Baton Rouge: Louisiana State Univ. Press, 1955), p. 39.

3. Daniel L. Delakas, *Thomas Wolfe: La France et les romanciers français* (Paris: Jouve E. Cie, 1950), p. 118.

4. *The Letters of Thomas Wolfe,* ed. Elizabeth Nowell (New York: Charles Scribner's Sons, 1956), pp. 194, 631, 648.

5. *Ibid.,* p. 586.

6. Thomas Wolfe, *Of Time and the River* (New York: Charles Scribner's Sons, 1944), p. 661.

7. Herbert J. Muller, *Thomas Wolfe* (Norfolk, Connecticut, 1947), p. 75.

8. Delakas, *op. cit.*, p. 132.

9. Karin Pfister, *Zeit und Wirklichkeit bei Thomas Wolfe* (Heidelberg: Carl Winter Universitätsverlag, 1954).

10. Marcel Brion, "Thomas Wolfe," *Revue des deux mondes*, XVI (August 15, 1952), 734.

11. P. E. Kilburn, *Ulysses in Catawba* (New York University, 1954),

12. Brion, *op. cit.*, p. 738.

13. Nathan L. Rothman, "Thomas Wolfe and James Joyce: A Study in Literary Influence," in *A Southern Vanguard*, ed. Allen Tate (New York: Prentice-Hall, 1947), p. 69.

14. B. R. McElderry, Jr., "Wolfe and Emerson on 'Flow,'" *Modern Fiction Studies*, II (May, 1956), 77–78.

15. W. P. Albrecht, "Time as Unity in Thomas Wolfe," *New Mexico Quarterly Review*, XIX (Autumn, 1949), 325.

16. Pfister, *op. cit.*, p. 51.

17. Rubin, *op. cit.*, p. 68

18. Thomas Wolfe, "The Story of a Novel," *Saturday Review of Literature* (December 14, 1935), 4.

19. *Letters*, ed. Nowell, p. 382.

20. *Ibid.*, p. 322.

21. *Ibid.*, p. 279.

22. "The Story of a Novel," *Saturday Review of Literature* (December 21, 1935), 3.

23. *Ibid.*

24. *Letters*, ed. Nowell, p. 254.

25. "The Story of a Novel," *Saturday Review of Literature* (December 21, 1935), 15.

26. *Letters*, ed. Nowell, p. 279.

27. "The Story of a Novel," *Saturday Review of Literature* (December 28, 1935), 3.

28. *Letters*, ed. Nowell, p. 280.

29. *Ibid.*, p. 323.

30. Thomas Wolfe, *Look Homeward, Angel* (New York: Charles Scribner's Sons, 1929), p. 3. Subsequent references to this volume appear in the text.

31. James Joyce, *A Portrait of the Artist As a Young Man* (New York: Random House, 1928), p. 299.

32. See above, and note 5.

33. Wolfe, *Of Time and the River*, p. 136. Subsequent references to this volume appear in the text.

34. Thomas Wolfe, *From Death to Morning* (New York: Charles Scribner's Sons, 1935), p. 121.

35. *Letters,* ed. Nowell, p. 377.

36. Richard Ellmann, *James Joyce* (New York: Oxford University Press, 1959), p. 565.

37. Thomas Wolfe, *The Web and the Rock* (New York: Charles Scribner's Sons, 1939), p. 8. Subsequent references to this volume appear in the text.

38. Wolfe, *Of Time and the River,* p. 200.

39. *Letters,* ed. Nowell, p. 631.

40. Thomas Wolfe, *You Can't Go Home Again* (New York: Harper and Brothers, 1942), p. 252.

41. *Ibid.,* p. 48.

42. Thomas Wolfe, "Boom Town," *American Mercury* (May, 1943), 21.

43. Thomas Wolfe, "A Western Journey," *Virginia Quarterly Review,* XV (Summer, 1939), 340.

44. Wolfe, *Of Time and the River,* p. 912.

Robert C. Slack

6. Thomas Wolfe: The Second Cycle

A GREAT DEAL has been said about the Thomas Wolfe hero as the throbbing romantic young man swinging across the earth with giant strides, scattering his emotions broadcast to the winds. The more severe critics of Wolfe emphasize the image of his hero as an uncontrolled adolescent, waving his arms wildly or beating his knuckles on the wall, wailing in despair one moment and yakking goat-cries of crude glee in the next. There is vitality here, they admit—but uncontrolled vitality, bursting at the seams, not integrated by a clearly perceived purpose, not fashioned by a careful artistic control.

There has been a good bit of such criticism of Wolfe, particularly among the high arbiters of literary taste. One of the most powerful early expressions of this view appeared in the *Saturday Review of Literature,* written by Bernard DeVoto.* His essay was based on the early writing of Wolfe, but it had a lot to do with crystallizing a pattern of reaction to Wolfe's work which has endured in several quarters even up to today.

I disagree with the evaluations of Wolfe as a novelist which are based upon such observations as these of the early Wolfe hero, even though I cannot deny that the observations, as far as they go, have some validity. Artistic control (especially that which is evinced by scrupulous omission) and immaculate literary craftsmanship are not the only valid measures of a novelist's accomplishment. Many of our greatest novelists have attained their stature far more because of their abounding vitality than because of their tight control. Wolfe's work

* See Chapter 8 in this book.

moves in large cycles; it is more justly looked at through a telescope than through a microscope. Moreover, a fair evaluation of his writing must take into account more than merely the first of these cycles.

It seems to me that there are at least two large cycles in the fiction of Thomas Wolfe. The first might be identified by a label which Wolfe himself supplies: "The Search for a Father." In a short book which he titled *The Story of a Novel,* Wolfe reveals the creative process out of which emerged his second novel, *Of Time and the River.* In this document he writes:

> . . . the central legend that I wished my book to express . . . was this: the deepest search in life, it seemed to me, . . . was man's search to find a father, not merely the father of his flesh, not merely the lost father of his youth, but the image of a strength and wisdom external to his need and superior to his hunger, to which the belief and power of his own life could be united.[1]

The first large cycle of Wolfe's writing is dominated by this search. It runs through the first two novels, *Look Homeward, Angel* and *Of Time and the River,* and gives them a kind of inner coherence which is tangible beneath the surface, at any point. These books constitute the saga of a man's "hunger in his youth," as Wolfe calls it. In them his hero, Eugene Gant, is driven by an immense desire to satisfy this huge and burning hunger. Eugene Gant is trying to take in all of life, in monstrous gulps. First, the flood of life that is his family: the vital and magnetic figure of his father, his loquacious and determined mother, the crude but immensely American-real characters of his brothers and sisters. Then there are widening contacts: the mountain-ringed town of Altamont, where his boyhood is spent; the state university; then graduate school at Harvard where he is a member of Professor Hatcher's famous playwriting workshop; next there is teaching at the university in New York, followed by his journey to Europe. Through all of this expanding experience, Eugene Gant moves with an immense and unsatisfied hunger. A marked instance is Eugene's frustration before the mountains of books in the Harvard library:

> The thought of these vast stacks of books would drive him mad: . . . the greater the number of the books he read, the greater the immense uncountable number of those which he could never read

would seem to be. Within a period of ten years he read at least 20,000 volumes . . . and opened the pages and looked through many times that number. . . .

He pictured himself as tearing the entrails from a book as from a fowl. . . . walking at night among the vast piled shelves of the library, he would read, watch in hand, muttering to himself in triumph or anger at the timing of each page: "Fifty seconds to do that one. Damn you, we'll see!" . . .—and he would tear through the next page in twenty seconds.

This fury which drove him on to read so many books had nothing to do with . . . formal learning. . . . He simply wanted to know about everything on earth . . . it was the same with everything he did. In the midst of a furious burst of reading in the enormous library, the thought of the streets outside and the great city all around him would drive through his body like a sword. It would now seem to him that every second that he passed among the books was being wasted—that at this moment something priceless, irrecoverable was happening in the streets, and that if he could only get to it in time and see it, he would somehow get the knowledge of the whole thing in him—the source, the well, the spring from which all men and words and actions, and every design upon this earth proceeds.

And he would rush out in the streets to find it, be hurled through the tunnel into Boston and then spend hours in driving himself savagely through a hundred streets, looking into the faces of a million people . . . until bone and brain and blood could stand no more. . . .[2]

This is the nature of the hunger that possessed Eugene Gant; and his movement in Wolfe's first two novels from the family ever farther into the outward world may well be characterized as a search—a search for some marvelous touchstone—for a leaf that is lost, or a stone that marks the place, or a door which opens to that certainty which a young man's faith assures him does beat at the heart of life.

To a large extent, this is the eternal Romantic Quest. It is Poe's traveler looking for his El Dorado; or the search that Thoreau speaks of in *Walden:*

I long ago lost a hound, a bay horse, and a turtledove, and am still on their trail. Many are the travellers I have spoken concerning them, describing their tracks and what calls they answered to. I have met one or two who had heard the hound, and the tramp of the horse, and even seen the dove disappear behind a cloud, and they seemed as anxious to recover them as if they had lost them themselves.[3]

(And Wolfe called it the young man's search for a father who shall be "the image of a strength and wisdom external to his need and superior to his hunger, to which the belief and power of his own life [can] be united.") The Romantic Quest, while valid for every youth and (it seems to me) an essential stage for every young person who aspires to be an artist, is by nature a self-centered one. The searcher is looking for something *for himself:* his concern is not to give, but to receive.

However, one may expect that the mature man, while retaining the idealistic curiosity and the desire for constant fulfillment, will grow beyond the binding self-centeredness of the romantic youth, will find his area of concern stretching further than his individual self, will begin to contribute to the world as well as receive from it. I think this kind of growth happened to Wolfe; and I think that the critics who identify him merely with an arm-waving and rhetorical adolescent, simply haven't taken his full measure.

Within the first cycle of Wolfe's work, which may be named the Search for a Father, there was growing up another cycle. This second one was of much larger dimension than the first, and it did not simply follow the first one in time, but grew large enough to include it. Wolfe became aware of the change while he was at work upon his second novel. He had produced an enormous manuscript, only a part of which seemed to continue the story of Eugene Gant. The rest of it contained something different. Wolfe had grown beyond the Eugene Gant outlook, and his awareness of this appears in the preface of his next book:

> *I hope that the protagonist will illustrate in his own experience every one of us. . . .*
> *This novel, then, marks not only a turning away from the books I have written in the past, but a genuine spiritual and artistic change. It is the most objective novel that I have written.*[4]

I believe that Wolfe really did effect a change in his later work. Of course, the last two novels are autobiographical, as are the first two; but there is a great deal more of another element in them. We have seen that Eugene Gant of the early works was digging into books and roaming the streets and looking into many faces, searching for sustenance that would feed his own hunger for life. But something else was happening, too. This Eugene Gant (Thomas Wolfe) was *seeing* the things he looked at. More and more he was becoming aware of them as objects outside himself and outside his own young, sensitive nature. The process grew; Wolfe was recording the world at it actually was. Particularly in his last book we have clear evidence that he was an acute and penetrating observer of his times. I believe that this area of his accomplishment has not been sufficiently explored. There is a rich and rewarding portrait of the America of the thirties in Wolfe's last novel; I am not sure that any other writer has given us a better one.

Let us consider some of the pictures of his time that he gives us. One of the major scenes in his last novel is the party at Jack's. Mrs. Esther Jack is the woman in her late forties who has befriended and fallen in love with the young Wolfean hero, now known as George Webber. She is a woman of many talents, one of the most accomplished stage-designers of the Theatre Guild. Also she is a woman of rich beauty, of great charm and social talents. Among her friends are many of the most important and powerful persons in the theatrical, literary, and social worlds of Manhattan. She has invited George Webber to the party in her luxurious aparement so that he, a neophyte novelist, may make the acquaintance of some of these distinguished leaders in the world of the arts. He has come unwillingly, even resentfully. Though in his youth he had once dreamed of coming to the golden Manhattan and mixing with such glamorous company, he now finds himself wretchedly uncomfortable, wretchedly awkward, nervous, and tongue-tied.

But whatever his own state of mind may be, he sees these people, and he makes us see them too. We see the tall smouldering beauty of Lily Mandell in her one-piece golden gown, swaying along with sleepy undulance, followed by the eyes of all the men—but followed with more particular intent by Mr. Lawrence Hirsch, the banker. Each time she pauses to speak to someone, Mr. Hirsch by chance strolls up and joins the conversation. After a few words he addresses a remark to Lily Mandell who surveys him slowly with a withering

look of loathing—"as one might look at a large worm within the
core of a chestnut" and moves away. Mr. Hirsch continues talking
a few minutes longer and then saunters on in the general direction
taken by Miss Mandell.

We see Stephen Hook, the writer of competent stories which
sell to magazines and of very fine books which have established his
high reputation (but which have almost no sale). He hides an
informed and perceptive mind behind a mask of weary disdain and
boredom; yet in an unguarded moment we are permitted to see a

> look of naked pleading in his hazel eyes . . . the look of a proud,
> noble, strangely twisted and tormented man—the look almost of a
> frightened child, who, even while it shrank away from the com-
> panionship and security it so desperately needed and wanted, was
> also pleading pitifully: "For God's sake, help me if you can! I am
> afraid!" [5]

We see Amy Carleton—or rather we hear her hoarse young
voice: "I *mean!* . . . You *know!* . . . But Esther! Darling, . . . !
It's the most . . . ! I *mean* . . ." Amy Carleton, who at this party
seems to be a "freckled, laughing image of happy innocence"—who
now in her middle twenties has already surpassed the ultimate limits
of notoriety, even for New York. Her first marriage had ended in
divorce, her second in annulment after twenty hours, her third when
her husband shot himself.

> And before and after that, and in between, . . . and now and
> then, and here and there, and at home and abroad, and on the
> seven seas, and across the length and breadth of the five continents,
> and yesterday and tomorrow and forever—could it be said of her
> that she had been promisc[u]ous? No, that could not be said of
> her. For she had been free as air, and one does not qualify the
> general atmosphere with such a paltry adjective as "promiscuous."
> (p. 247)

And so, with her present lover, and her former one also, panting
at her heels, the "freckled, laughing image of happy innocence"
joins the party at Jack's.

There are many others at this remarkable party. We meet the
cherubic Mr. Samuel Fetzer, the connoisseur of rare books, crying
out "*Beddoes!* Oh, *Beddoes* by all means!" smacking his lips over the

name of this little-read poet, as though the word itself were a sip of old port. We see Miss Roberta Heilprinn, the shrewd director of a celebrated art theatre, who has demonstrated that she is more than a match for all the wolves of Broadway and has thrived on it.

The star attraction, hired for the entertainment of the guests, is the rage of the social season, the celebrated Piggy Logan and his circus of wire dolls. Piggy prepares for his act by donning his thick blue turtleneck sweater with an enormous homemade Y sewn across its front, his tennis sneakers, his old battered kneepads, and his ancient football helmet. Then he clears the center of the living room floor of its furniture, hangs up some big circus posters, yellow with age, reading "Barnum & Bailey—May 7th and 8th," "Ringling Brothers—July 31st."

First, Wolfe tells us, there was a grand procession of the performers, Mr. Logan solemnly walking each one around the ring in turn. This took some time. Then came an exhibition of bareback riders, an interlude of clowns, and next a procession of wire elephants.

This performance gained particular applause because of the clever way in which Mr. Logan made the figures imitate the swaying, ponderous lurch of elephants—and also because people were not always sure what each act meant, and when they were able to identify something, a pleasant little laugh of recognition would sweep the crowd and they would clap their hands to show they had got it.

There were a good many acts of one kind or another, and at last the trapeze performers were brought on. It took a little while to get this act going because Mr. Logan, with his punctilious fidelity to reality, had first to string up a little net below the trapezes. And when the act did begin it was unconscionably long, chiefly because Mr. Logan was not able to make it work. He set the little wire figures to swinging and dangling from their perches. This part went all right. Then he tried to make one little figure leave its trapeze, swing through the air, and catch another figure by its downswept hands. This wouldn't work. Again and again the little wire figure soared through the air, caught at the outstretched hands of the other doll—and missed ingloriously. It became painful. People craned their necks and looked embarrassed. He giggled happily with each new failure and tried again. It went on and on. . . . But nothing happened. At length, when it became obvious that nothing was going to happen, Mr. Logan settled the whole matter himself by taking one little figure firmly between two fat fingers, conveying it to the other, and carefully hooking it onto the other's arms. Then he looked up at his audience and giggled cheerfully, to be greeted after a puzzled pause by perfunctory applause. (pp. 279–80)

The grand climax is the sword-swallowing act. Mr. Logan picked up a small rag doll, bent a long hairpin more or less straight, and began to force the hairpin down the rag throat. It became rather horrible. "It was a curious spectacle," writes Wolfe, "and would have furnished interesting material for the speculations of a thoughtful historian of life and customs in this golden age" (p. 280).

The party is a microcosm of the illustrious and powerful seen in an evening of relaxation; and in George Webber's eyes they do not come off very well. The party moves to an unscheduled climax when fire breaks out somewhere in the apartment building, the lights fail, an acrid smoke drifts through the halls, and the party of the illustrious with candles in their hands proceed in ghostlike procession down nine flights to the open courtyard. For an awkward hour the polished surface of their lives has left their control. By way of symbolic overtone, it may be noted that this party occurred in October of 1929, one week before the thunderous crash in the Stock Market which brought the golden era to its end. Wolfe has given us a perceptive account of the moral disorder in the world of privilege just before its collapse.

He lets us see another world, too, during the autumn of 1929— the world of the Southern town in which he was raised, the town called Libya Hill in the novel. Just before the publication of his first book, George Webber returns on a visit; but he finds that it is no longer home for him. The whole town has gone mad with real-estate speculation.

The barbers, the lawyers, the grocers, the butchers, the builders, the clothiers—all were engaged now in this single interest and obsession. . . . Along all the streets in town the ownership of the land was constantly changing; and when the supply of streets was exhausted, new streets were feverishly created in the surrounding wilderness; and even before these streets were paved or a house had been built upon them, the land was being sold, and then resold, by the acre, by the lot, by the foot, for hundreds of thousands of dollars. (pp. 110–11)

George is astonished to find that the most honored figure in town is now Tim Wagner, whom he remembered as the town sot. Tim had run through two fortunes in alcoholic debauchery before he was twenty-five and used to live in an ancient abandoned horse-drawn hearse. But now—fifteen years later—Tim is raised to the position of high priest and prophet of the land madness. The citizens of Libya Hill believe that in his addled brain lies some power of intuition that makes all his judgments infallible.

While on this brief return to Libya Hill, George is also given an insight into the workings of the great business corporation. His friend Randy Shepperton is the district agent for a national concern known as the Federal Weight, Scales, and Computing Company. The "Company's man," Mr. Merrit, pays one of his calls, and spends a few days at the Sheppertons'. From Mr. Merrit, George hears the saga of the great business empire which he represents—particularly its sales organization. The institution had a modest beginning when its founder expressed his hopes by saying, "I should like to see one of my machines in every store, shop, or business that needs one, and that can afford to pay for one." Mr. Merrit shakes his head pityingly over the limited vision of the old man, and then his eyes light up as he tells of the great moment of poetic inspiration that visited the present head of the company, Mr. Paul S. Appleton, III:

The idea had come to him in a single blinding flash . . . and Mr. Merrit still remembered the momentous occasion as vividly as if it had been only yesterday. It was at one of the meetings of the assembled parliaments of the Company that Mr. Appleton, soaring in an impassioned flight of oratory, became so intoxicated with the grandeur of his own vision that he stopped abruptly in the middle of a sentence and stood there as one entranced, gazing out dreamily into the unknown vistas of magic Canaan; and when he at last went on again, it was in a voice surcharged with quivering emotion:

"My friends," he said, "the possibilities of the market, now that we see how to create it, are practically unlimited!" Here he was silent for a moment, and Mr. Merrit said that the Great Man actually paled and seemed to stagger as he tried to speak, and that his voice faltered and sank to an almost inaudible whisper, as if he himself could hardly comprehend the magnitude of his own conception. "My friends—" he muttered thickly, and was seen to clutch the rostrum for support—"my friends—seen properly—" he whispered and moistened his dry lips—"seen properly—the market we shall create being what it is—" his voice grew stronger, and the clarion words now rang forth—"there is no reason why one of our machines should not be in the possession of every man, woman, and child in the United States!" Then came the grand, familiar gesture to the map: "There's your market, boys. Go out and sell them!" (p. 133)

And Mr. Merrit loves to tell of the Company Heaven, known as the Hundred Club. Each salesman was assigned a quota, and his membership depended upon his meeting his quota one hundred per cent. If he did better than that, the rewards were high. (Of course, when he had met his quota for one year, he must be prepared to find it raised the next.)

While it was quite true that membership in the Hundred Club was not compulsory, it was also true that Mr. Paul S. Appleton, III, was a theologian who, like Calvin, knew how to combine free will and predestination. If one did *not* belong to the Hundred Club, the time was not far distant when one would not belong to Mr. Appleton. (p. 135)

Every year, the members of the Hundred Club were brought together for what was known as "The Week of Play"—a glorious alcoholic spree in one of the great cities of the nation, all at the Company's expense. However, Wolfe tells us,

. . . as Mr. Merrit painted his glowing picture of the fun they had on these occasions, George Webber saw quite another image. It was an image of twelve or fifteen hundred men . . . Americans, most of them in their middle years, exhausted, overwrought, their nerves frayed down and stretched to the breaking point, met from all quarters of the continent "at The Company's expense" for one brief, wild, gaudy week of riot. And George thought grimly what this tragic spectacle of business men at play meant in terms of the entire scheme of things and the plan of life that had produced it. (pp. 136–37)

Yes, the Wolfean hero began to see the world outside himself. He saw the high world of the great cities and the common, next-door-neighbor world of his home town in the mountains. He saw within them both an eating cancer of corruption and of greed.

And he saw both these worlds fall in the great crash of 1929. He heard how Randy Shepperton lost his job, could not get another, lived on his savings, sold his home, and existed on that money for a year, and then, broken in spirit, had to move in with his older sister's family. He heard how the bank failed at home, and how the mayor, having invested city government funds in the mad real-estate bubble, shot himself in the City Hall. More affecting even than these reports from a distance, were the homeless men that George saw on his nightly ramblings through New York. He saw them in the vicinity of restaurants lifting the lids of garbage cans and searching for morsels of food. He saw them huddled in corridors of a subway station—as many as thirty-four huddled together on the cold concrete, wrapped up in old newspaper. He saw many of them in the public latrine in front of New York City Hall, the

> flotsam of the general ruin of the time. . . . These were the wanderers from town to town, the riders of freight trains, the thumbers of rides on highways, the uprooted, unwanted male population of America. They drifted across the land and gathered in the big cities when winter came, hungry, defeated, empty, hopeless, restless, driven by they knew not what, always on the move, looking everywhere for work, for the bare crumbs to support their miserable lives, and finding neither work nor crumbs. Here in New York, to this obscene meeting place, these derelicts came, drawn into a common stew of rest and warmth and a little surcease from their desperation. (pp. 413–14)

He looked upon the great amount of writing and the great numbers of writers producing it in his time, and he castigated many of them as false—as special pleaders for things as they are, or escapists, or banders into little cults and isms. Wolfe writes admiringly of George's great editor Foxhall Edwards that he

> had no part in the fine horse-manure with which we have allowed ourselves to be bored, maddened, whiff-sniffed, hound-and-hornered, nationed, new-republicked, dialed, spectatored, mercuried, storied, anviled, new-massed, new-yorkered, vogued, vanity-faired, timed, broomed, transitioned . . . by the elegant, refined, and snobified Concentrated Blotters of the Arts. . . . He was none of your . . . groupy-croupy, cliquey-triquey, meachy-teachy, devoto-bloato wire-pullers and back-scratchers of the world. (pp. 485–86)

Unsympathetic criticism had always stung Wolfe, even in his undergraduate college days; and he did not hesitate to strike back. In the passage above, he was by no means lashing out at nothing at all. Here are a few of the judgments that Mr. DeVoto had uttered. Of *Look Homeward, Angel,* he suggested that it "looked like a document in psychic disintegration" containing in large quantities "raw gobs of emotion, aimless and quite meaningless jabber, claptrap, belches, grunts and Tarzan-like screams." Of Wolfe's second novel, *Of Time and the River,* Mr. DeVoto suggested that the hero was "clearly a borderline manic-depressive" and that whatever organization the book had was supplied not by the author but by his editor, Mr. Perkins, and the assembly-line at Scribner's. This last charge eventually led to Wolfe's breaking his relationship with Maxwell Perkins and Scribner's, and transferring his publishing to Harper's for the last two novels.—But this is another story, and aside from our present concern.

I have been emphasizing a side of Wolfe that is not a part of the image fostered by many critics with whom he is out of favor. He saw many of the weaknesses of his society, and he ridiculed them in sustained satire and irony. His portraits of life in Brooklyn, for instance, are rarely surpassed.

There is a great deal more evidence, not satirical, that Wolfe was a keen observer of his times. Being a Southerner himself, he saw and felt that

there was something wounded in the South. . . . something twisted dark, and full of pain which Southerners have known with all their lives. . . .

Perhaps it came from their old war, and from the ruin of their great defeat and its degraded aftermath. Perhaps it came from causes yet more ancient—from the evil of man's slavery, and the hurt and shame of human conscience in its struggle with the fierce desire to own. It came, too, perhaps, from the lusts of the hot South, tormented and repressed below the harsh and outward patterns of a bigot and intolerant theology, yet prowling always, stirring stealthily, as hushed and secret as the thickets of swamp-darkness. And most of all, perhaps, it came out of the very weather of their lives, out of the forms that shaped them and the food that fed them, out of the unknown terrors of the skies above them, out of the dark, mysterious pineland all around them with its haunting sorrow. (pp. 327–28)

This passage inevitably makes me think of William Faulkner, whose fictional world it suggests, and who himself ranked Wolfe in the very top bracket among modern writers.

Wolfe takes his hero to Europe in his last novel. First, he visits England where he comes into contact with a variety of Dickensesque Londoners. Wolfe calls them "the Little People . . . a race of gnomes who look as if they have burrowed in tunnels and lived for so many centuries in underground mines that they have all become pale and small and wizened" (p. 531). In London, George Webber, the writer of a single book, is sought out by the famous novelist, Lloyd McHarg, who has recently been awarded the Nobel prize. Lloyd McHarg, of course, is the representation of Sinclair Lewis, who really did look up Wolfe in London, and who in his speech of acceptance of the Nobel prize had publicly praised the younger writer's work. Wolfe gives a memorable portrait of the writer who stands on the pinnacle of success—and what such fame and success have brought him: a set of crackling nerves, a physical frame that is being driven to the ragged edge by the nervous vitality that is burning within him, a man "lashing himself into a state of frenzied bafflement" (p. 562). It is a memorable portrait, sharply drawn, all the harsh lines seen, yet with an undertone of respect and sympathetic understanding.

After England, George Webber visits Germany. It is the spring of 1936, the spring of the Olympic Games in Berlin. Hitler has been in power for three years; but George is only dimly aware of the significance of that. In his earlier visits to Europe, Germany seemed to be the home-land of his spirit. This time, it is May, his novel has been translated into German and has drawn rave reviews; George finds himself nationally famous. But beneath the glory of this hour, George gradually becomes aware of the poisonous evil which is infecting the land that has been the home of his spirit. It can no longer be home for him. Finally all the pieces of the novel fall together. George Webber sees that you can't go home again.

You can't go back home to your family, back home to your child-
hood, back home to romantic love, back home to a young man's

> *dreams of glory and fame, back home to* . . . *escape to Europe and*
> *some foreign land,* . . . *back home to the father you have lost*
> *and have been looking for,* . . . *back home to the old forms and*
> *systems of things which once seemed everlasting but which are*
> *changing all the time.* . . . (p. 706)

"*You can't go home again*": this phrase gave Wolfe the title of his last novel. It crystallized his later vision of life; and I propose to use it as the name of the second large cycle of Wolfe's fiction. It seems to me that Wolfe began as the romantic young man, feeding himself hungrily on the rich and varied experiences of his expanding world, seeking in them some sense of security for his own need. I have spoken of this cycle of his work as "The Search for a Father." But a larger cycle was beginning to take form and to expand beyond the limits of the first one. The social criticism that appears so markedly in Wolfe's later writing more than suggests that his Search for a Father in our society was not crowned with success. The seeker did not find the lasting and secure goal that he was looking for. He found that love, and success, and fame, and all the various apparent "homes" of the spirit are really not fixed and abiding. They change, and we change; and it is an illusion that we can "go home again" to some golden age that is lost in a buried past.

Matthew Arnold, you may remember, perceived something very like this, and it brought him a profound sadness. In *Dover Beach* he wrote:

> The Sea of Faith
> Was once, too, at the full, and round earth's shore
> Lay like the folds of a bright girdle furl'd.
> But now I only hear
> Its melancholy, long, withdrawing roar . . .
>
> . . . the world, which seems
> To lie before us like a land of dreams,
> So various, so beautiful, so new,
> Hath really neither joy, nor love, nor light,
> Nor certitude, nor peace, nor help for pain. . . .[6]

This perception deeply saddened Matthew Arnold; the very admission of it was a kind of defeat.

But the perception that "you can't go home again" did not break the spirit of Thomas Wolfe; indeed, strangely enough, it heartened him. For if life is change, he felt, then we can improve it. His final credo, on the last page of his last novel, is no defeated whine or whimper. The loss of a false illusion is only the way to a new belief. Here is Wolfe's conclusion:

> I believe that we are lost here in America, but I believe we shall be found. And this belief . . . is . . . not only our own hope, but America's everlasting, living dream. I think the life which we have fashioned in America, and which has fashioned us . . . was self-destructive in its nature, and must be destroyed. I think these forms are dying, and must die, just as I know that America and the people in it are deathless, undiscovered, and immortal, and must live.
>
> I think the true discovery of America is before us. I think the true fulfillment of our spirit, of our people, of our mighty and immortal land, is yet to come. I think the true discovery of our own democracy is still before us. And I think that all these things are certain as the morning, as inevitable as noon . . . our America is Here, is Now, and beckons on before us, and . . . this glorious assurance is not only our living hope, but our dream to be accomplished. (p. 741)

Wolfe brings us an image of the America he lived in and knew, without slurring over its faults, without sparing his criticism of it. He wrote in the thirties; the social concerns that he dealt with are with us still: the awkwardness of having and acknowledging a special privileged class in our democratic society; the materialistic greed that infects every area of our lives; the still painful wound in the Southland; and the threat of totalitarianism abroad. These are live concerns today, and Wolfe's portrait of them is still deeply meaningful.

Furthermore, it seems to me, Wolfe gives us an image of America that we recognize in our hearts is a true one; and it is an image that we can be proud to hold before the world. This is an accomplishment which is very hard to match in the work of any other modern American novelist. Go down the list: Faulkner—Hemingway—Jones—Kerouac. . . . Do any of these portray an America that you feel is as true to your own experience?

If you can agree with me that Wolfe's portrayal is indeed far closer to the land and the life that we ourselves have known, then I am confident that you will also feel the symbolic appropriateness of the concluding detail of Elizabeth Nowell's biography: that, when he died, they could not in Baltimore, Maryland, or in all of the region around, find a coffin "big enough to hold Thomas Wolfe."

Notes

1. Thomas Wolfe, *The Story of a Novel* (New York: Charles Scribner's Sons, 1936), p. 39.

2. Thomas Wolfe, *Of Time and the River* (New York: Charles Scribner's Sons, 1935), pp. 91–92.

3. Henry David Thoreau, *Walden* (New York: Random House, 1937), p. 15.

4. Thomas Wolfe, *The Web and the Rock* (New York, 1939), p. v. Copyright 1937, 1938, 1939 by Maxwell Perkins as Executor. Reprinted with permission of Harper & Row, Publishers.

5. Thomas Wolfe, *You Can't Go Home Again* (New York, 1940), p. 234. Copyright 1934, 1937, 1938, 1939, 1940, 1941 by Maxwell Perkins as Executor. Reprinted with permission of Harper & Row, Publishers.

6. Matthew Arnold, *Selected Poetry and Prose* (New York: Holt, Rinehart and Winston, Inc., 1953), p. 90.

PART II   *His Style*

Thomas Wolfe

7. From Thomas Wolfe's Purdue Speech: "Writing and Living"*

IT HAS SEEMED to me for some time that there is a kind of significance in the fact that my first book appeared in October, 1929. For me, it seemed that in a way my life—my working life—had just begun; but in so many different ways I did not know about, or even suspect at that time, so many things that I believed in, or thought that I believed in, were ended. Many people see in the last great war a kind of great dividing line in their own lives—a kind of great tale of two worlds, a world before the War, and a world after the War; but in my own experience, if I had to write my own tale of two worlds, I think I should be more inclined to use 1929 as the dividing line. Certainly, that has been the most memorable division in my own life that I can now recall.

Before that, as we have seen, my experience as a man and as a writer had passed through certain well-defined stages, all of which were very familiar to the times and to the lives of many other young men of the times. The son of an average small-town family, I had in the early Twenties embarked upon a writing career—had decided to be a writer—a fact which was not only in complete variance with the lives of all my other people before me, but was also symptomatic of a marked social tendency of the time—the desire of thousands of young men everywhere to write. I had passed through progressive stages of change and of development which were also characteristic of the time: I had gone through the stage of aesthetic preciosity, of talking about "art" and "beauty," and about "the artist"; of scorning

* Edited by William Braswell and Leslie A. Field.

"the bourgeoisie," the Philistines and Babbitts, who were not only not artists, but who could never understand "the artist," but belonged to a completely different, separate world. From this, which was a time, I am afraid, in which I talked a great deal more about "beauty" and "art" than I created it, expended a great deal more time in scorning and in ridiculing "the bourgeoisie" than in trying to find out who they were and what they were like—I passed into the period when I had to go to work, and where I learned for the first time what work—hard, creative work—was like, and where at last I began to spend more time in an effort to create "art" and "beauty" than in talking about it. And now finally, I had reached the stage of first accomplishment—where at last I had accomplished something, got it completed, accepted, printed, and put between the covers of a book, where for the first time the general public, if it so desired, could look at it.

This is certainly a definite and closely linked chain of clear development, and for me it marked the end of one great cycle. Although perhaps I did not know much in 1929, I did know a good deal more than I knew in 1920. I knew, first of all, that writing was hard work—desperately hard work—and whoever accomplishes a good piece of writing must work hard and constantly, with exhausting concentration, and not depend upon sporadic flashes of casual inspiration to do the job for him. I knew furthermore, and finally, that I could write—that I was able to see a job through to the end, and able to get it published by a good publisher. It is not necessary to point out what an inestimable comfort this knowledge was to me, for it had served to establish some confidence in my own abilities which I had never had before, and to restore my self-respect and my belief in myself and in what I wanted to do, which had been shaken by years of failure and frustration. I was certainly a wiser man in 1929 than I was in 1920, and I think I was also a stronger and surer one. I no longer had so big a chip upon my shoulder, I was no longer so truculent and occasionally arrogant in my relations to other people, because I no longer felt such inner need to prove to myself that I could do what I wanted to do. But I suppose a good deal of the old foolishness still remained: I would have smiled in 1929 at some of the aesthetic snobberies and preciosities of the young men at Harvard in 1923, but if anyone had asked me why I wrote, Why

I wanted to be a writer and continue to write books, I would have said some of the same things that I had said years before: I would have talked about "the artist," and I suppose I might still have had a romantic and fanciful notion of him, and of his relations to society. I am afraid I might also have talked a good deal about "art" and "beauty"—perhaps I shouldn't have been so hard on "the Babbitts and the Philistines," and as arrogantly scornful of "the bourgeoisie" as I had been in 1923—but I would have still looked down on them from a kind of aesthetic altitude and felt that they belonged to a separate order of things, in a different world. I was a lot closer to life, to people, to the world around me, to America in 1929, than I had ever been before; although I was still too detached from it, not nearly close enough. But the experience of the last few years—the experience of work—the necessity of work—the fact that I really had worked had now brought me much closer to life, much closer to an understanding of the lives of people, as I think work always does. And for the last three years, before the publication of my first book, the work I had been doing had taught me much—that work, in substance, had demanded a kind of spiritual and emotional excavation of the deepest and intensest sort into the life I had known and of which I had been a part—the life of my home town, of my family, of the people I had come from—of the whole structure and frame of things that had produced me. I knew more about all of this than I had ever known before, but, as I was to discover, I did not know enough. For one thing, the book still showed unmistakably the evidence of the stages I had gone through, the periods of development, the special aesthetic faiths and creeds of the time. It is what is called an autobiographical novel—a definition with which I have never agreed, simply because it seems to me every novel, every piece of creative writing that anyone can do, is autobiographical. Nevertheless, it is true that this book was autobiographical in the personal and special sense: it was possible, for example, to identify the life of the hero with the life of the author—to suspect that a great many of the characters and incidents in the book were drawn pretty closely and directly from the writer's own experience. And, although I have not read the book for years, I believe that in this sense of the word —in this special autobiographical sense—was the book's greatest weakness: I believe the character of the hero was the weakest and least convincing one in the whole book, because he had been derived not only from experience but colored a good deal by the romantic aestheticism of the period. He was, in short, "the artist" in pretty much the Harvard Forty-seven Workshop sense of the word—the wounded sensitive, the extraordinary creature in conflict with his environment, with the Babbitt, the Philistine, the small town, the family. I know that I was not satisfied with this character even at the time: he seemed to me to be uneasy and self-conscious, probably because I was myself uneasy and self-conscious about him. In this sense, therefore, the book followed a familiar pattern—a pattern made familiar by Joyce in *A Portrait of the Artist as a Young Man,* and later in *Ulysses*—a book which at that time strongly influenced my own work. But I think the book also had been conceived and created with some of the blazing intensity of youth: although I did not know it at the time, in that sense of the word the book was a kind of passionate expletive—a fiery ejaculation hurled down upon a page of print because it had to come out, it had to be said. Here, too, my real education was beginning, for as yet I did not know these things. Again, the book had a rather extraordinary career: although it was on the whole well-reviewed and well-received throughout the rest of the country, and had, for a first book, a moderately good sale, in my own home town it was received with an outburst of fury and indignation that in my own experience has not been surpassed, and that I believe is even extraordinary in anyone's experience. Briefly, the people of the town read the book as if it had been the pages of the *World Almanac;* and seeing that some things were true, they became almost immediately convinced that everything was literally true and literally intended; and from this they became so outraged that they denounced me and my book individually and in the mass— from the pulpits, from the street corners, and from the public press; in letters signed, and in letters anonymous; and in threats that included tar and feathers, hanging, gun-shot, and all other forms of sudden death. Their outrage and anger, although mistaken, were unmistakable: there is no doubt that from the moment of the book's publication, I became an exile from my native town. I could not have come back at that time, and it was seven years, in fact, before I wanted to come back, and did return.

This was bewildering and overwhelming: it was all different from what I had expected—so different from the reception that I had hoped to have in my home town that for a time my own sense of grief, disappointment and chagrin were very great; for one of the things it is hard to lose is the desire for the approbation and applause of one's own neighbors—the knowledge that one has succeeded in the estimation of the people of his own town. Moreover, it did do something to strengthen me in a further belief in what was perhaps the fundamental theme of the whole book—the story of the sensitive young man in conflict with his environment, driven out at last, forced to flee and escape from his own town. For now that had happened to me, and if that had been all that had happened, it might have embittered me into further belief and confirmation of my earlier error. Fortunately, there were other compensations: if I had been driven out at home, I had been accepted elsewhere; if my own townspeople had read my book with outrage and indignation, the larger public had read it as I had intended it to be read, as a book, as a work of fiction, as a product of the creative imagination which, if it had any value at all, had value because it was just as true of Portland, or Des Moines, of people everywhere, as it was of my own town.

So there I was in 1929, at the end of one route, at the beginning of another, at the end and the beginning of so many different things I then did not know or suspect, that looking back now, I seem to have been a guileless innocent. On the whole, my view of things was pretty hopeful, pretty cheerful, for although I did have the desolating and rather desperate sense of exile, of having pulled up my roots completely as far as the old life was concerned, I had a feeling now of new beginning, too—of being launched at last, of having before me the happy prospect of an established and productive career. At that time, among the many other things I did not know, I did not know that for a man who wants to continue with the creative life, to keep on growing and developing, this cheerful idea of happy establishment, of continuing now as one has started, is nothing but a delusion and a snare. I did not know that if a man really has in him the desire and the capacity to create, the power of further growth and further development, there can be no such thing as an easy road. I did not know that so far from having found out about writing, I had really found out almost nothing: I had made a bare beginning, I had learned at best that I could do it. I had made a first and simple utterance; but I did not know that each succeeding one would not only be harder and more difficult than the last, but would be completely different—that with each new effort would come new desperation, the new, and old, sense of having to begin from the beginning all over again, of being face to face again with the old naked facts of self and work, of realizing again that there is no help anywhere save the help and strength that one can find within himself.

Again—and now I was moving to another deeper stage—I had not realized yet that the world changes, that the world is changing all the time, that the world, indeed, is in a constant and perpetual state of revolution—and that a man, a creative man most of all, if he is going to live and grow, must change with the world. I did not realize, in fact, even in 1929, that those images and figures of my experience and training—the image of "the artist" and of "art," of "beauty" and of "love," of the wounded sensitive, driven out and fleeing away from the Philistines of the tribe—all of which had seemed so fixed and everlasting in the scheme of things, were really just the transient images of the times, a portion of the aesthetic belief and doctrine of the period. I did not realize that the year 1929, which was so important to me in such immediate personal ways concerning my own life and my immediate career, was to be a fatal and important year in so many other ways I did not even know about at that time, in so many ways affecting the life of the nation and of all the people in it, affecting human beliefs, that it seems now to mark a dividing line between two worlds. About the organized structure of society in 1929—its systems of finance, economy, politics and government—and how they shaped and affected the lives of people, I knew almost nothing, and had never considered it a part of my interest to question or examine them. Certainly, if anyone should have suggested to me, in 1929, that it was not only a part of the purpose and function of an artist to examine them, but that if he continued to produce, his participation and examination would be inescapable, I should have denied the proposition utterly. I should have said that the purpose and the function of the artist was to create, to create what was true and beautiful, without reference to its social implications as regards the world around him; I think that I should probably have further said that the interest of the artist in such things as economics, politics, government, the organized structure of society, was not only outside the province of his life and work—to create the beautiful and true—but would probably be alien and injurious to it, if he allowed it to intrude in what he did.

The fact that I no longer feel this way, and how and why, and by what degrees and stages I have come to feel differently, marks the last stage of my development at which I have now arrived. . . .

Bernard DeVoto

8. Genius Is Not Enough

SOME MONTHS AGO *The Saturday Review* serialized Mr. Thomas
Wolfe's account of the conception, gestation, and as yet uncompleted
delivery of his Novel, and Scribners are now publishing the three
articles as a book.* It is one of the most appealing books of our time.
No one who reads it can doubt Mr. Wolfe's complete dedication to
his job or regard with anything but respect his attempt to describe
the dark and nameless fury of the million-footed life swarming in his
dark and unknown soul. So honest or so exhaustive an effort at self-
analysis in the interest of aesthetics has seldom been made in the
history of American literature, and "The Story of a Novel" is likely
to have a long life as a source-book for students of literature and for
psychologists as well. But also it brings into the public domain material that has been hitherto outside the privilege of criticism. Our
first essay must be to examine it in relation to Mr. Wolfe's novels, to
see what continuities and determinants it may reveal, and to inquire
into their bearing on the art of fiction.

Let us begin with one of many aspects of Mr. Wolfe's novels
that impress the reader, the frequent recurrence of material to
which one must apply the adjective placental. (The birth metaphors
are imposed by Mr. Wolfe himself. In *The Story of a Novel* he
finds himself big with first a thunder cloud and then a river. The
symbolism of waters is obviously important to him, and the title of
his latest novel is to be that of the series as a whole.) A great part of

* *The Story of a Novel,* by Thomas Wolfe (New York: Charles Scribner's Sons,
1936), $1.50.

Look Homeward, Angel was just the routine first novel of the period, which many novelists had published and many others had suppressed, the story of a sensitive and rebellious adolescent who was headed toward the writing of novels. The rest of it was not so easily cataloged. Parts of it showed intuition, understanding, and ecstasy, and an ability to realize all three in character and scene, whose equal it would have been hard to point out anywhere in the fiction of the time. These looked like great talent, and in such passages as the lunchroom scene in the dawn that Mr. Wolfe called nacreous some fifty times, they seemed to exist on both a higher and a deeper level of realization than any of Mr. Wolfe's contemporaries had attained. But also there were parts that looked very dubious indeed—long, whirling discharges of words, unabsorbed in the novel, unrelated to the proper business of fiction, badly if not altogether unacceptably written, raw gobs of emotion, aimless and quite meaningless jabber, claptrap, belches, grunts, and Tarzanlike screams. Their rawness, their unshaped quality, must be insisted upon; it was as if the birth of the novel had been accompanied by a lot of the material that had nourished its gestation. The material which nature and most novelists discard when its use has been served. It looked like one of two things, there was no telling which. It looked like the self-consciously literary posturing of a novelist too young and too naïve to have learned his trade. Or, from another point of view, it looked like a document in psychic disintegration. And one of the most important questions in contemporary literature was: would the proportion of fiction to placenta increase or decrease in Mr. Wolfe's next book?

It decreased. If fiction of the quality of that lunchroom scene made up one-fifth of *Look Homeward, Angel,* it constituted, in *Of Time and the River,* hardly more than a tenth. The placental material had enormously grown and, what was even more ominous, it now had a rationalization. It was as unshaped as before, but it had now been retroactively associated with the dark and nameless heaving of the voiceless and unknown womb of Time, and with the unknown and voiceless fury of the dark and lonely and lost America. There were still passages where Mr. Wolfe was a novelist not only better than most of his contemporaries but altogether out of their class. But they were pushed farther apart and even diluted when they occurred by this dark substance which may have been nameless but was certainly far from voiceless.

Certain other aspects of the new book seemed revealing. For one thing, there was a shocking contempt of the medium. Some passages were not completely translated from the "I" in which they had apparently been written to the "he" of Eugene Gant. Other passages alluded to incidents which had probably appeared in an earlier draft but could not be found in the final one. Others contradictorily reported scenes which had already appeared, and at least once a passage that had seen service already was reenlisted for a second hitch in a quite different context, apparently with no recollection that it had been used before.

Again, a state of mind that had been appropriate to the puberty of Eugene seemed inappropriate as the boy grew older, and might therefore be significant. I mean the giantism of the characters. Eugene himself, in *Of Time and the River,* was clearly a borderline manic-depressive: he exhibited the classic cycle in his alternation between "fury" and "despair," and the classic accompaniment of obsessional neurosis in the compulsions he was under to read all the books in the world, see all the people in Boston, observe all the lives of the man-swarm, and list all the names and places in America. That was simple enough, but practically every other character in the book also suffered from fury and compulsions; and, what was more suggestive, they were all twenty feet tall, spoke with the voice of trumpets and the thunder, ate like Pantagruel, wept like Niobe, laughed like Falstaff, and bellowed like the bulls of Bashan. The significant thing was that we were seeing them all through Eugene's eyes. To a child all adults are giants: their voices are thunderous, their actions are portentous and grotesquely magnified, and all their exhibited emotions are seismic. It looked as if part of Eugene's condition was an infantile regression.

This appearance was reinforced by what seemed to be another stigma of infantilism: that all the experiences in *Of Time and the River* were on the same level and had the same value. When Mr. Gant died (of enough cancer to have exterminated an army corps), the reader accepted the accompanying frenzy as proper to the death of a man's father—which is one of the most important events in anyone's life. But when the same frenzy accompanied nearly everything else in the book—a ride on a railroad train, a literary tea-fight, a midnight lunch in the kitchen, a quarrel between friends, a walk at night, the rejection of a play, an automobile trip, a seduction that misfired, the discovery of Eugene's true love—one could only decide that something was dreadfully wrong. If the death of one's father comes out emotionally even with a ham-on-rye, then the art of fiction is cockeyed.

Well, *The Story of a Novel* puts an end to speculation and supplies some unexpected but very welcome light. To think of these matters as contempt of the medium, regression, and infantilism is to be too complex and subtle. The truth shows up in two much simpler facts: that Mr. Wolfe is still astonishingly immature, and that he has mastered neither the psychic material out of which a novel is made nor the technique of writing fiction. He does not seem aware of the first fact, but he acknowledges the second with a frankness and an understanding that are the finest promise to date for his future books. How far either defect is reparable it is idle to speculate. But at least Mr. Wolfe realizes that he is, as yet, by no means a complete novelist.

The most flagrant evidence of his incompleteness is the fact that, so far, one indispensable part of the artist has existed not in Mr. Wolfe but in Maxwell Perkins. Such organizing faculty and such critical intelligence as have been applied to the book have come not from inside the artist, not from the artist's feeling for form and aesthetic integrity, but from the office of Charles Scribner's Sons. For five years the artist pours out words "like burning lava from a volcano" —with little or no idea what their purpose is, which book they belong in, what the relation of part to part is, what is organic and what irrelevant, or what emphasis or coloration in the completed work of art is being served by the job at hand. Then Mr. Perkins decides these questions—from without, and by a process to which rumor applies the word "assembly." But works of art cannot be assembled like a carburetor—they must be grown like a plant, or in Mr. Wolfe's favorite simile, like an embryo. The artist writes a hundred thousand words about a train: Mr. Perkins decides that the train is worth only five thousand words. But such a decision as this is properly not within Mr. Perkins' power; it must be made by the highly conscious self-criticism of the artist in relation to the pulse of the book itself. Worse still, the artist goes on writing till Mr. Perkins tells him that the novel is finished. But the end of a novel is, properly, dictated by the internal pressure, osmosis, metabolism—what you will—of the novel itself, of which only the novelist can have a first-hand knowledge. There comes a point where the necessities of the book are satisfied, where its organic processes have reached completion. It is hard to see how awareness of that point can manifest itself at an editor's desk—and harder still to trust the integrity of a work of art in which not the artist but the publisher has determined where the true ends and the false begins.

All this is made more ominous by Mr. Wolfe's almost incredibly youthful attitude toward revision. No novel is written till it is revised—the process is organic, it is one of the processes of art. It is, furthermore, the process above all others that requires objectivity, a feeling for form, a knowledge of what the necessities of the book are, a determination that those necessities shall outweigh and dominate everything else. It is, if not the highest functioning of the artistic intelligence, at least a fundamental and culminating one. But the process appears to Mr. Wolfe not one which will free his book from falsity, irrelevance, and its private incumbrances, not one which will justify and so exalt the artist—but one that makes his spirit quiver "at the bloody execution" and his soul "recoil from the carnage of so many lovely things." But superfluous and mistaken things are lovely to only a very young writer, and the excision of them is bloody carnage only if the artist has not learned to subdue his ego in favor of his book. And the same juvenility makes him prowl "the streets of Paris like a maddened animal" because—for God's sake!—the reviewers may not like the job.

The placental passages are now explained. They consist of psychic material which the novelist has proved unable to shape into fiction. The failure may be due either to immature understanding or to insufficient technical skill: probably both causes operate here and cannot be separated. The principle is very simple. When Mr. Wolfe gives us his doctors, undertakers, and newspapermen talking in a lunchroom at dawn, he does his job—magnificently. There they are, and the reader revels in the dynamic presentation of human beings, and in something else as well that should have the greatest possible significance for Mr. Wolfe. For while the doctors and undertakers are chaffing one another, the reader gets that feeling of the glamour and mystery of American life which Mr. Wolfe elsewhere unsuccessfully labors to evoke in thousands of rhapsodic words. The novelist makes his point in the lives of his characters, not in tidal surges of rhetoric.

Is America lost, lonely, nameless, and unknown? Maybe, and maybe not. But if it is, the condition of the novelist's medium requires him to make it lost and lonely in the lives of his characters, not in blank verse, bombast, and apocalyptic delirium. You cannot represent America by hurling adjectives at it. Do "the rats of death and age and dark oblivion feed forever at the roots of sleep?" It sounds like a high school valedictory, but if in fact they do, then the novelist is constrained to show them feeding so by means of what his characters do and say and feel in relation to one another, and not by chasing the ghosts of Whitman and Ezekiel through fifty pages of disembodied emotion. Such emotion is certainly the material that fiction works with, but until it is embodied in character and scene it is not fiction—it is only logorrhea. A poem should not mean but be, Mr. MacLeish tells us, and poetry is always proving that fundamental. In a homelier aphorism Mr. Cohan has expressed the same imperative of the drama: "Don't tell 'em, show 'em." In the art of fiction the *thing* is not only an imperative, it is a primary condition. A novel *is*—it cannot be asserted, ranted, or even detonated. A novelist represents life. When he does anything else, no matter how beautiful or furious or ecstatic the way in which he does it, he is not writing fiction. Mr. Wolfe can write fiction—has written some of the finest fiction of our day. But a great part of what he writes is not fiction at all: it is only material with which the novelist has struggled but which has defeated him. The most important question in American fiction today, probably, is whether he can win that encounter in his next book. It may be that *The October Fair* and *The Hills Beyond Pentland* will show him winning it, but one remembers the dilution from *Look Homeward, Angel* to *Of Time and the River* and is apprehensive. If he does win it, he must do so inside himself; Mr. Perkins and the assembly line at Scribners' can do nothing to help him.

That struggle has another aspect. A novelist utilizes the mechanism of fantasy for the creation of a novel, and there are three kinds of fantasy with which he works. One of them is unconscious fantasy, about which Dr. Kubie was writing in these columns something over a year ago. A novelist is wholly subject to its emphases and can do nothing whatever about them—though when Mr. Wolfe says that the center of all living is reconciliation with one's father he comes close to revealing its pattern in him. There remain two kinds of fantasy which every novelist employs—but which every one employs in a different ratio. Call them identification and projection, call them automatic and directed, call them proliferating and objectified—the names do not matter. The novelist surrenders himself to the first kind, but dominates and directs the second kind. In the first kind he says "I am Napoleon" and examines himself to see how he feels. In the second kind, he wonders how Napoleon feels, and instead of identifying himself with him, he tries to discover Napoleon's necessities. If he is excessively endowed with the first kind of fantasy, he is likely to be a genius. But if he learns to utilize the second kind in the manifold interrelationships of a novel he is certain to be an artist. Whatever Mr. Wolfe's future in the wider and looser interest of Literature, his future in the far more rigorous interest of fiction just about comes down to the question of whether he can increase his facility at the second kind of fantasy. People would stop idiotically calling him autobiographical, if he gave us less identification and more understanding. And we could do with a lot less genius, if we got a little more artist.

For the truth is that Mr. Wolfe is presented to us, and to himself, as a genius. There is no more dissent from that judgment in his thinking about himself than in Scribner's publicity. And, what is more, a genius of the good old-fashioned, romantic kind—possessed by a demon, driven by the gales of his own fury, helpless before the lava-flood of his own passion, selected and set apart for greatness, his lips touched by a live coal, consequently unable to exercise any control over what he does and in fact likely to be damaged or diminished by any effort at control. Chaos is everything if you have enough of it in you to make a world. Yes, but what if you don't make a world—what if you just make a noise? There was chaos in Stephen Dedalus's soul, but he thought of that soul not as sufficient in itself but merely as a smithy wherein he might forge his novel. And listen to Mr. Thomas Mann:

When I think of the masterpiece of the twentieth century, I have an idea of something that differs essentially and, in my opinion, with profit from the Wagnerian masterpiece—something exceptionally logical, clear, and well developed in form, something at once austere and serene, with no less intensity of will than his, but of cooler, nobler, even healthier spirituality, something that seeks its greatness not in the colossal, the baroque, and its beauty not in intoxication.

Something, in other words, with inescapable form, something which exists as the imposition of order on chaos, something that *is,* not is merely asserted.

One can only respect Mr. Wolfe for his determination to realize himself on the highest level and to be satisfied with nothing short of greatness. But, however useful genius may be in the writing of novels, it is not enough in itself—it never has been enough, in any art, and it never will be. At the very least it must be supported by an ability to impart shape to material, simple competence in the use of tools. Until Mr. Wolfe develops more craftsmanship, he will not be the important novelist he is now widely accepted as being. In order to be a great novelist he must also mature his emotions till he can see more profoundly into character than he now does, and he must learn to put a corset on his prose. Once more: his smithy is the only possible place for these developments—they cannot occur in the office of any editor whom he will ever know.

Maxwell E. Perkins

9. Thomas Wolfe*

I THINK that there is not in any one place so nearly complete a collection of an author's writings and records as that of Thomas Wolfe's now in the Harvard Library. When he died on that sad day in September 1938, when war was impending, or soon after that, I learned that I was his executor and that he had actually left little—as he would have thought, and as it seemed then—besides his manuscripts. It was my obligation to dispose of them to the advantage of his beneficiaries and his memory, and though the times were bad, and Wolfe had not then been recognized as what he now is, I could have sold them commercially, piecemeal, through dealers, for more money than they ever brought. I was determined that this literary estate should remain a unit, available to writers and students, and I tried to sell it as such; but at that time, with war clouds gathering and soon bursting, I could find no adequate buyer.

Then Aline Bernstein, to whom Wolfe had given the manuscript of *Look Homeward, Angel,* sold it by auction for the relief of her people in misfortune, on the understanding that it would be given to Harvard. Not long after that William B. Wisdom, who had recognized Wolfe as a writer of genius on the publication of the *Angel,* and whose faith in him had never wavered, offered to purchase all of his manuscripts and records. He had already accumulated a notable collection of Wolfeana. His correspondence showed me that he thought as I did—that the point of supreme importance was that

---

*The article is printed in the form received from Mr. Perkins's secretary two days after his death, with some slight modifications in punctuation and with the addition of a title.

these records and writings should not be scattered to the four winds, that they be kept intact. And so the whole great packing case of material—letters, bills, documents, notebooks, and manuscripts— went to him on the stipulation, which I never need have asked for, that he would will it all to one institution. Since *Look Homeward, Angel,* was already in Harvard, since Tom Wolfe had loved the reading room of the Library where, as he so often told me, he devoured his hundreds of books and spent most of his Harvard years, Mr. Wisdom made a gift of all this to Harvard. And there it now is.

Though I had worked as an editor with Thomas Wolfe on two huge manuscripts, *Look Homeward, Angel* and *Of Time and the River,* I was astonished on that Spring evening of 1935 when Tom, about to sail for England, brought to our house on East 49th Street, because Scribner's was closed, the huge packing case containing all his literary material. Tom and I and the taxi man carried it in and set it down. Then Tom said to the man, "What is your name?" He said, "Lucky." "Lucky!" said Tom—I think it was perhaps an Americanization of some Italian name—and grasped his hand. It It seemed a good omen. We three had done something together. We were together for that moment. We all shook hands. But for days, that huge packing case blocked our hall, until I got it removed to Scribner's.

The first time I heard of Thomas Wolfe I had a sense of foreboding. I who loved the man say this. Every good thing that comes is accompanied by trouble. It was in 1928 when Madeleine Boyd, a literary agent, came in. She talked of several manuscripts which did not much interest me, but frequently interrupted herself to tell of a wonderful novel about an American boy. I several times said to her, "Why don't you bring it in here, Madeleine?" and she seemed to evade the question. But finally she said, "I will bring it, if you promise to read every word of it." I did promise, but she told me other things that made me realize that Wolfe was a turbulent spirit, and that we were in for turbulence. When the manuscript came, I was fascinated by the first scene where Eugene's father, Oliver W. Gant, with his brother, two little boys, stood by a roadside in Pennsylvania and saw a division of Lee's Army on the march to Gettysburg.

But then there came some ninety-odd pages about Oliver Gant's life in Newport News, and Baltimore, and elsewhere. All this was what Wolfe had heard, and had no actual association with which to reconcile it, and it was inferior to the first episode, and in fact to all the rest of the book. I was turned off to other work and gave the manuscript to Wallace Meyer, thinking, "Here is another promising novel that probably will come to nothing." Then Meyer showed me that wonderful night scene in the café where Ben was with the Doctors, and Horse Hines, the undertaker, came in. I dropped everything and began to read again, and all of us were reading the book simultaneously, you might say, including John Hall Wheelock, and there never was the slightest disagreement among us as to its importance.

After some correspondence between me and Wolfe, and between him and Madeleine Boyd, from which we learned how at the October Fair in Germany he had been almost beaten to death—when I realized again that we had a Moby Dick to deal with—Wolfe arrived in New York and stood in the doorway of my boxstall of an office leaning against the door jamb. When I looked up and saw his wild hair and bright countenance—although he was so altogether different physically—I though of Shelley. *He* was fair, but his hair was wild, and his face was bright, and his head disproportionately small.

We then began to work upon the book and the first thing we did, to give it unity, was to cut out that wonderful scene it began with and the ninety-odd pages that followed, because it seemed to me, and he agreed, that the whole tale should be unfolded through the memories and senses of the boy, Eugene, who was born in Asheville. We both thought that the story was compassed by that child's realization; that it was life and the world as he came to realize them. When he had tried to go back into the life of his father before he arrived in Asheville, without the inherent memory of events, the reality and the poignance were diminished—but for years it was on my conscience that I had persuaded Tom to cut out that first scene of the two little boys on the roadside with Gettysburg impending.

And then what happened? In *Of Time and the River* he brought the scene back to greater effect when old Gant was dying on the gallery of the hospital in Baltimore and in memory recalled his olden days. After that occurred I felt much less anxiety in suggesting cuts: I began then to realize that nothing Wolfe wrote was ever lost, that omissions from one book were restored in a later one. An extreme example of this is the fact that the whole second half of *The Web and the Rock* was originally intended to be the concluding episode in *Of Time and the River*. But most, and perhaps almost all, of those early incidents of Gant's life were worked into *The Web and the Rock* and *You Can't Go Home Again*.

I had realized, for Tom had prefaced his manuscript with a statement to that effect, that *Look Homeward, Angel* was autobiographical, but I had come to think of it as being so in the sense that *David Copperfield* is, or *War and Peace*, or *Pendennis*. But when we were working together, I suddenly saw that it was often almost literally autobiographical—that these people in it were his people. I am sure my face took on a look of alarm, and Tom saw it and he said, "But Mr. Perkins, you don't understand. I think these people are great people and that they should be told about." He was right. He had written a great book, and it had to be taken substantially as it was. And in truth, the extent of cutting in that book has somehow come to be greatly exaggerated. Really, it was more a matter of reorganization. For instance, Tom had that wonderful episode when Gant came back from his far-wandering and rode in early morning on the trolley car through the town and heard about who had died and who had been born and saw all the scenes that were so familiar to Tom or Eugene, as the old trolley rumbled along. This was immediately followed by an episode of a similar kind where Eugene, with his friends, walked home from school through the town of Asheville. That was presented in a Joycean way, but it was the same sort of thing—someone going through the town and through his perceptions revealing it to the reader. By putting these episodes next to each other the effect of each was diminished, and I think we gave both much greater value by separating them. We did a great deal of detailed cutting, but it was such things as that I speak of that constituted perhaps the greater part of the work.

Of Time and the River was a much greater struggle for Tom. Eventually, I think it was on Thanksviging Day 1933, he brought me in desperation about two feet of typescript. The first scene in this was the platform of the railroad station in Asheville when Eugene was about to set out for Harvard, and his family had come to see him off. It must have run to about 30,000 words and I cut it to perhaps 10,000 and showed it to Tom. He approved it. When you are waiting for a train to come in, there is suspense. Something is going to happen. You must, it seemed to me, maintain that sense of suspense and you can't to the extent of 30,000 words. There never was any cutting that Tom did not agree to. He knew that cutting was necessary. His whole impulse was to utter what he felt and he had no time to revise and compress.

So then we began a year of nights of work, including Sundays, and every cut, and change, and interpolation, was argued about and about. The principle that I was working on was that this book, too, got its unity and its form through the senses of Eugene, and I remember how, if I had had my way, we should, by sticking to that principle, have lost one of the most wonderful episodes Wolfe ever wrote—the death of Gant. One night we agreed that certain transitions should be written in, but instead of doing them Wolfe brought on the next night some five thousand words about Eugene's sister in Asheville when her father was ill, and a doctor there and a nurse. I said, "Tom, this is all outside the story, and you know it. Eugene was not there, he was in Cambridge; all of this was outside his perception and knowledge at the time." Tom agreed with me, but the next night, he brought me another five thousand words or so which got up into the death of Gant. And then I realized I was wrong, even if right in theory. What he was doing was too good to let any rule of form impede him.

It is said that Tolstoy never willingly parted with the manuscript of *War and Peace*. One could imagine him working on it all through his life. Certainly Thomas Wolfe never willingly parted from the proofs of *Of Time and the River*. He sat brooding over them for weeks in the Scribner library and not reading. John Wheelock read them and we sent them to the printer and told Tom it had been done. I could believe that otherwise he might have clung to them to the end.

He dedicated that book to me in most extravagant terms. I never saw the dedication until the book was published and though I was most grateful for it, I had forebodings when I heard of his intention. I think it was that dedication that threw him off his stride and broke his magnificent scheme. It gave shallow people the impression that Wolfe could not function as a writer without collaboration, and one critic even used some such phrases as, "Wolfe and Perkins—Perkins and Wolfe, what way is that to write a novel." Nobody with the slightest comprehension of the nature of a writer could accept such an assumption. No writer could possibly tolerate the assumption, which perhaps Tom almost himself did, that he was dependent as a writer upon anyone else. He had to prove to himself and to the world that this was not so.

And that was the fundamental reason that he turned to another publisher. If he had not—but by the time he did it was plain that he had to tell, in the medium of fiction and through the transmutation of his amazing imagination, the story of his own life—he never would have broken his own great plan by distorting Eugene Gant into George Webber. That was a horrible mistake. I think Edward Aswell, of Harper & Brothers, agrees with me in this, but when the manuscript that came to form *The Web and the Rock* and *You Can't Go Home Again* got to him to work on, and in some degree to me, as Wolfe's executor, Tom was dead, and things had to be taken as they were.

The trouble began after the publication of *Of Time and the River,* which the reviewers enormously praised—but many of them asserted that Wolfe could only write about himself, that he could not see the world or anything objectively, with detachment—that he was always autobiographical. Wolfe was extremely sensitive to criticism, for all his tremendous faith in his genius as an obligation put upon him to fulfill. One day when I lived on East 49th Street near Second Avenue, and he on First Avenue, just off the corner of 49th, I met him as I was going home. He said he wanted to talk to me, as we did talk every evening about that time, and we went into the Waldorf. He referred to the criticisms against him, and said that he wanted to write a completely objective, unautobiographical book, and that it would show how strangely different everything is from what a person expects it to be. One might say that he was thinking of the theme that has run through so many great books, such as *Pickwick Papers* and *Don Quixote,* where a man, young or old, goes hopefully out into the world slap into the face of outrageous reality. He was going to put on the title page what was said by Prince Andrei, in *War and Peace,* after his first battle, when the praise fell upon those who had done nothing and blame almost fell upon one who had done everything. Prince Andrei, who saved the battery commander who most of all had held back the French from the blame that Little Tushin would have accepted, walked out with him into the night. Then as Tushin left, Tolstoy said, "Prince Andrei looked up at the stars and sighed; everything was so different from what he thought it was going to be."

Tom was in a desperate state. It was not only what the critics said that made him wish to write objectively, but that he knew that what he had written had given great pain even to those he loved the most. The conclusion of our talk was that if he could write such an objective book on this theme within a year, say, to the extent of perhaps a hundred thousand words, it might be well to do it. It was this that turned him to George Webber, but once he began on that he really and irresistibly resumed the one story he was destined to write, which was that of himself, or Eugene Gant.

And so, the first half of *The Web and the Rock,* of which there is only a typescript, is a re-telling in different terms of *Look Homeward, Angel.* Wolfe was diverted from his natural purpose—and even had he lived, what could have been done? Some of his finest writing is that first half of *The Web and the Rock.* Could anybody have just tossed it out?

But, if Tom had held to his scheme and completed the whole story of his life as transmuted into fiction through his imagination, I think the accusation that he had no sense of form could not have stood. He wrote one long story, "The Web of Earth," which had perfect form, for all its intricacy. I remember saying to him, "Not one word of this should be changed." One might say that as his own physical dimensions were huge so was his conception of a book. He had one book to write about a vast, sprawling, turbulent land—America—as perceived by Eugene Gant. Even when he was in Europe, it was of America he thought. If he had not been diverted and had lived to complete it, I think it would have had the form that was suited to the subject.

His detractors say he could only write about himself, but all that he wrote of was transformed by his imagination. For instance, in *You Can't Go Home Again* he shows the character Foxhall Edwards at breakfast. Edwards's young daughter enters "as swiftly and silently as a ray of light." She is very shy and in a hurry to get to school. She tells of a theme she has written on Walt Whitman and what the teacher said of Whitman. When Edwards urges her not to hurry and makes various observations, she says, "Oh, Daddy, you're so funny!" What Tom did was to make one unforgettable little character out of three daughters of Foxhall Edwards.

He got the ray of light many years ago when he was with me in my house in New Canaan, Connecticut, and one daughter, at the age of about eight or ten, came in and met this gigantic stranger. After she was introduced she fluttered all about the room in her embarrassment, but radiant, like a sunbeam. Then Tom was present when another daughter, in Radcliffe, consulted me about a paper she was writing on Whitman, but he put this back into her school days. The third, of which he composed a single character, was the youngest, who often did say, partly perhaps because she was not at ease when Tom was there, "Oh, Daddy, you're so silly." That is how Tom worked. He created something new and something meaningful through a transmutation of what he saw, heard, and realized.

I think no one could understand Thomas Wolfe who had not seen or properly imagined the place in which he was born and grew up. Asheville, N. C., is encircled by mountains. The trains wind in and out through labyrinths of passes. A boy of Wolfe's imagination imprisoned there could think that what was beyond was all wonderful— different from what it was where there was not for him enough of anything. Whatever happened, Wolfe would have been what he was. I remember on the day of his death saying to his sister Mabel that I thought it amazing in an American family that one of the sons who wanted to be a writer should have been given the support that was given Tom, and that they all deserved great credit for that. She said it didn't matter, that nothing could have prevented Tom from doing what he did.

That is true, but I think that those mountainous walls which his imagination vaulted gave him the vision of an America with which his books are fundamentally concerned. He often spoke of the artist in America—how the whole color and character of the country was completely new—never interpreted; how in England, for instance, the writer inherited a long accretion of accepted expression from which he could start. But Tom would say—and he had seen the world— "who has ever made you know the color of an American box car?" Wolfe was in those mountains—he tells of the train whistles at night —the trains were winding their way out into the great world where it seemed to the boy there was everything desirable, and vast, and wonderful.

It was partly that which made him want to see everything, and read everything, and experience everything, and say everything. There was a night when he lived on First Avenue that Nancy Hale, who lived on East 49th Street near Third Avenue, heard a kind of chant, which grew louder. She got up and looked out of the window at two or three in the morning and there was the great figure of Thomas Wolfe, advancing in his long country-man's stride, with his swaying black raincoat, and what he was chanting was, "I wrote ten thousand words today—I wrote ten thousand words today."

Tom must have lived in eight or nine different parts of New York and Brooklyn for a year or more. He knew in the end every aspect of the City—he walked the streets endlessly—but he was not a city man. The city fascinated him but he did not really belong in it and was never satisfied to live in it. He was always thinking of America as a whole and planning trips to some part that he had not yet seen, and in the end taking them. His various quarters in town always looked as if he had just moved in, to camp for awhile. This was partly because he really had no interest in possessions of any kind, but it was also because he was in his very nature a Far Wanderer, bent upon seeing all places, and his rooms were just necessities into which he never settled. Even when he was there his mind was not. He needed a continent to range over, actually and in imagination. And his place was all America. It was with America he was most deeply concerned and I believe he opened it up as no other writer ever did for the people of his time and for the writers and artists and poets of tomorrow. Surely he had a thing to tell us.

Edward C. Aswell

10. From "A Note on Thomas Wolfe"

MANY CRITICS have observed that the literary style of his posthumous books is often quite different from that of his earlier books. Much of the writing is more objective in tone, its lyricism more restrained. This was first noticeable in the opening half of *The Web and the Rock,* but not in the latter half (for reasons to be explained later). His objectivity was still more apparent in *You Can't Go Home Again* as a whole. It is most striking of all in the title piece of the present volume.* What is the explanation of this change? What lay behind it? What does it indicate about Wolfe's growth as an artist?

These questions can best be answered by telling what I know of his purposes and of the techniques he used to achieve them. Of course there is nothing mysterious about the ends which his writing was meant to serve. The motives which drove him to write, and which lent such singular integrity to everything he wrote, can be read clearly enough in his books. But his techniques are more obscure, and often cannot be derived from the evidence that is visible in his printed pages. His methods were certainly unusual, if not unique in literature. Very few people know anything about them. Perhaps that is one reason why there are so many misconceptions about Thomas Wolfe.

For example, some of his readers seem to think that when Tom was in the throes of composition, all he had to do was to open the sluice gates and the words tumbled forth in an irresistible torrent like the surge of pent-up waters suddenly released. True, he wrote like one possessed. His first drafts were always done in longhand with a pencil,

---

* *The Hills Beyond.*

and when he had a secretary, as he did throughout his last year, one of her chores was to keep a dozen pencils sharpened and ready for his need. With amazing speed he would fill innumerable sheets of paper with his vigorous scrawl, and toss them aside to fall on the floor for his secretary to pick up, put in order, and transcribe. He never hesitated for a word: the words came too fast for him, and in his effort to keep up with them he would often form only the first letter and the last with a wriggle between, so that only the initiated could decode his sentences.

But the analogy by which this process has been compared to the opening of sluice gates becomes very misleading if left without qualification. To understand what was happening with Tom when he was writing, one needs to remember all the years through which his experience and observation had slowly accumulated. One also needs to be reminded of his acute self-tortures of thought and feeling about everything he had experienced and observed. He could not put anything that had happened to him out of his consciousness until he had rehearsed it in memory a thousand times, going back over it again and again in every detail until he had got at the core of it and had extracted the last shred of meaning out of it on every level. One needs to be told, too, of his ingenious experiments with different ways of saying what he wanted to say, sometimes only worked out in his head, sometimes roughly sketched on paper. All of this preceded the moment of spate-writing and made it possible.

Beyond this, one needs to know—and the fact may come as a surprise—that Tom had become a tireless reviser and rewriter. Whether this was true of him in his younger days I cannot say, but it was certainly true of him later. Much as he had told me and shown me of what he had been doing in those last years, I was not quite prepared to discover, when I came to deal with the whole manuscript, how vitally essential rewriting had become to his whole method. Far more often than not I found that there would be at least two different versions of the same episode, and sometimes there were as many as four or five versions. There would be a first draft hastily sketched out, then later drafts that filled in the details, and it was fascinating to see how the thing had changed and grown under his hand. When he was dissatisfied with a scene or character he would not, as a rule, simply revise his draft and get it recopied: he would put it aside and rewrite it some different way from start to finish. He would pace the floor over it, and he might dictate the revision straight to the typewriter— then his secretary would have an exhausting day trying to keep up. In editing the manuscript it was very puzzling to come upon these variant versions because they were not marked (the pages were frequently out of order and were not even numbered), and only a careful comparison of the internal evidence could determine which was the last draft and the most complete realization of his intentions.

Martin Maloney

11. A Study of Semantic States: Thomas Wolfe and the Faustian Sickness

TO READ fiction or drama is, generally speaking, to examine a set of verbalizations which deal with conflicts the author was unable to solve, except on paper: this statement is a commonplace to most literary critics. It has been used as a starting point for many excellent critical studies; some of the best recent examples may be found in Edmund Wilson's *The Wound and the Bow* (New York: Oxford University Press, 1947). No doubt this formula might be successfully applied to the work of almost any professional writer of serious intent and reasonable literary stature, and certainly the resultant criticism should prove interesting as "semantic" analysis.

A somewhat similar but much more special formula is suggested by Alfred Korzybski's "An Extensional Analysis of the Process of Abstracting from an Electro-colloidal Non-aristotelian Point of View" (issued in mimeographed "preliminary draft" in 1944; for a revised version, see *General Semantics Bulletin* Nos. 4 and 5 [Autumn-Winter, 1950–51], pp. 9–12). In this brief sketch, Korzybski shows diagrammatically four "levels" of abstraction: 1) happenings, internal or external; 2) nervous impact of the happenings; 3) feelings, organismal reactions to the nervous impact; and 4) verbal reactions to the feelings, implying, identifying, etc. all four "levels." Of this diagram Korzybski says in part,

> The dangers of this actual situation are in the fact that [levels] II and III, without consciousness of abstracting and extensional attitudes, are disregarded completely, missing the interrelations of these four phases of human living reactions, with the result that I and IV are identified in value, which may be a fatal mistake. . . .

What has been said here has much broader significance than is realized. . . . So far unfortunately the public in general, scientists included, disregard [levels] II and III, and take IV seriously as representing I. Most of the time this is not the case, and may lead only to heated debates, hostilities and whatnot, through such identifications of I and IV, and disregard of II and III.

This ingenious insight into human behavior seems to have interesting implications for literary criticism. There are many theories about and explanations of the "creative process" by which a novelist, for example, produces his fictions. There is a fairly common belief that such writers are, or ought to be, "imaginative," which is to say that their writing relates to level III, the level of "organismal reactions." This is no doubt correct as far as it goes, but tends to slight, or to omit any reference to levels II or I, making literary creation a self-generative process, independent of events in the world or of perceptions of events. Since this attitude, as stated, is manifest nonsense, its exponents are likely to nurse a belief in "inspiration"—the breath of the muse—as a stimulus to imagination. A very different "concept" of this process is expounded by those writers and critics who conceive that the writer's function is to reproduce with "photographic" accuracy and precision the life around him. Korzybski's sketch of the process of abstracting (evaluation) not only permits us to point out the incorrect evaluations in these theories and in others, it also suggests an approach to literary criticism which seems both novel and promising. A good deal of literary criticism deals primarily, or even exclusively, with the verbal output of the writer. Some criticism takes into account the complex of events which surround him. Relatively little is aimed at the third level, of "feelings," "organismal reactions," etc. Yet this, if Korzybski's formulation is correct, is what the writer writes about. This is, in short, the writer's private world, the next-to-last stage of the chain reaction which results in literature. When we discuss the writing of fiction, essays, plays or poetry, it is this level of "organismal reactions" which is peculiarly important.

This approach to literary criticism obviously requires rather special data, chiefly autobiographical and critical, which is not available in all cases. Perhaps only a few writers—those who deal in "autobiographical" fiction and who produce introspective accounts, formal or otherwise, of the creative process—can be adequately studied in this way. Yet it seems probable that wherever this method can be applied at all, it will produce novel and valuable insights into creative behavior.

We shall attempt, in this paper, to study some aspects of the life and literary work of Thomas Wolfe, an American novelist and short-story writer. Wolfe was born in Asheville, North Carolina, in 1901. He was educated at the University of North Carolina, where he became interested in playwriting, and at Harvard, where he studied under the late George Pierce Baker. A play which he wrote during this period was seriously considered for production by the Theater Guild, but was eventually rejected. After leaving Harvard, Wolfe taught for some time at New York University. In 1929, his first novel, *Look Homeward, Angel,* was published. He continued to write, and eventually was able to devote all his time to this pursuit. He published, in 1935, a second long novel, *Of Time and the River,* and a collection of short pieces entitled *From Death to Morning.* In 1936 he published a short book dealing with his methods as a writer, *The Story of a Novel.* He died September 15, 1938. He left an enormous collection of miscellaneous manuscript amounting to over a million words. From this manuscript his publishers edited two novels, *The Web and the Rock* and *You Can't Go Home Again,* and a partially completed novel plus some short pieces published as *The Hills Beyond.*

Wolfe's books were extraordinary, as one might judge even from this brief sketch. They seem to have been—with the possible exception of *The Hills Beyond*—autobiographical in an almost literal sense. The "hero" of the first two novels is Eugene Gant, "a huge, frenzied fellow . . . who had an insane passion to walk a million streets, read a million books, make love to a million women—to eat, see, know, feel everything under the sun." The hero of the two posthumous novels is a huge, frenzied fellow named George Webber who is at least a blood brother to Eugene Gant and who—like Eugene—is scarcely to be distinguished from Wolfe himself.[1] The novels are vast, sprawling works which many critics have called "formless." The latter epithet is incorrect; the books, taken together, have a form—the structure of Wolfe's own experience as he was able to relive it.[2]

Wolfe's method of writing these works is revealing. He was an energetic and fertile writer, and he was gifted with an extraordinary memory. It was apparently not his practice to plan his novels, as novels. He thought in terms of a single work which was to stretch over several thousands of printed pages, over several generations of human experience, and to include in its cast some thousands of characters.[3] Actually, a great deal of the writing he published grew out of his own immediate experience and recollections. Since he was his own hero, and since the incidents of his tale depended on what he could remember and dramatize, he was free to range the whole period of his life, writing today what happened last week, and tomorrow an event which took place twenty years ago.[4] When he had thus accumulated a huge mass of manuscript, he sorted it out in chronological sequence, and lo! he had a novel. The preparation of the book, *Of Time and the River,* was accomplished in this fashion. In the case of the two posthumous novels, the sorting-weaving task was accomplished by the Harpers editor, Edward Aswell.

Wolfe's method of composing fiction was at once introspective and reminiscent. Consequently, he devoted a great deal of thought and creative effort to his own experience and techniques as a writer. In his second book, *Of Time and the River,* which follows closely his own experiences at Harvard and abroad, Wolfe dramatizes his state of being as "Faustianism" (the second section of this volume, dealing with his life at Harvard, is called "Young Faustus," while the concluding section is entitled "Faust and Helen"). In the entire book, Wolfe portrays—through Eugene Gant—the "Faustian life" with its raging hungers, world-shaking passions, mad pursuits of the unattainable, etc. The "Faustian" sickness, to Wolfe, seems equated with the abnormal and unquenchable thirst and hunger for *all* achievement, *all* experience. This is a theme which runs through Wolfe's fiction, and his life, out to the end. Though, as we shall see, he came to understand the nature of his problem, apparently he never managed to resolve it completely.

Let us try to suggest some of the evaluations which relate to Wolfe's "Faustian" life. The purest statement of these evaluations we may find in some of his earliest letters. As a young man of twenty-two, a would be playwright, Wolfe wrote to his mother:

I know this now: I am inevitable. I sincerely believe the only thing that can stop me now is insanity, disease or death. . . . I want to know life and understand it and interpret it without fear or favor. This, I feel, is a man's work and worthy of a man's dignity. For life is not made up of sugary, sticky, sickening Edgar A. Guest sentimentality, it is not made up of dishonest optimism, God is *not* always in his Heaven, all is *not* always right with the world. It is not all bad, but it is not all good, it is not all ugly, but it is not all beautiful, it is life, life, life—the only thing that matters. It is savage, cruel, kind, noble, passionate, selfish, generous, stupid, ugly, beautiful, painful, joyous,—it is all these, and more, and it's all these I want to know and, by God, I shall, though they crucify me for it. I will go to the ends of the earth to find it, to understand it. I will know this country when I am through as I know the palm of my hand, and I will put it on paper, and make it true and beautiful.

And later in the letter:

And I intend to wreak out my soul on paper and express it all. This is what my life means to me: I am at the mercy of this thing and I will do it or die. I never forget; I have never forgotten. I have tried to make myself conscious of the whole of my life . . .[5]

From these brief statements alone much might be inferred. The term "I" is equated with "inevitable," so as to endow the "I" with an heroic, superhuman quality. "I" is set in opposition to "life"— an endlessly variable term characterized in a long series of contradictory adjectives. But I, Wolfe writes, am determined to master and dominate this magnificent complexity and translate it to paper. At this point, Wolfe encounters in a mild form a serious obstacle to his system. How can one dominate "life"? What is the process? How can one even talk plausibly about it? In order to be able even to set forth his program in the abstract, Wolfe is obliged to reduce the term "life" to a term of less scope. So, although the two terms are not obviously equated, "life" becomes "this country" for the purpose of slightly more specific discussion. One feels in these lines a distinct uncertainty which Wolfe carefully separates from himself and personifies as "the enemy." An undefined but obviously inimical "they" may "crucify me for it"—i.e., the successful mastery of "life." It is indicated, though not very convincingly, that "they" are Edgar A. Guest sentimentalists, dishonest optimists, etc. which hardly makes the threat of crucifixion very meaningful. In the second quotation, the enemy has become "this thing," i.e., the self-imposed task of complete self-expression and so complete mastery of "life": "I intend to wreak out my soul on paper and express it all."

We are prepared here, not to inquire into the experiences which preceded and related to this curious "philosophy," but to attempt to describe it and the succeeding events in Wolfe's life to which it relates. It is very evident, however, that Wolfe's term "life" represents a motive, in the sense that mastery of "life" through creative writing is his goal. The term is undefined and multiordinal, and as a result the goal exists only in cloud-cuckoo-land. The impossibility of realizing "all life" verbally, the impossibility of even knowing what progress one has made toward the goal: these obvious facts make it difficult to handle such terms even as higher order abstractions, without any special reference to the practical difficulties of their application. Wolfe himself realizes this, though not clearly. He does what he can to make his "philosophy" verbally plausible. He inflates himself to semi-heroic size, suggests that—like an epic hero—he can be touched only by insanity, disease or death. But this is not enough. The picture is not complete without an enemy. Here the enemy is first anonymous (the reference to "dishonest optimists" is merely a trial flight, and probably stems from Wolfe's reading of H. L. Mencken) and then, surprisingly, becomes personified in the task he has undertaken and especially in his memory, which like an old man of the sea will destroy him if he does not triumph over it. It seems clear enough that the figure of the enemy at this stage of Wolfe's career was a sort of preparation for the failure he anticipated and struggled against. He could always say, at need, "It was not my failure; I was betrayed, I was destroyed." In short, Wolfe kept the paraphernalia of martyrdom close at hand.

Crude and naïve as the statements in these letters seem, one may find in them the seeds of Wolfe's major obstacle to success as a writer. His talk, it appears, was not mere talk; he tried to make this distorted map apply to the world of his experience. He was at constant pains, for example, to preserve the heroic—or at least, the more-than-life-size quality of those alter egos of his, Eugene Gant and George Webber.[6] The "Faustian" life which he makes his heroes lead, and which he himself undoubtedly led, is hardly more than a record of a determined effort to work out an illegitimate totality to the end. The enemy appears in his works almost to the day of his death, in myriad forms; indeed, one is inclined to believe that Wolfe's search for a scapegoat led him to his prejudices against Jews, literary critics, aesthetes and "intellectuals," etc.

One might, from this beginning, infer the course of Wolfe's "Faustian sickness," provided one had a trifle of additional data to command. Had Wolfe been a feeble fellow, without real strength or capacity or talent, his "philosophy" would have ended in quick frustration and defeat, and would have come to nothing. But he was not feeble in any sense; he needed to exaggerate very little to inflate himself to heroic size. He was possessed of great physical vigor, his perceptions were keen, and he had an extraordinary memory. His natural capacity for the task he had set himself was of a quality impressive enough to be described as "genius." Thus, although failure is implicit in the very nature of the terms he chose to describe his lifework, he might have been expected, with luck, to make some noise in the world. And so he did. One could predict the great physical and intellectual appetites, the endless travels, the titanic bursts of creation, the questionings, the doubts, the suspicions and fears. One might have predicted, too, that the literary remains of such a man would be like the statue of Ozymandias—monumental ruins.

The evidence by which such predictions must be tested is extensive—too much so to be rehearsed thoroughly here. We can, however, glance at one phase of Wolfe's activities—his attitudes toward books and learning. Here, as elsewhere, Wolfe suffered from the illegitimate totality in an unusual way. Quite simply, he wanted to read all the books in the world, in whatever language, on the evident assumption that this experience would put at his command all recorded knowledge; he was indeed a kind of apprentice Faust. In *Of Time and the River,* Wolfe portrays Eugene Gant caught in the Faustian net, driven half mad by his efforts to engulf a totality which was forever multiplying itself. At least one of the passages in question is worth quoting at length:

Now he would prowl the stacks of the library at night, pulling books out of a thousand shelves and reading in them like a madman. The thought of these vast stacks of books would drive him mad: the more he read, the less he seemed to know—the greater the number of the books he read, the greater the immense uncountable number of those which he could never read would seem to be. Within a period of ten years he read at least 20,000 volumes —deliberately the number is set low—and opened the pages and looked through many times that number. This may seem unbelievable, but it happened. Dryden said this about Ben Jonson: "Other men read books but he read libraries"—and so now was it with this boy. Yet this terrific orgy of the books brought him no comfort, peace, or wisdom of the mind and heart. Instead, his fury and despair increased from what they fed upon, his hunger mounted with the food it ate.

He read insanely, by the hundreds, the thousands, the ten thousands, yet he had no desire to be bookish; no one could describe this mad assault upon print as scholarly: a ravening appetite in him demanded that he read everything that had ever been written about human experience. He read no more from pleasure—the thought that other books were waiting for him tore at his heart forever. He pictured himself as tearing the entrails from a book as from a fowl. At first, hovering over book stalls, or walking at night among the vast piled shelves of the library, he would read, watch in hand, muttering to himself in triumph or anger at the timing of each page: "Fifty seconds to do that one. Damn you, we'll see! You will, will you?"—and he would tear through the next page in twenty seconds.[7]

Then, says Wolfe, in the midst of this furious attack upon the books, he would suddenly become convinced that "something priceless, irrecoverable was happening in the streets, and if he could somehow get to this event and encompass it and master it, he would have the key to universal understanding, complete knowledge of mankind."

This picture is no doubt over-dramatized—recollection for Wolfe was anything but tranquil—but there can be little doubt that it is basically true. Geismar speaks of Wolfe as a young man being "driven wild" by the endless volumes in the library at Harvard,[8] and Wolfe himself, in a letter to Mrs. J. M. Roberts, writes: "I suppose I made a mistake in trying to eat all the plums at once, for instead of peace it has awakened a good sized volcano in me. I wander through the stacks of that great library there like some damned soul; never at rest—even leaping ahead from the pages I read to thoughts of those I want to read." [9]

This habit persisted some years later when Wolfe visited France, and was even complicated by his lack of familiarity with the French language or with French literature.

The hopeless and unprofitable struggle of the Faustian life had never been so horribly evident as it now was—the futility of his insane efforts to memorize every stone and paving brick in Paris, to burn the vision of his eyes through walls and straight into the lives and hearts of a million people, to read all the books, eat all the food, drink all the wine, to hold the whole gigantic panorama of the universe within his memory . . . and somehow to use it all for one final, perfect, all-inclusive work—his life's purpose, his heart's last pulse and anguish, and his soul's desire.

This passage occurs in *Of Time and the River* (p. 660). Later, in a passage transferred from Wolfe's own journal to this novel, he remarks "I am getting a new sense of control—millions of books don't annoy me so much—went along the Seine today after Louvre—most of it worthless old rubbish I must begin to put up my fences now—I can't take the world or this city with me." (p. 666) But this was more wishful thinking than a true reformation; two days later he records, "Old Books—Seem to be millions of these too—*Essais de l'Abbe Chose sur la Morale,* etc. The Faustian hell again!" (p. 667) So swamped and drowned in his ill-learned French and the new, unknown literature did Wolfe become that the books, the life of Paris, and the names of the writers took on an air of fantasy: he imagined these graceful, elegant, Frenchified fellows—Feuillet, Capus, Courteline, Boylesve, Prevost, and the rest—gathering in the cafés, drinking their wine or their bock, rapidly, easily, gracefully dashing off book after book, an endless stream of perfect, charming, and above all effortless literary works. He knew it was fantastic and impossible, but he could not help believing in it, in a way. In a diary entry of somewhat later date, he remarks that the European has learned control —or rather, indifference. "Each man writes his own book without worrying very much about what the other has written—he reads little or if he reads much, it is only a trifle—a spoonful of the ocean of print that inundates everything—Picture Anatole France—with a reputation for omniscience—picking daintily here and there among the bookstalls of the Seine. To go by them affects me with horror and weariness—as it does Paul Valéry—but I lack his power to resist. . . . I cannot keep away from them." (p. 677)

Wolfe never learned this "European" moderation. It was the same when he went to Germany: the food, the liquor, the paintings, the books—he was obsessed with the impossibility of consuming them all. He even found out how many books were published in Germany at that time: "There were over 30,000," he writes. "It was appalling." [10]

This inordinate desire to know and experience everything seems to have extended to nearly every phase of his activity: to eating and drinking, to travel, to his relations with the rest of humanity. And of course, to writing; for the end of all his experience was to be that act of translation into words. Even when he had analyzed and dramatized his own problems, when he had set forth a saner and more temperate program for himself, he could still write in *The Story of a Novel,* "Out of the billion forms of America, out of the savage violence and the dense complexity of all its swarming life; from the unique and single substance of this land and life of ours, must we draw the power and energy of our own life, the articulation of our speech, the substance of our art." [11] As Muller points out, it was characteristic of Wolfe to magnify the "physical task," the necessity of comprehending a "billion forms." He adds, with wry understatement, "The great American novel need not contain all of America." [12]

There is even some evidence to suggest that Wolfe pondered the possibility of *being* everybody as well as *knowing* everybody. The evidence is by no means conclusive, and probably Wolfe never formulated this purpose as bluntly as we have here. I would, however, mention the section of *Look Homeward, Angel* in which Wolfe describes his curious, half-serious play acting when he became, to strangers, sometimes Christ, sometimes Thomas Chatterton, sometimes John Milton.[13] There is also this passage of fantasy from the same book:

> Me! Me! Bruce-Eugene, the Scourge of the Greasers, and the greatest fullback Yale ever had! Marshall Gant, the saviour of his country! Ace Gant, the hawk of the sky, the man who brought Richthofen down! Senator Gant, Governor Gant, President Gant, the restorer and uniter of a broken nation, retiring quietly to private life in spite of the weeping protest of one hundred million people, until, like Arthur or Barbarossa, he shall again hear the drums of need and peril.

Jesus of Nazareth Gant, mocked, reviled, spat upon, and imprisoned for the sins of others, but nobly silent, preferring death rather than cause pain to the woman he loves. Gant, the Unknown Soldier, the Martyred President, the Slain God of Harvest, the Bringer of Good Crops. Duke Gant of Westmoreland . . .

and so on through a dozen or so other roles, ending with "Anubis and Osiris and Mumbo-Jumbo Gant." (pp. 591–92)

Pamela Johnson quotes Wolfe's words, "Could I make tongue say more than tongue could utter! Could I make brain grasp more than brain could think!" and adds that

> All his life Wolfe tried to do this impossible thing, and in trying burned himself out. His entire work is a forcing process. With every word he wrote he was trying to say more than any human being had ever said of the marvel of the earth and of man. He wanted to capture in words the experience of *nearly understanding* and, more preposterous and more wonderful, to be the first man in the world to understand completely. This was the ideal by which he lived and by which he laboured, an unsophisticated, incorrupt and terrifying ideal. . . . Yet all Wolfe succeeded in producing was a history of violent endeavour. (*Hungry Gulliver*, p. 153)

The phrase, "violent endeavour," in Wolfe's case, seems almost an understatement. The Faustian ideal produced its inevitable corollary of frustration and a sense of failure. In Wolfe this frustration seems to have taken the form of enormous rages, sometimes meaningless physical activity and even violence. There is also evidence that the frustration in its turn gave way to nausea and depression and despair. In judging Wolfe's life, we are obliged to draw heavily on his own testimony, which is, necessarily, dramatized. However, there is some reason to believe that the states of rage and depression he sometimes describes occurred in a very real sense. Muller, in a different context, speaks of "the notorious excesses of Eugene Gant" (the Wolfe-figure in the early novels).

> Eugene is forever beside himself, which is where he wants to be. He "yells," "howls," "bellows madly," "snarls like a wild beast"; he is repeatedly "choked with fury," "white with constricted rage," "frantic with horror"; when he broods in silence it is to contemplate

things "intolerable," "implacable," "unutterable"; when he nevertheless utters the unutterable, his favorite adjectives are "wild," "tormented," "demented," "demonic," "maniacal"; and at the end of such bouts with himself or the world, he "beats his knuckles bloody on the stamped-out walls." (*Thomas Wolfe,* p. 34)

All this may be exaggerated, but it is not baseless. Geismar, for example, probably underestimates these phenomena when he writes,

> While he was teaching at New York University he noted that his eyes had gone bad. "I hope it is the cold, I don't know."—"I haven't wasted time by sleeping," he wrote again, "I am worked to a frazzle, and my left eye went bad about ten days ago." And his physical ailments, as Wolfe knew, were accentuated by his working habits—that is, by the fits of nervous frenzy and the spells of nervous exhaustion that followed each other during his work days, by his increasing sense of being deserted and alone ("I suppose I am one of the loneliest people in the world"), and by the dreams of time and guilt which now began to mark his nights: by all these symptoms of the heightened physical and spiritual intensity which had now become his normal routine. (*The Portable Thomas Wolfe,* p. 14)

But neither Muller's casual assumption that Wolfe exaggerates, nor Geismar's suggestion that Wolfe's state resulted from a combination of mild hypochondria and bad working habits, seems adequate to explain the reactions hinted at in these passages.

The dreams of time and guilt to which Geismar refers seem to be part and parcel of a deeper unease than that resulting from overwork or fear for one's health. Wolfe himself, I believe, understood the nature of these dreams better than his critics. His report of them can be found in *The Story of a Novel,* and is too long to quote here. Instead, let us glance quickly at his summary of the dreams and their significance:

> There was a kind of dream which I can only summarize as dreams of Guilt and Time. Chameleon-like in all their damnable and unending fecundities, they restored to me the whole huge world that I had known, the billion faces and the million tongues, and they restored it to me with the malevolent triumph of a passive and unwanted ease. My daily conflict with Amount and Number, the huge accumulations of my years of struggle with the forms of life,

my brutal and unending efforts to record upon my memory every brick and paving stone of every street that I had ever walked upon, each face of every thronging crowd in every city, every country with which my spirit had contested its savage and uneven struggle for supremacy—they all returned now—each stone, each street, each town, each country—yes, even every book in the library whose loaded shelves I had vainly tried to devour at colleges—they returned upon the wings of these mighty, sad, and somehow quietly demented dreams—I saw and heard and knew them all at once, was instantly without pain or anguish, with the calm consciousness of God, master of the whole universe of life against whose elements I had contended vainly for all-knowledge for so many years. And the fruit of that enormous triumph, the calm and instant passivity of that inhuman and demented immortality, was somehow sadder and more bitter than the most galling bitterness of defeat in my contention with the multitudes of life had ever been. (pp. 594–95)

If these dreams appear symptomatic of a deeply rooted emotional disturbance, they hardly seem morbid or dangerous. What does strike one immediately as dangerous and un-sane is Wolfe's proliferation of the "enemy" term in his philosophy. Muller remarks that "At this stage the frustration of the struggling young writer in the city had developed into a feeling of persecution that approached downright mania. All around him he saw not merely indifference but hatred, malice, venom—a calculated plot to destroy him. He had to have enemies; nothing else could explain his frustrations." (p. 103) This development of the "enemy" term had been in process for years, probably since the earliest formulation of his goals in life. An investigation of Wolfe's letters to his mother produced an abundance of revealing data on this score. There are eight references suggesting persecution by residents of Wolfe's home town; two references dealing with old friends who have now "turned against" him; fourteen references to persecution by his family and by family responsibilities; five references to persecution by Rotarians, Kiwanians, and other "dishonest optimists"; and seven references to persecution by unspecified persons (the "they" reference noted previously is a good example). In addition, we may find no less than thirteen references to a kind of persecution by disease, a half dozen references to extreme loneliness, and two or three meditations upon death. It should be remembered, in connection with these passages, that many of them are quite lengthy and detailed.

Whether by way of dramatizing his own situation (which might be pardonable, as his own life was the material of his writing), or by way of a kind of linguistic self-deception, Wolfe was given to exaggeration in matters of amount and number. In his novels, he sometimes attributes to his hero prodigious feats of eating, reading, writing, etc. In *Of Time and the River,* as we have seen, Eugene is alleged to have read 20,000 books in the space of ten years. Yet we learn that, while he was accomplishing this prodigy, he ate hundreds of steaks in a given restaurant (over a period of a year or two), spent thousands of hours admiring a single waitress who worked there, and so forth. He, Wolfe, apparently carried this same habit over to his writing, reporting to his editor that he had prepared a fifty-thousand-word outline of a book when actually he had written fewer than ten thousand words; had written a million words of narrative when actually he had written less than a fifth of that amount. Aswell (the editor) commented that he became able to translate these terms of Wolfe's, rendering "I have written a million words" as "I have written a great deal," "I have written fifty thousand words" as "I have just started writing." (Muller, *Thomas Wolfe,* p. 35) Perhaps Wolfe had found here the only palliative for the Faustian sickness; having set up a goal of "allness" which exists verbally but not in fact, one is obliged to achieve the goal verbally but not in fact.

The aims and methods of Wolfe's writing were of a piece with his aims and methods in living. He was gifted with an uncommonly retentive memory, and motivated by a belief that one's goal in writing should be the reproduction on the printed page of "life." Wolfe's memory, says John Peale Bishop,

> was anything but common. He could—and it is the source of what is most authentic in his talent—displace the present so completely by the past that its sights and sounds all but destroyed surrounding circumstance. He then lost the sense of time. For Wolfe, sitting at a table on a terrace in Paris, contained within himself not only the America he had known; he also held, within his body, both his parents. They were there, not only in his memory, but more portentiously in the makeup of his mind.[14]

In his earlier years, Wolfe was not modest about his memory, at least when he wrote his mother from Harvard that "I never forget: I have never forgotten." He spoke more temperately, yet with a quiet certainty he had earlier lacked, when a dozen years later he composed *The Story of a Novel*:

> The quality of my memory is characterized, I believe, in a more than ordinary degree by the intensity of its sense impressions, its power to evoke and bring back the odors, sounds, colors, shapes, and feel of things with concrete vividness. Now my memory was at work night and day, in a way that at first I could neither check nor control and that swarmed unbidden in a stream of blazing pageantry across my mind, with the million forms and substances of the life that I had left, which was my own, America. I would be sitting, for example, on the terrace of a cafe watching the flash and play of life before me on the Avenue de l'Opera, and suddenly I would remember the iron railing that goes along the boardwalk at Atlantic City. I could see it instantly just the way it was, the heavy iron pipe; its raw, galvanized look; the way the joints were fitted together. It was all so vivid and concrete that I could feel my hand upon it and know the exact dimensions, its size and weight and shape. And suddenly I would realize that I had never seen any railing that looked like this in Europe. And this utterly familiar, common thing would suddenly be revealed to me with all the wonder with which we discover a thing which we have seen all our life and yet have never known before. (Geismar, p. 578)

Clearly, then, Wolfe's Faustianism was dual: his observation and recollection not only reached out to embrace an enormously vast number of items, but would have understood each trifling occurrence in the infinite complexity of its own detail. The amazing thing is, that Wolfe really did remember and perceive an enormous quantity of phenomena, that he did remember and react to the trifles in sometimes startlingly precise detail, and that he did suggest a surprising amount of his experience in his writing. Consider, for example, this curious anecdote from *The Story of a Novel*. Wolfe remarks that one of his faults in writing is "that I have often attempted to reproduce in its entirety the full flood and fabric of a scene in life itself." It appears that in one of his manuscripts he included an incident of minor importance, along these lines. A young woman drives with her husband to her mother's house. She goes in, leaving the husband in the car, and begins to talk to the mother and to her two brothers. The husband becomes irritable and honks his car horn. The woman calls that she will be out at once. The talk continues. It continues, in fact, for four hours, with the infuriated husband continuing to honk, and the wife impatiently putting him off. Wolfe says, "I put it all down in the original manuscript just as I had seen and known and lived it a thousand times, and even if I do say so myself, the nature of the talk, the living vitality and character of the language, the utter naturalness, the floodtide river of it all was wonderful, but I had made four people talk 80,000 words—200 printed pages of close type in a minor scene of an enormous book." (Geismar, p. 605)

In Wolfe's Faustian world, "stories" (meaning the common conventions of modern fiction) did not and probably could not exist; "life" alone mattered. Wolfe did not write "stories," but instead produced a single, long, complex narrative, imposing no formal structure on it, but trying by repetition and analysis and accurate statement to make the structure of the living phenomena apparent. Wolfe wrote no "novels," although four books describable as novels have been published from the huge, homogeneous mass of manuscript he produced. Aswell remarks that "Tom always spoke of the whole mass of manuscript from which these later volumes were taken simply as 'the book.' He did not know whether in the end it would make one book or a dozen, and he didn't much care. That seemed to him the publisher's problem, and he was right about it." [15] He felt strongly—was sometimes oppressed and baffled and enraged by—a sense of the story's growth. When he wrote, the process often seems to have been more an evacuation than a creation.

> Seated at a table in his cold, little room that overlooked the old cobbled court of the hotel, he wrote ceaselessly from dawn to dark, sometimes from darkness on to dawn again—hurling himself upon the bed to dream; in a state of comatose awareness, strange sleeping-wakeful visions, dreams mad and terrible as the blinding imagery that now swept constantly across his brain its blaze of fire. The words were wrung out of him in a kind of bloody sweat, they poured out of his finger tips, spat out of his snarling throat like writhing snakes; he wrote them with his heart, his brain, his sweat,

his guts; he wrote them with his blood, his spirit; they were wrenched out of the last secret source and substance of his life. (*Of Time and the River*, pp. 858–59)

And again and again he speaks of his work—the endless tide of his recollections, observations and knowledge—as damming up, as choking and destroying him. "I've got too much material," says George Webber. "It keeps backing up on me . . . until sometimes I wonder what in the name of God I'm going to do with it all—how I'm going to find a frame for it, a channel, a way to make it flow!" [16]

Critics almost inevitably comment on the crudity of some of Wolfe's creative techniques, on the "formlessness" of his work, on the chaotic way in which he wrote. Bishop, for example, says, ". . . he did not find for that novel, nor do I believe he ever could have found, a structure of form which would have been capable of giving shape and meaning to his emotional experience." (*Essays*, p. 134) Aswell, of course, is obliged to believe the opposite. He says that Wolfe's novels have no "artificialities of plot," but rather "the form of life itself." He suggests that Wolfe was both scientist and artist, recalling the notes which Wolfe kept during the course of his last continental journey. (pp. 361 *et seq.*) Wolfe himself discussed this point, and with a good deal of common sense. But what seemed to some critics and even to Wolfe worthy of special comment will hardly prove surprising to the student of general semantics. It was the striving after an impossible goal that produced and determined so much in Wolfe's books, the attempt to experience and write about "everything," the occasional confusion of levels so that he tried to duplicate in language the structure of "all" the facts. This, one must conclude, was the key evaluation in Wolfe's life and his writing. In the light of this hypothesis, it is not surprising that his manuscripts are incomplete, "formless," chaotic; or that he was in no sense a literary technician.

The Faustian sickness seems to have plagued Wolfe most grievously when he started out to "create" fictitious characters. He tried to get the nonverbal phenomena of life directly and literally into his work. He was frequently autobiographical in the strict reporting sense. He says, with reference to *Look Homeward, Angel*, that "the young writer is often led through inexperience to a use of the materials of life which are, perhaps, somewhat too crude and naked for the purposes of a work of art." (Geismar, pp. 572–73) In many cases he evidently did produce easily recognizable portraits in his first novel. After the book was published, one of the neighbors complained gently. It's all right to put us in the book, he said, but you might have left out our address and telephone number (Muller, p. 1). Wolfe was simply unable, in this early writing, to escape the burden of his literal knowledge; he could not change even minor and trivial details, apparently because "they happened that way." Thus, Wolfe's father, W. O. Wolfe, becomes W. O. Gant in the *Angel;* his mother, Julia Elizabeth, becomes Eliza; his brother Ben remains Ben. Wolfe, in short, tends to forget that he is talking about his reactions to his perceptions of living persons, and above all to forget that there are many varied and interesting and adequate ways of talking about such things. Although Wolfe himself would probably have denied it, this habit persisted; even after he had published his excellent self-analysis and self-criticism in *The Story of a Novel,* he must surely have written some portions of *The Web and the Rock* and *You Can't Go Home Again.* And these books are almost as solidly based on his literal experience as was *Look Homeward, Angel.* He learned slowly, and only through repeated error.

One might wonder how Wolfe contrived to "know" so many people intimately enough to derive his characterizations. Bishop offers an interesting insight in this connection. He remarks that "at the center of Wolfe's writing is a single character, and it was certainly the aim of that writing to present this character in all his manifold contacts with the world of our time." Yet when we come to understand this character, we see that—aside from his contacts with his family— his relationships with other people are casual and fleeting. "For Eugene Gant, the only satisfactory relationship with another human creature is one which can have no continuity." (*Essays,* pp. 134–35) From a careful reading of Wolfe's works, one might readily agree with this opinion. A surprising number of his characters are created through the process known as "tagging," i.e., attributing to a person in the story two or three simple, distinctive characteristics of appearance or behavior which are then referred to whenever the character appears. Thus, Luke Gant in *Look Homeward, Angel* is tagged by his stutter, his idiotic laugh, his curly, golden hair and his beaming face —features which are played upon whenever Luke appears. Wolfe's fondness for this device may represent a compromise between his Faustianism (which would certainly demand supernaturally vivid, multi-dimensional characters *and* an impossibly vast number of them) and the practical necessities of living and writing. The mechanism involved is no doubt classifiable as another "escape" from the impossible Faustian world. Wolfe's life and writings, one begins to realize, abound in such mechanisms.

The result of this literal but curiously limited kind of characterization was that Wolfe failed in one way and succeeded too well in another. His first two books, *Look Homeward, Angel* and *Of Time and the River*, were probably failures in the sense that they did not measure up to his ideal. Judging by the totality of what Wolfe has written about these two books, one would say that he behaved typically in getting as little sense of accomplishment and success out of their writing and publication as possible, and in indulging in worries and fears and frustrations over his "talent," his forthcoming books, his future. Indeed, *Of Time and the River* was published almost without Wolfe's knowledge; his editor [Maxwell Evarts Perkins, to whom the book is dedicated] finally took the necessary action when Wolfe was away from New York, over his insistence that the book was not yet ready for printing. When Wolfe demanded six more months to work on it, his editor replied that "the book was not only finished, but that if I took six months more on it, I would then demand another six months and six months more beyond that, and that I might very well become obsessed with this one work that I would never get it published. . . . I was not, he said, a Flaubert kind of writer. I was not a perfectionist." (Geismar, p. 42) The last phrase is almost ridiculous. Wolfe was certainly not another Flaubert. Yet he might have delayed forever the publication of his work, not because he wanted to polish and perfect it, but because he was haunted by the knowledge that he had not gotten *all* the universe between its two covers.

But although Wolfe "failed" in this sense, his Faustianism succeeded all too well in another direction. A good many of Wolfe's friends and former neighbors were able to find themselves represented in his first book with what they feared was photographic accuracy. The response was as violent as it was surprising to Wolfe. The book was denounced vigorously in public and in private by the citizens of Asheville. A number of persons wrote Wolfe venomous letters, anonymous and otherwise, filled with obscenity, threats of private murder and public lynching.[17] These individuals were by no means guiltless of misevaluation; they confused fiction with fact; they insisted that the book was not only "true," but true in all details. One instance of this misevaluation was rather curious. In *Look Homeward, Angel,* the elder Gant, toward the end of his life, sells his prized stone angel to the proprietor of a local house of prostitution, and the angel is duly placed over the grave of one of this lady's ex-employees. Wolfe says this incident is pure fiction, "yet I was informed by several people later that they not only remembered the incident perfectly, but had actually been witnesses to the transaction." After the publication of the book, a newspaper sent a reporter to the Asheville cemetery to find the original angel. This confused fellow returned with photographs and a feature story, which were duly published. The result was unhappy. The photographed angel had been erected over the grave of a "well known Methodist lady who had died a few years before." Her indignant family found the implications of this story "infamous" and very properly demanded a retraction (Geismar, p. 574).

In a sense, then, and from time to time, Wolfe seems to have thought of his language as a map of "reality" so literal and accurate as to be almost identical with reality. He frequently forgot that there are levels of abstraction in discourse, and that any writer is obliged to be selective when reporting, and that writers (especially writers of fiction) frequently talk more about themselves than about the world outside them. He was indeed aware that any good writer bases his creation on "the truth," i.e., on certain abstractions of the way life is lived; but he too often was unaware that there are various ways of abstracting, various orders of abstraction, or various aspects of phenomena which might be legitimately discussed in fiction. This is not to say that Wolfe was always unaware, or completely unaware, of these matters. But he had not mastered or integrated these attitudes; they were not a functioning part of his working equipment; he had made some progress, it is true, but at the time of his death he had a long way to travel.

By the time his first two books had been published, Wolfe believed that he had learned certain lessons from his editors and critics.

He came to acknowledge the impossibility of achieving total experience in living or total expression in writing. He says,

> It may be objected . . . that in such research as I have here attempted to describe there is a quality of intemperate excess, an almost insane hunger to devour the entire body of human experience, to attempt to include more, experience more, than the measure of one life can hold, or than the limits of a single work of art can well define. I readily admit the validity of this criticism. I think I realize as well as anyone the fatal dangers that are consequent to such a ravenous desire, the damage it may wreak upon one's life and on one's work. . . . And now I really believe that so far as the artist is concerned, the unlimited extent of human experience is not so important for him as the depth and intensity with which he experiences things. I also know now that it is a great deal more important to have known one hundred living men and women in New York, to have understood their lives, to have got, somehow, at the root and source from which their natures came than to have seen or passed or talked with 7,000,000 people upon the city streets. (Geismar, pp. 586–87)

While one notes even in this passage a kind of tamed intemperateness, a sort of half-disguised uncertainty like that of a confirmed alcoholic taking the pledge (I *really* believe), still the understanding is there and the concession is a considerable one. About this time, too, Wolfe began to create characters by "free invention"; that is, he created persons in his fiction who corresponded in detail to his observations, but whose total pattern was an invention. Nebraska Crane and Judge Rumford Bland, who appear in *The Web and the Rock* and *You Can't Go Home Again,* are examples. In his fragmentary novel, *The Hills Beyond,* Wolfe makes an attempt to abandon his old Faustianism; the book seems to be constructed on the theory that total experience is impossible and that, after all, one can only suggest in words a few of the details about any given person or experience. The result, as it stands, is not impressive. As Muller says, "Here we see the new, sober, impersonal Wolfe, who is consciously practicing restraint, who has profited by criticism; and, we must add, regrettably, that the gains are outweighed by a considerable loss in natural wealth and power." (Muller, p. 20) It is no doubt unfair to evaluate Wolfe's work of this period. *The Hills Beyond* is fragmentary, and would certainly have been rewritten had the author lived. Even *The Web and the Rock* and *You Can't Go Home Again* are, practically speaking, rough drafts of the novels they might have been.

Nevertheless, it is true that during the last two or three years of his life, Wolfe believed that he had conquered the Faustian sickness, had achieved—if not a completely accurate evaluation of his problems and conflicts—at least a more sane and healthy one. What was the result?

The immediate result was that his writing suffered. The strife, the waste of his life, the impossible pursuit of an ill-defined and unachievable goal had surely released his energies and extended his powers in a way quite uncommon to most men in our time. The wild but magnificent chants, the rich profusion of character and incident, the feeling of overwhelming and chaotic growth which informs his earlier work, are missing from what he wrote last. All too frequently he will simply remark that one cannot get this character or that incident into words—and then demonstrate the truth of his remark. "At times," says Muller, "he is calm to the point of banality." (p. 118) The uncommon and remarkable characteristics of his early writing seem to have been by-products of the Faustian sickness; and when the sickness abated somewhat, the by-products diminished, whether temporarily or forever no man can say. In trying to rely on sanity and temperateness and skill in his writing, Wolfe characteristically went too far and achieved little more than pedestrianism. His new and hard-learned attitudes he found but poor substitutes for the nonsanity, the impossible ideals and bitter frustrations which had made him a writer in the first place.

In the final chapter of *You Can't Go Home Again,* in a long letter ostensibly addressed by George Webber to his editor, Wolfe writes:

> That was a giant web in which I was caught, the product of my huge inheritance—the torrential recollectiveness, derived out of my mother's stock, which became a living, million-fibered integument that bound me to the past, not only of my own life, but of the very earth from which I came, so that nothing in the end escaped from its inrooted and all-feeling explorativeness. . . . You stayed beside me like the rock you are until I unearthed the plant,

followed it back through every fiber of its pattern to its last and tiniest enrootment in the blind, dumb earth. And now that it is finished, and the circle come full swing—we, too, are finished. (pp. 740–41)

So Wolfe brought his Faustian life (verbally, at least) to its close. No doubt he meant what he said. He burned several obvious bridges behind him; he changed publishers, breaking with the editor who had been his friend through the long years of writing; as we have seen, he began at least to experiment with a new style and with a new handling of materials.

What Wolfe expected of this new life, of this new "cycle" of work that lay before him, is difficult to say. Even his basic attitudes are difficult to determine; his new "philosophy" was not really phrased at the time of his death. The formal conclusion to Wolfe's Faustian life which we have quoted in part above was also, in fact, the conclusion to his physical existence. He died before he could be effectively reborn. There is evidence—see the final paragraphs of *You Can't Go Home Again*—that he expects as much. So perhaps it is quite pointless to speculate on what he might have done, had he lived.

It is possible, though not highly probable, that Wolfe might have developed as a technician, and might have come to dominate his materials instead of being possessed by them. No one can say. His work and career, as they are now concluded, must stand as a classic example of creative activity motivated, shaped and limited by a singularly dramatic pattern of misevaluations.

Notes

1. Herbert J. Muller, *Thomas Wolfe* (Norfolk, Conn.: New Directions Books, 1947), p. 6.

2. *Ibid.*, p. 26. See also Edward Aswell, "A Note on Thomas Wolfe," in Wolfe, *The Hills Beyond* (Garden City, New York: The Sun Dial Press, 1943), p. 360 *et seq.*

3. See Aswell, *op. cit.*, p. 364.

4. See Pamela Hansford Johnson, *Hungry Gulliver: An English Critical Appraisal of Thomas Wolfe* (New York: Charles Scribner's Sons, 1948), pp. 1–2.

5. John S. Terry, *Thomas Wolfe's Letters to His Mother* (New York, 1945), pp. 49–50 and pp. 52–53.

6. Compare with this reading the one suggested by Pamela Hansford Johnson, in *Hungry Gulliver*, pp. 97–98. Eugene Gant "yells of his triumphs with women because he is not so sure of himself as a lover; of his genius as an artist because he is not quite confident that any noise will be made about it elsewhere. Wolfe's height and Eugene's height is the source of a mania; it is the blessed compensation for the sense of personal inferiority. 'Look how huge I am,' the hero cries, 'look how much food, rich gorgeous, ogreish food I can cram into this giant frame.' " No doubt Miss Johnson's explanation explains a good deal, and with a certain justice; Wolfe was by no means sure of himself, specially in his earlier years, and some of his behavior may represent an over-reaction to this uncertainty. Yet the "inferiority complex" explanation is over-simple and after all explains very little. For that reason I have preferred the somewhat less conventional hypothesis which appears in the text of this paper.

7. Thomas Wolfe, *Of Time and the River* (New York, 1944), pp. 91–92.

8. Maxwell Geismar, ed., *The Portable Thomas Wolfe* (New York, 1946), p. 2.

9. "Writing Is My Life: Letters of Thomas Wolfe," *The Atlantic Monthly* (December, 1946), p. 61.

10. Thomas Wolfe, *The Web and the Rock* (New York, 1939), p. 660.

11. Wolfe, "The Story of a Novel," in Geismar, editor, *The Portable Thomas Wolfe*, p. 611.

12. Muller, *op. cit.*, p. 10.

13. Thomas Wolfe, *Look Homeward, Angel: A Story of the Buried Life* (New York: Charles Scribner's Sons, 1929), Chapter XXXVIII.

14. Edmund Wilson, ed., *The Collected Essays of John Peale Bishop* (New York: Charles Scribner's Sons, 1948), p. 130.

15. Aswell, *op. cit.*, p. 365.

16. Thomas Wolfe, *You Can't Go Home Again* (New York: Harper and Brothers, 1940), p. 386.

17. Cf. "The Story of a Novel," p. 571 *et seq.*; also, *You Can't Go Home Again*, Chapter XXII, "A Question of Guilt."

Floyd C. Watkins

12. Rhetoric in Southern Writing: Wolfe

THE CLAIMS that Thomas Wolfe was an expatriate Southerner who fouled his own nest are matched by claims that he befouled his own books with "turbulent and undisciplined rhetoric"—and no ten-minute paper can even clarify the issues between the attackers and the defenders of his style. Some judge him the greatest writer of modern times, some the worst, and some both the best and the worst. Faulkner, Wolfe's fellow Southern rhetorician, has "rated Wolfe first" although he was, says Faulkner, "willing to throw away style." Robert Penn Warren finds the rhetoric "astonishingly loose," "sometimes grand, . . . more often tedious and tinged with hysteria." * Edwin Berry Burgum maintains that in "the periodic sentences and the consolation of abstract statement . . . indubitably Wolfe becomes one of the great stylists in the English language." If the critics disagree, the Wolfe cultists are certain that his style is one of his great accomplishments. Indeed, his poetic rhetoric has attracted the large audience to which many modern poets claim they cannot appeal.

The varying judgments by different critics, the frequent changes in the attitude of the reader toward Wolfe, and the tendency to like a passage from Wolfe at one time and to dislike it at another—all these are understandable if we view him as a poet—particularly a primitive or natural poet. Perhaps the most basic characteristic of Wolfe's prose is that it reveals a love for primitivistic sound and phrase. As a college student he once recited for days a single line from one of the penny dreadfuls of his time: "The arm was hairy, hairy beyond

* See Chapter 16 in this book.

all description." Much of his writing reveals an attraction to the mere words and rhythms of a sentence not entirely unlike the appeal to the primitive in Vachel Lindsay's "The Congo." His elaborate repetitions and pointing words and phrases are occasionally as inept as the dull reiterations of a freshman theme, often as primitive as the incremental repetition of a folk ballad, and sometimes as infinitely various as the work of a careful poet.

The long description of Altamont waking at dawn in *Look Homeward, Angel* contains an example of how Wolfe repeated phrases and figures and achieved an unusual effect by varying the combinations of colors and images. "Spring," he wrote, "lay strewn lightly like a fragrant gauzy scarf upon the earth; the night was a cool bowl of lilac darkness, filled with fresh orchard scents." In the following twelve pages he repeats in many combinations such terms as "lilac darkness," "pearl light," "nacreous dawn," and "blue-pearl" until the repetitions lead gradually to the full light of day, which appears suddenly in the new term "virginal sunlight." Without such extended development, some of the descriptive passages would seem overwritten, but the activities of the waking citizens as well as the repetitions prepare for a rhapsody like the following: "Nacreous pearl light swam faintly about the hem of the lilac darkness; the edges of light and darkness were stitched upon the hills. Morning moved like a pearl-gray tide across the fields and up the hillflanks, flowing rapidly down into the soluble dark." This is one of the best examples of Wolfe's characteristic rhetorical patterning of phrases throughout a unified passage. Similarly, in the description of the death of Ben Gant, the images of the "bright and stricken thing," the cock, and the leaves are repeated with great power and accumulating effect.

Look Homeward, Angel is Wolfe's most subtle novel in imagery. He describes wonder as "the union of the ordinary and the miraculous," and in many instances he succeeds in blending the two poetically and almost metaphysically in the poetic sense. Destiny, he says for example in the first paragraph, leads "into the hills that shut in Altamont over the proud coral cry of the cock, and the soft stone smile of an angel. . . ." "Coral cry" metaphysically yokes heterogeneous elements by violence together; it may involve a description of the color of the cock, or the description of the sound as a color, or the description of the color of the dawn. And "the soft stone smile of the angel" merges paradoxical terms. Oxymorons and conceits of this kind are almost omnipresent in the first novel but rather infrequent in the later works.

Wolfe's turbulent emotions and extravagant figures of speech often counterbalance his successes. That cow in *Look Homeward, Angel* which is "singing in her strong deep voice her Sunday exuberance" is an unhappy example of Wolfe's own occasional bovine mooings; and she even suggests the ineptness of the squeal and the goat-cry in the love story in *The Web and the Rock* or of characters "holding [their] . . . entrails thoughtfully in [their] . . . hands" in *Of Time and the River*. The most overdone passages in *Look Homeward, Angel* at times make the hero more ridiculous than adolescent. If the description of Eugene's paper route is on the whole a masterful accomplishment, the hero is excessively afflicted with emotions while carrying the papers: "he burst into maniacal laughter. He leaped high into the air with a scream of insane exultancy, burred in his throat idiot-animal squeals, and shot his papers terrifically into the flimsy boarding of the shacks."

What most of us too often fail to see, however, is Wolfe's frequent comic intent in his rhetorical passages. Often he succeeds in making his adult readers nostalgically long for childhood, and he amuses them in the same passages by creating comic melodrama about childhood, using deliberately high-flown rhetoric. When young Eugene Gant visualizes himself as the Dixie Ghost in a motion picture, Wolfe is not only portraying a child's imagination but also sympathetically laughing at the child and the movie. When the Ghost "found himself face to face with the little dancing girl," there was as much comedy as childhood romance: "Two smoking globes of brine welled from the pellucid depths of her pure eyes and fell with a hot splash on his bronzed hand." Later, the Ghost "pondered on love's mystery. Pure but passionate. Appearances against her, 'tis true. The foul breath of slander. She worked in a bawdy-house but her heart was clean. Outside of that, what can one say against her?"

If Wolfe depicts W. O. Gant as a tragic hero of almost gigantic proportions in some scenes, he also frequently uses rhetoric to make him a boisterous clown. When, for example, ladies compliment him because he votes for prohibition, Wolfe describes him mock-heroically: "With far-seeing statesmanship he looked westward toward Pisgah."

And then W. O. launches into a political oration extolling his own virtues and damning the evil whisky he loves. But this pose is shaken by his cronies' crudeness, expressed in a style characteristic of the writings of the Old Southwest humorists: "Go on, W. O., but for God's sake, don't belch!" And Tim O'Doyle, the bartender, adds a tall tale in the homely speech of Southern folk: "I've seen him start for the door and step through the windey. When we see him coming we hire two extra bottle openers. He used to give the barman a bonus to get up early."

Look Homeward, Angel exhibits the major tendencies in Wolfe's rhetoric. It is his best book, because his rhetorical flourishes are most happily employed to describe the emotions and the imagination of a sensitive child or youth. In the next two books, the rhetoric frequently becomes bombastic descriptions of adolescent emotions of an older if not more mature hero. You Can't Go Home Again marks in many respects a new stage. The rhetoric appears in panoramic descriptions of the landscape of America and in passages where a lyrical style is appropriate.

The decline evident in Of Time and the River and The Web and the Rock is significantly offset by Wolfe's increasing use of his Southern origins and of Southern speech and oratory. "The Web of Earth" is one of his best works because Wolfe presents so ably the mountaineer rhetoric of Eliza Gant in what might be called a stream of conversation. Uncle John's account of the battle of Chickamauga in The Hills Beyond is one of the most effective representations of mountaineer speech in American literature. And the political oratory and backwoods humor of Zachariah Joyner in The Hills Beyond are other examples of Wolfe's growing consciousness of his Southern heritage, including Southern rhetoric.

Wolfe must be viewed as a Southern rhetorician. He was a poet in his love of sound and his use of sensuous imagery. At his worst, he is "full of sound and fury, signifying nothing"; at his best, as one of his characters says of W. O. Gant, he could "tie a knot in the tail of the English language."

Richard Walser

13. From Thomas Wolfe: An Introduction and Interpretation

IN DESIGNING his vision of life, Wolfe perceived that never were there ready-made outlines to follow. Wolfe felt that he had to begin all over again, and often it meant sounding out ways unknown to writers of the past. *His* traditions, *his* world, *his* self were not those of others, but demanded, in their very difference, new patterns and new structures. Like all genuine authors, Wolfe had to discover his own way, his own technique. Thus he had to build a new form (it was new to him) by means of which he might be able to detail his vision. Emerson would have understood and approved an organic structure based not upon tradition but upon natural insight. The act of creation in itself provides its own ordering.

Wolfe's novels, then, constitute a reaction against the *romans bien faits* with their neat, proper, thin-blooded outlines. True, Wolfe did not often think of himself as a novelist, and he did not write in terms of stories supplied with the expected pseudo-plots and conventional paraphernalia. He wished, rather, to follow life with its seemingly patternless movements, and he did not push for answers with which experience had not provided him. Nothing must be implied; everything must be told. Yet his pattern, as it turned out, was a constant progression from romanticism toward realism, from rebellion toward maturity, from youth toward responsibility.

To give unity to this progression throughout the four major novels and all the shorter pieces, Wolfe evolved a theme inherent in the material itself. In America—strange, vast, poetic—the individual was a wanderer, lonely and set apart. The autobiographical heroes Eugene Gant and George Webber were artists spurned by a collective society whose prosperous, callous mechanization had forced them into exile. The heroes struggled with town and family and school, with New York esthetes and Brooklyn philistines, with all those elements forgetful of their American heritage.

The image of the lonely, ostracized wanderer moving here and there, touching life passionately yet always readying himself for departure, is a constant one beginning with *Look Homeward, Angel*.

".... The first move I ever made, after the cradle, was to crawl for the door [said Eugene Gant at the age of seventeen], and every move I have made since has been an effort to escape. . . . If I am not free, I am at least locked up in my own prison, but I shall get me some beauty, . . . I shall find my way out of it yet, though it take me twenty years more—alone."

"Alone?" said Eliza, with the old suspicion. "Where are you going?"

"Ah," he said, "you were not looking, were you? I've gone."

Wolfe's "going" gradually assumed a purposefulness more significant than mere flight from disdained environments and influence; it became a retreat into discovery of self, and from self into that which made up self—America. America had been surveyed, Wolfe said, but it had never been explored. To tell its shapes and colors, a new language had to be invented, a speech different from that of the statistician and the realist, a lyric tongue to express the interior spirit of a people and a continent. He was aware of Whitman's language, but clearly Whitman's way was not what he had in mind. Something else again was needed to catch the beauty, awe, spaciousness, and frightening loneliness of America.

Everywhere were insignia of the boundless land. There were the trains moving through the darkness, the sounds of the boats in the harbors, the vast rivers draining the mighty states, and the terrible endless skies. And there were the arrogant multi-peopled cities, and the little courthouse towns, and the men and women—fearing, hoping, hating, loving. All these things had to be told. They had to be told because no writers, with the exception of Whitman and Dos Passos, had made any attempt to deal with the expanse of America or to get at an understanding of the scope and proportions and capacious life of a land using the English tongue but un-European in its enormous and sequestered insularity. It was a land of paradoxes, of course, a land of poverty and bounty, of defeat and success, of unfruitfulness and raw fecundity, of downcast hopes and bright promise. Wolfe saw it as a land of sophisticated Bostonians and Southern colored folk from Old Catawba, of luscious Jewish women and destitute jobless drunks, of despicable sycophants and strong-armed Paul Bunyans. It was a nation constantly on the move—the trains, always the trains, shooting across high trestles in the nighttime and curling around the hillsides, the whistles blowing a message to the solitary farmhouses beyond the valley.

It is movement, perhaps, which most characterizes Wolfe's novels. Automobiles, boats, and trains hurl Eugene-George on to new experience. The seductive woman smoothing her legs in an upper Pullman berth is image and part of the fantasy and wish fulfillment of America. "Through you," Wolfe wrote Aline Bernstein after his first voyage to Europe, "I slid back into America again."

On the move, somewhere, would be found the glorious dream, symbolized by that beautiful, enticing woman. She (the idea of America, the woman) would be security against all degradations and failures. In her were longing and love, and Wolfe poured into his books a return of that love, even when she had to bear up under his chastisement; for only through love and desire was fulfillment possible.

Wolfe found out that love of land was not inherent, that "the way to discover one's own country was to leave it; that the way to find America was to find it in one's heart, one's memory, and one's spirit, and in a foreign land." He perceived this truth on seven trips to Europe. It was then that, from sheer separation, he loved America most. Away from it, always he was drawn back by memory and some unexplained urge within.

Wolfe's exploration of America was an emotional voyage, undertaken not by listing and describing from hearsay and imagination the various aspects of a land too broad to be encompassed within the experience and life of one man. Often he chose the little, touching, unnoticed thing—"the sound of a milk wagon as it entered an American street just at the first gray of the morning"—sending off a stream of recollection into the past too tender for the rough jags of the unreal and made-up. A recollection such as this stirred the affections, not the intellect. It glowed and warmed him. In 1930 from London he wrote: "My longing for America amounts to a constant ache." From its tangible substance, Wolfe was able to evoke the emotional personality of his country, bringing it out of memory with all its haunting beauty.

It was filtered through his own consciousness, and from it he drew his strength—his strength as an artist. For Wolfe found, eventually, that America was in himself. "He was not 'celebrating' America, as Whitman had done," writes Alfred Kazin; "he was trying to echo it in himself." From it he had need to draw his life, his art, and his speech. It was no easy discovery, no easy task; but by 1936 he was able to proclaim:

> I have at last discovered my own America, I believe I have found my language, I think I know my way. And I shall wreak out my vision of this life, this way, this world and this America, to the top of my bent, to the height of my ability, but with an unswerving devotion, integrity and purity of purpose that shall not be menaced, altered or weakened by any one.

Fortunately, the language to wreak out his vision was already at his disposal. For the straight narrative scenes he had the tried-and-true techniques of realistic fiction, valid and versatile enough to carry the burden of his intention. Infused with Wolfe's peculiar ironic commentary, it served well. Yet, for those pages where a more rhapsodic expression was indicated to unfold emotional themes, he turned to poetry. He did not use the word poetry. Instead he was often heard to say: "I'd rather be a poet than anything else in the world. God, what wouldn't I give to be one!" Seemingly he had not equated with poetry a personal emotionality to which he was even then giving expression. But whether he understood or not, in the spontaneous quality of his lyric passages there were imagery and rhythm and frequently even meter.

> Who has seen fury riding in the mountains?
> Who has known fury striding in the storm?
> Who has been mad with fury in his youth,
> given no rest or peace or certitude by fury,
> driven on across the earth by fury,
> until the great vine of the heart has broke,

the sinews wrenched, the little tenement of bone,
blood, marrow, brain, and feeling in which great fury
raged, was twisted, wrung, depleted, worn out,
and exhausted by the fury which it could not lose
or put away? Who has known fury, how it came?

This paragraph from *Of Time and the River,* extracted verbatim and rearranged only by the breaking up of sentences into lines, exhibits the melody and luxury of speech Wolfe permitted himself.

When America itself was the subject, he adopted a less stilted pattern and a more rigid vocabulary.

I will go up and down the country,
and back and forth across the country
on the great trains that thunder over America.
I will go out West where States are square;
Oh, I will go to Boise, and Helena and Albuquerque.
I will go to Montana and the two Dakotas
and the unknown places.

The opulence of prose-poetry, even with Wolfe's alert ear for speech and words, had its drawback: it was not fashionable in a decade which paid tribute to the starker vogue of journalistic Hemingwayese.

Still, heritage would not be denied. When he was a boy, he was "raised" on poetry. At home, Wolfe's father declaimed the famous passages from Shakespeare, and the two often conversed in measured phrases. From his mother the lad learned how to embellish a story with simile and metaphor. For all three, Southern rhetoric—the high sounding locutions, the delight of a series of four- and five-syllable adjectives—glittered and flourished. In school and college, Wolfe sat to the rhythm of the great English masters. He was captivated by the Cavalier and Swinburnian schools, by Donne and Sir Thomas Browne and Milton, and later by James Joyce. There were, too, the resounding cadences of the Bible, rich and lavish.

If Wolfe made no claim to being a poet—and he assuredly did not—the effects of a tradition and the admirations of student days had nevertheless their impact on his prose. In poetry he satisfied his yearning for emotional release, his eargerness for music. "I almost never attend a concert or symphony," he wrote. "My real interest has been in poetry." So, in his novels, he opened the floodgates; and as he did it, like D. H. Lawrence and Henry Miller, he uplifted fiction to a plane where it shared an identity with poetry. As one thinks about the matter, it is not really so unusual that the poet's techniques and art should be adapted to prose fiction. Poetry is the most primitive of literatures. Since historically the novel is but an offshoot of traditional poetry, the writers of English fiction of the last four hundred years, in abjuring rhyme and meter, have not necessarily abjured the language and style of poetry. The only strange twist is that hard upon such writers as Theodore Dreiser and Sinclair Lewis there could have been a Thomas Wolfe at all, or further that he was impelled to fling his dithyrambic passages across the stretch of America. In his paeans to Time and America, his hymns to Death, Loneliness, and Sleep, his salutes to trains and rivers, and his tributes to night, Wolfe swept past the lyric optimism of Whitman into an epic abundance. The picture was completely there, as it always has been in the best poetry.

Perhaps he was able to write in rhapsodic vein because he was willing to be neglectful of current trends and fashionable dicta. But the reason is more that he was young with a young man's vision. It has been said that Wolfe retained his adolescence until the end, that he never worked away from a boyhood with its ideals and hopes, that he kept the pain and poetry of youth even when, in the later novels, he tried to send them on their way. There is some truth in the observation. Poetry—the best lyric poetry—is concomitant with morning, and Wolfe wrote out of the morning of his life. Disillusionments which eventually disturbed him were soon replaced by faith.

The prose poems introducing each of the four major novels return and ring and give emphasis to the stories to be told. In them and in the colors they create, one may observe Wolfe's essential quality.

PART III   *Specific Novels*

PART III

Bruce R. McElderry, Jr.

14. The Durable Humor of Look Homeward, Angel

WHEN WOLFE's first novel appeared in 1929 it contrasted sharply with the drab realism and despairing naturalism so prevalent in the decade since the war. The really typical book of 1929 was Ernest Hemingway's *Farewell to Arms,* which leaves its central figure numb with grief for his dead wartime love, without a shred of faith in life, in country, or in himself. *Look Homeward, Angel* was a different book. With confident good humor it turned back to an older America, primarily to the America of 1900 to 1917. That older America, as Wolfe represented it, was far from ideal. It was provincial, it was naïve, it was crude. But it was exuberantly alive, and it believed in itself. It was that belief in itself that America needed to recover in the nineteen-thirties, and the popularity of Wolfe's books in the ten years from 1929 to 1939 is a testimony to the service he rendered. His untimely death in 1938 cast a Keatsian halo around his memory, and in 1939 Wolfe was a minor literary cult.

The Keatsian halo has proved unfortunate, for it has prevented recognition of Wolfe as one of the finest humorous writers in America since Mark Twain, perhaps even better than Twain in range and variety. *A Subtreasury of American Humor* (1941), for example, included no selection from Wolfe. There has been an overzealous concern with the "serious" side of his work: the autobiographical nature of his fiction, the importance of editorial revision by Max Perkins, the question of whether Wolfe developed an adequate "philosophy," and the extent to which he mastered artistic form. It is time to re-read *Look Homeward, Angel,* his best novel, not so much as the agonizing search for maturity by an adolescent genius, as for the wonderful gallery of comic characters remembered and created from Wolfe's journey through the early years of this century. Eugene Gant's struggle to escape from family and environment is a thoroughly American pattern, and it gives intelligible direction to the story, but it is not the main attraction, any more than the freeing of the negro slave Jim is the main attraction of *Huckleberry Finn*. In both books it is the rich panorama and the lively episodes that enthrall.

In the comfortable old times pictured in *Look Homeward, Angel* a boy's heroes were Theodore Roosevelt, Admiral Dewey, and Woodrow Wilson. William Jennings Bryan actually appears in one scene of the novel, sonorously praising to a newspaper reporter the charms of Altamont (Asheville). Veterans of the Civil War looked back over the long years with sad pride, and the Spanish-American War was a recent event, of glorious memory. Ridpath's *History of the World* was serious reading, and for entertainment there were dozens of Alger books with alliterative titles like *Sink or Swim,* the endless adventures of the Rover Boys, and *Stover at Yale*. It was the era of the *Police Gazette,* the minstrel show, and the early silent movies. Young people of a certain age—and older ones, too—sang "I Wonder Who's Kissing Her Now," "Till the Sands of the Desert Grow Cold," and "The End of a Perfect Day." All these delights, and many more, are set down in Wolfe's novel as they really were. They are amusing, as old snapshots always are, but they are true, too, and they are worth remembering without the malice that so distorts Sinclair Lewis's description of provincial America in *Main Street*.

It is the tolerance, the lack of malice, that gives distinction to Wolfe's humor in this novel. In this he is often superior to Twain, for much of Twain's humor is overshadowed by his obvious desire to score off somebody else as more stupid than himself, or sometimes to get even with himself for being stupid. Either way the temptation to bludgeon his way is strong. Wolfe is more natural, and more varied. How easily he gets his effect as he describes the meeting of Eliza Pentland and W. O. Gant. Eliza introduces herself as a representative of the Larkin Publishing Company:

> She spoke the words proudly, with dignified gusto. Merciful God! A book-agent! thought Gant.
> "We are offering," said Eliza, opening a huge yellow book

with a fancy design of spears and flags and laurel wreaths, "a book of poems called *Gems of Verse for Hearth and Fireside* as well as *Larkin's Domestic Doctor and Book of Household Remedies*, giving directions for the cure and prevention of over five hundred diseases."

"Well," said Gant, with a faint grin, wetting his big thumb briefly, "I ought to find one that I've got out of that."

"Why, yes," said Eliza, nodding smartly, "as the fellows says, you can read poetry for the good of your soul and Larkin for the good of your body." (p. 11) [1]

This is humor drawn from nature, requiring nothing but selection and the restraint of accurate reporting. Another passage illustrates humorous interpretation. Gant has just called his four sons for breakfast:

> "When I was your age, I had milked four cows, done all the chores, and walked eight miles through the snow by this time."

Indeed, when he described his early schooling he furnished a landscape that was constantly three feet deep in snow, and frozen hard. He seemed never to have attended school save under polar conditions. (p. 50)

Sometimes the humorous effect is finely dramatic, as when one of Gant's sprees makes it appear that he is actually dead. Eugene's brother Ben turns to Eliza in fright:

> "Well," she said, picking her language with deliberate choosiness, "the pitcher went to the well once too often. I knew it would happen sooner or later."
>
> Through a slotted eye Gant glared murderously at her. Judicially, with folded hands, she studied him. Her calm eye caught the slow movement of a stealthy inhalation.
>
> "You get his purse, son, and any papers he may have," she directed. "I'll call the undertaker."
>
> With an infuriate scream the dead awakened.
>
> "I thought that would bring you to," she said complacently.
> He scrambled to his feet.
>
> "You hell-hound!" he yelled. "You would drink my heart's blood. You are without mercy and without pity—inhuman and bloody monster that you are." (p. 280)

Subtler, however, is the remarkable scene in which "Queen" Elizabeth, the town madam, orders from Gant a tombstone for one of her girls:

> "And she was such a fine girl, Mr. Gant," said Elizabeth, weeping softly. "She had such a bright future before her. She had more opportunities than I ever had, and I suppose you know"— she spoke modestly—"what I've done." (p. 266)

Elizabeth insists on purchasing the angel, Gant's favorite piece of statuary, and together they select a suitable inscription for the young prostitute's monument:

> She went away in beauty's flower,
> Before her youth was spent;
> Ere life and love had lived their hour
> God called her, and she went.

No excerpt can convey a sense of the delicate balance that prevents this scene from falling into burlesque. Gant and Elizabeth are humorous characters in a humorous situation. Wolfe lets them have their scene without satirical interjections.

Old man Gant is Wolfe's greatest character, and it is time to recognize him as one of the most varied comic characters in American literature. Beside him, Twain's Beriah Sellers is a shallow and tiresome stereotype. Gant's feud with Eliza is counterpointed by his even greater rage at her brother, Major Will Pentland. Gant's tirades, his passion for food and drink, his fear of the automobile he absentmindedly purchased, his unblinking support of the temperance movement, his pride in his children—these are but a few of the comic materials. But Gant is not the only source of humor. Eliza herself, literal-minded and obsessed with greed, is a wonderful foil to her turbulent husband. When Gant returned without warning from his long ramble in the west she "explains" his return:

> "I was saying to Steve last night, 'It wouldn't surprise me if your papa would come rolling in at any minute now'—I just had a feeling. I don't know what you'd call it," she said, her face plucked inward by her sudden fabrication of legend, "but it's pretty strange when you come to think about it. I was in Garret's

the other day ordering some things, some vanilla extract, soda, and a pound of coffee . . ."

Jesus God! thought Gant. It's begun again. (p. 78)

Besides Gant and Eliza, there is young Luke Gant, energetically stuttering the townspeople into buying the *Saturday Evening Post.* There are Doc Maguire and Horse Hines (the undertaker), frequently found at Uneeda Lunch No. 3. There are Eugene's teachers: Mr. Leonard clumsily justifying the study of the classics he so unimaginatively taught; Professor Torrington, the pompous Rhodes Scholar who thought Barrie more important than Shaw; and Buck Benson, who said, "Mister Gant, you make me so damned mad I could throw you out the window," but left Eugene with a permanent love of Greek. There is a wonderful account of a Shakespeare pageant (1916):

> The pageant had opened with the Voices of Past and Present—voices a trifle out of harmony with the tenor of the event—but necessary to the commercial success of the enterprise. These voices now moved voicelessly past—four frightened sales-ladies from Schwartzberg's, clad decently in cheese-cloth and sandals, who came by bearing the banner of their concern. Or, as the doctor's more eloquent iambics had it:
>
> > Fair Commerce, sister of the arts, thou, too,
> > Shalt take thy lawful place upon our stage.
>
> They came and passed: Ginsberg's—"the glass of fashion and the mould of form"; Bradley the Grocer—"When first Pomona held her fruity horn"; The Buick Agency—"the chariots of Oxus and of Ind." (p. 374)

And—years before Walter Mitty—there are the skillful parodies of youthful daydreaming in which Eugene Gant sees himself as Mainwaring the young minister, declaring his love to Grace the beautiful parishioner before he goes "out west"; as Bruce Glendenning, the beachcomber who saves Veronica from a band of yelling natives; and as "The Dixie Ghost," beating Faro Jim to the draw.

Despite these shining riches, there remains what Kipling called "The Conundrum of the Workshops." The work may be clever, striking, human—but "Is it Art?" It is a hard question with respect to humor. Even admirers of Dickens are embarrassed by it. And as for *Huckleberry Finn,* Twain himself authorized the shooting of persons attempting to find a motive, moral, or plot in it. It is generally thought that without these you cannot have Art. Whether they are in fact present in *Huckleberry Finn* I shall not go into, but motive, moral, and plot are reasonably in evidence in *Look Homeward, Angel.* Eugene Gant is a sensitive boy, and his journey to adulthood has point and interest. For readers today it has more point than Huck's journey on the raft. At any rate it is a more difficult journey, for Twain took care that Huck never underwent the pangs of adolescence, in which, as Keats said, "the soul is in ferment." Whatever defects in Art there may be, *Look Homeward, Angel* has many pages as funny as any in the *Subtreasury of American Humor.* If we begin with them, and tolerantly recognize that the perfect novel has not yet been written, we may come to agree with Wolfe's mother. After she read her son's novel she said: "It's not bad at all—not bad at all."

Note

1. Page references are to the Modern Library edition.

Richard S. Kennedy

15. Wolfe's Look Homeward, Angel as a Novel of Development

THE GERMAN TERM, *Bildungsroman,* which can best be translated as "novel of development" or "novel of growth" has never, to my knowledge, been adequately defined or characterized as a subcategory of the novel. We recognize in the term itself the core of its meaning. It refers to a novel which has as its subject the story of a young man or young woman who goes through the struggles of growing up and in the end reaches maturity, a point at which he has sufficient understanding of life that he can bring his career somewhat under control, free from the mistakes of the past. This kind of novel has a very strong appeal for readers because the experience is common to us all and is important to us all. The appeal is not only to young people but to everyone, for we are always, all our life long, going through the process of maturing. We are always learning from experience, we are always seeking to understand the life around us, we are always wrestling with problems that affect our destinies. I would even venture to say that the reader who is tired of stories about the process of maturing is tired of life.

The theme of passing from innocence to knowing is found in many short stories which treat of a climactic episode that changes the way the central character looks at life. Katherine Mansfield's *The Garden Party,* for instance, brings Laura to the point at which she has a new insight into the complexity and strangeness of the world around her. After viewing the dead body of the young working man and offering apologies for her hat, she can declare to her brother, "Isn't life—?" and she, wordless at this point, lets us supply the many words that can fit—fascinating, bewildering, enigmatic, surprising, and so on. A novel, however, will have a whole series of these illuminating experiences. The usual sequence is to bring the hero or heroine from birth up through adolescence. But the important point is that the struggle toward understanding must be dominant and the movement must be from confusion toward control. Thus *The Red Badge of Courage,* although it begins at the point the hero is going into the army, would be properly called a novel of development because the hero is put through many tests until at last he achieves manliness and courage. Wouk's *The Caine Mutiny,* which covers about the same age span for the hero and places him in the military service, does not fall in the category of the *Bildungsroman.* The great bulk of the book is devoted to questions of authority and justice. Dickens' *Great Expectations* has a complicated mystery which winds through its plot, yet it is a good example of the novel of development. Pip goes through moral floundering from which he gradually emerges toward the end of the book. On the other hand, Dostoevsky's *Crime and Punishment,* which deals with a young man and his moral groping, cannot be called a novel of development because its focus is on a social theme and a religious theme which arise out of the misapplication of a theory that has led to murder. The first half of Dreiser's *An American Tragedy* follows the pattern of the novel of growth but the last half does not. The defining characteristic, then, of the *Bildungsroman* is a series of ordeals and learning experiences through which the hero passes as if going through initiation rites at the brink of manhood.

The thematic pattern itself is very old. For example, the maturing of Telemachus is an important part of Homer's *Odyssey.* But the pattern does not turn up often until the Romantic Movement when self-consciousness became common practice in literature. Most of the great examples of the *Bildungsroman* appear in the nineteenth and twentieth centuries: Thackeray's *Pendennis,* Meredith's *Ordeal of Richard Feverel,* Melville's *Redburn,* Maugham's *Of Human Bondage,* Lawrence's *Sons and Lovers.* The list could be very long.

Thomas Wolfe's *Look Homeward, Angel* is almost a classic example. Indeed Thomas Wolfe was very perceptive about the features of the *Bildungsroman* because it was the kind of book he could handle best. He recognized, for instance, that the novel of development was actually another form of the journey novel—with life as the journey and a certain psychological geography as the ground to be covered. In the manuscript of *Look Homeward, Angel,* he placed at the beginning of his narrative the word "Anabasis," which means in Greek "a going up." [1] He took the term from Xenophon's account of the journey "up-country" of Cyrus the Persian in pursuit of the Greeks. Wolfe recognized, too, the sense of quest in the reaching out toward maturity. When he began work on his book *Of Time and the River,* he decided that the theme would be the search for a father—it was to be a symbolic search for a figure of authority. In his last book,* *The Web and the Rock,* he intended that it would be about "the innocent man discovering life." [2] He planned to put on the title page a quotation from *War and Peace,* "Prince Andrei looked up at the stars and sighed; everything was so different from what he thought it was going to be." [3]

Look Homeward, Angel contains all the experiences that the apprentice-hero usually passes through, except the religious ordeal. The story presents the struggle of young Eugene Gant to free himself from his environment and particularly to break free of a possessive mother. He passes through common childhood experiences in conflict with his brothers and sisters. He opens up his imagination through the world of books. He develops sexual curiosity. He reaches out for wider horizons under the guidance of sympathetic teachers in school. He gets his first job. He finds new intellectual freedoms and bewilderments in college. He undergoes sexual initiation. He is introduced to alcohol (the sacred brew of twentieth-century initiation rites). He faces the problem of death when his favorite brother is swept away in the influenza epidemic. He falls in love and endures loss of love. He makes the break from home, and, as the book comes to a close, he reaches an interpretation of life and finds a way of life that he can follow.

But the mere presence of this subject matter (or this archetypal pattern, as one may call it) is no demonstration of the literary value of the work. A novel like *The End of Roaming* by Alexander Laing or one like *A Tree Grows in Brooklyn* by Betty Smith would have this

---

* *The Web and the Rock* is the title Wolfe gave to the autobiographical novel he was working on at the time of his death. Edward Aswell divided up the manuscript and published it in three separate volumes, only the first of which was entitled *The Web and the Rock.*

pattern too, for any autobiographical novelist or any commercial novelist can adopt the pattern and, for his ephemeral purposes, draw upon the appeals which the pattern offers. A work must have something more if we will class it as a work of art worthy of being read more than once or worthy of being studied and of being discussed. The something more will be philosophic breadth, perhaps the kind of treatment that turns the hero into Everyman (or, one should say, Every Young Man). Or to put it another way, the something more will be the handling of the material in such a way as to create an intricate and harmonious literary complex which will enhance the significance of the book as well as provide the aesthetic pleasure of the successful work of art.

In another place, I have discussed the complexity of ideas that provide a framework for the story of Eugene Gant in *Look Homeward, Angel,* and I have also tried to show how, by means of symbol and structural arrangement, Wolfe created a full and ordered world for his hero to operate in.[4] Now I would like in this study to take just one other element of Wolfe's literary endeavor and point out how it makes its contribution to the richness of this work. I want to talk about Wolfe's style. I will begin with a reminder that the American writer has a good knack for taking lowly materials and surrounding them with an aura of the great and important. Melville takes a rough crew and an odoriferous whaling vessel and by means of style and structure creates a prose epic. Tennessee Williams takes a nymphomaniac and a thug and with symbol and technical manipulation creates a profound and moving tragedy. Wolfe takes the story of a lower-middle-class boy who lives in a Southern town and creates a novel of development that transcends its restricted lineaments. By various devices, Wolfe enlarges his scene beyond the family circle and beyond town life to make us aware that Eugene is part of a very large and complex world and that he is one of the participants in the history of man. Style is one of the means by which he creates a sense of variety and abundance in the book, for Wolfe has a variety of styles that he employs.

One of the narrative styles may be described as rich, sometimes overflorid, arranged in long, loose sentences, frequently made up of elements piled in a series:

Eugene was loose now in the limitless meadows of sensation: his sensory equipment was so complete that at the moment of perception of a single thing, the whole background of color, warmth, odor, sound, taste established itself, so that later, the breath of hot dandelion brought back the grass-warm banks of Spring, a day, a place, the rustling of young leaves[;] or a page of a book, the thin exotic smell of tangerine, the wintry bite of great apples; or, as with *Gulliver's Travels,* a bright windy day in March, the spurting moments of warmth, the drip and reek of the earth-thaw, the feel of the fire.[5]

When the diction is concrete, as it is in this example, the style is very effective, particularly for communicating an atmosphere of plenitude—of a world that has so much in it that because of abundance itself it must be very good.

At times, Wolfe's prose takes on some of the qualities of the poetry of the Imagists. There are passages which are simple, metaphorical, and rhythmical in which an impression in the mind of Eugene is carried vividly to us—as, for example, when the boy thinks of his brother:

My Brother Ben's face, thought Eugene, is like a piece of slightly yellow ivory; his high white head is knotted fiercely by his old man's scowl; his mouth is like a knife, his smile the flicker of light across a blade. His face is like a blade, and a knife, and a flicker of light: it is delicate and fierce, and scowls beautifully forever, and when he fastens his hard white fingers and his scowling eyes upon a thing he wants to fix, he sniffs with sharp and private concentration through his long pointed nose. (p. 165)

The effect of passages like this is to create the impression that life is full of vivid little moments of illumination which can be responded to and experienced intensely.

I have called passages like these poetic because they have rhythm and highly-charged language, but they are just one of Wolfe's characteristic ways of saying things. There are times, however, when he is consciously being "poetic": that is when he writes short, set pieces (he later called them dithyrambs) that have an elevated manner and a formality of address and of arrangement in his sentences. We find these inserted in various places in the book. Here is one which Wolfe has placed at the end of a scene about Eugene's first love affair:

Come up into the hills, O my young love. Return! O lost, and by the wind grieved, ghost, come back again, as first I knew you in the timeless valley, where we shall feel ourselves anew, bedded on magic in the month of June. There was a place where all the sun went glistering in your hair, and from the hill we could have put a finger on a star. Where is the day that melted into one rich noise? Where is the music of your flesh, the rhyme of your teeth, the dainty languor of your legs, your small firm arms, your slender fingers, to be bitten like an apple, and the little cherry-teats of your white breasts? And where are all the tiny wires of finespun maidenhair? Quick are the months of earth, and quick the teeth that fed upon this loveliness. You who were made for music, will hear music no more: in your dark house the winds are silent. (p. 456)

When a prose lyric like this elegy is very personal to Wolfe, it is an intrusion, but one would never want to banish it. It becomes a memorable passage. It remains a beautiful excrescence on the work. Its general function then is only its presence as part of the encyclopedic profusion of the book. More often, such passages are formal apostrophes, and the effect is rather of oratory than poetry. The reader has a feeling that a public spokesman is giving voice to a communal emotion or attitude. Again there is a sense of a larger world which surrounds the hero and with which he must come to terms.

There are other passages in which the style combines both the grand and the commonplace. The effect is to elevate or to ennoble the commonplace. When old Mr. Gant returns from a trip and looks over the home town, Wolfe begins the whole section with an epic style, even employing epithet: "How looked the home-earth then to Gant the Far Wanderer?" (p. 71) The verbal contrasts that Wolfe plays with are many: he combines the rich and the spare; he exaggerates and then follows up with understatement; he joins the majestic and the vulgar, the formal and the colloquial. The effects are varied. Sometimes he is highly comical. At other times, he makes ordinary details seem to be recurrences in the endless cycles of time. For example, here is a passage which makes use of mythological allusion and high flown language about the coming of spring—when little boys play games in the street:

> Yes, and in the month when Proserpine comes back, and Ceres' dead heart rekindles, when all the woods are a tender smoky blur, and birds no bigger than a budding leaf dart through the singing trees, and when odorous tar comes spongy in the streets, and boys roll balls of it upon their tongues, and they are lumpy with tops and agated marbles; and there is blasting thunder in the night, and the soaking millionfooted rain. . . . (p. 95).

In *Look Homeward, Angel* style is used for depth as well as for breadth. Wolfe uses the stream-of-consciousness style quite frequently in the book—usually a series of phrases and images that are supposed to represent the thought-stream of the characters. Here is an example. But I will spell out the movement of thought before quoting it. Old Mr. Gant is riding through Altamont. He thinks of some of the chamber of commerce booster slogans about the town. His thought jumps to Los Angeles and its growth. He thinks then of Mr. Bowman who lives in California and who used to be in love with Mrs. Gant. This makes him think about himself and an experience with a woman in New Orleans. This then makes him remember a time long ago in New Orleans when he was robbed in a hotel room. He thinks of prostitutes in New Orleans. He then thinks of fictional heroines in stories about New Orleans. This makes him spin out a fantasy in which he plays a heroic part:

> America's Switzerland. The Beautiful Land of the Sky. Jesus God! Old Bowman said he'll be a rich man some day. Built up all the way to Pasadena. Come on out. Too late now. Think he was in love with her. No matter. Too old. Wants her out there. No fool like—White bellies of the fish. A spring somewhere to wash me through. Clean as a baby once more. New Orleans, the night Jim Corbett knocked out John L. Sullivan. The man who tried to rob me. My clothes and my watch. Five blocks down Canal Street in my nightgown. Two A. M. Threw them all in a heap—watch landed on top. Fight in my room. Town full of crooks and pickpockets for prizefight. Make good story. Policeman half hour later. They come out and beg you to come in. Frenchwomen. Creoles. Beautiful Creole heiress. Steamboat race. Captain, they are gaining.

I will not be beaten. Out of wood. Use the bacon she said proudly. There was a terrific explosion. He got her as she sank the third time and swam to shore. (pp. 74–75)

Stream-of-consciousness passages amplify the characterizations in a book. But the general impression of the excursions through the minds of the characters in *Look Homeward, Angel* is that the hidden life of the psyche, the buried life as Wolfe calls it, is teeming with activity and that human life, such as that developing in Eugene, is a mysterious but wonderful thing.

These are some examples of the narrative styles. The presence of many different dialogue styles, of course, increases the stylistic variety, particularly because most of the characters are quite distinctive in the way they speak: W. O. Gant is full of exaggeration and rhetorical flourish; Mrs. Gant carries on in the rambling, interminable manner of free association; Ben is sharp and laconic; Luke stutters. In addition there are the currents and eddies of talk in the town— the words of clerks, servants, loafers, politicians, gatherers at the lunch counters. Much of this town talk, seemingly insignificant, is like that in Wilder's *Our Town:* it reflects the rhythms of life, comings and goings, deaths and entrances. Moreover, it is good talk, with a marked colloquial flavor. Here, for example, is Gant on the street-car:

"Jim Bowles died while you were gone, I reckon," said the motorman.

"What!" howled Gant. "Merciful God!" he clucked mournfully downward. "What did he die of?" he asked.

"Pneumonia," said the motorman. "He was dead four days after he was took down."

"Why, he was a big healthy man in the prime of life," said Gant. "I was talking to him the day before I went away," he lied convincing himself permanently that this was true. "He looked as if he had never known a day's sickness in his life."

"He went home one Friday night with a chill," said the motorman, "and the next Tuesday he was gone." (p. 72)

Beyond this, *Look Homeward, Angel* has a number of other evidences of Wolfe's linguistic interest such as parodies of pulp fiction stories with Eugene as the hero—like the one about Bruce-

Eugene Glendenning, international vagabond, who fights off the dangerous natives, and keeps back two cartridges for himself and the beautiful Veronica Mullins; or Eugene's fantasies when he comes from the motion picture theater—Eugene Gant, the Dixie Ghost, who shoots it out with Faro Jim in the Triple Y Saloon. In this book, Wolfe plays with language in dozens of ways.

What I have been trying to establish is that by means of style Wolfe has done two important things. First, he has provided a swirl of experience around his hero and made the whole experience of life and of growing up seem exciting and valuable. Second, the linguistic variety has contributed to the complexity of the little universe in which Wolfe has placed Eugene Gant and which the boy is trying to understand. In his search for understanding, Eugene has been impelled to look to the city and its crowded streets and to the multiplicity of social experience that travel and wandering seem to offer. But at the end of the book, the ghost of his brother Ben, returned from the dead, tells Eugene that he is wrong. Eugene should look inside himself for the way to understanding. "*You* are your world," says Ben. The quality and the amplitude of that world has been partly conveyed to us by means of style.

Notes

1. Harvard College Library, MS 326 F. A photostat of the first page has been reproduced in George R. Preston, Jr., *Thomas Wolfe, A Bibliography* (New York: Charles S. Boesen, 1943), p. 24. Wolfe had translated Xenophon's *Anabasis* in his school days at the North State Fitting School in Asheville.

2. "Author's Note" in *The Web and the Rock* (New York: Harper and Brothers, 1940).

3. See Maxwell Perkins' account in the Introduction to *Look Homeward, Angel*, "The Scribner Library" (New York: Charles Scribner's Sons, 1957), p. xii. (See also the essay by Maxwell Perkins in this collection.)

4. Richard S. Kennedy, *The Window of Memory: The Literary Career of Thomas Wolfe*, "The Design of *Look Homeward, Angel*" (Chapel Hill: Univ. of North Carolina Press, 1962), Chapter 9.

5. *Look Homeward, Angel* (New York: Charles Scribner's Sons, 1929), p. 81. All other page references are to this edition and will be placed in parentheses after the quotation.

Robert Penn Warren

16. A Note on the Hamlet of Thomas Wolfe

THOMAS WOLFE owns an enormous talent; and chooses to exercise it on an enormous scale. This talent was recognized promptly enough several years ago when his first novel, *Look Homeward, Angel,* came from the press to overwhelm a high percentage of the critics. Nor was this sensational success for a first novel undeserved, even if the book was not, as Hugh Walpole suggested, as "near perfect as a novel can be." Now Mr. Wolfe's second novel, *Of Time and the River,* appears, and the enthusiasm of the reception of the first will probably be repeated; though not, I venture to predict, on a scale scarcely so magnificent. That remains to be seen; but it may not be too early to attempt a definition of the special excellence and the special limitations of the enormous talent that has produced two big books and threatens to produce others in the near future.

If Mr. Wolfe's talent is enormous, his energies are more enormous, and fortunately so. A big book is forbidding, but at the same time it carries a challenge in its very pretension. It seems to say, "This is a serious project and demands serious attention from serious minds." There is, of course, the snobbery of the three-decker. Mr. Wolfe is prolific. His publishers assure the public that he has written in the neighborhood of two million words. In his scheme of six novels, two are now published (*Look Homeward, Angel,* 1884–1920, and *Of Time and the River,* 1920–1925); two more are already written (*The October Fair,* 1925–1928, and *The Hills Beyond Pentland,* 1838–1926); and two more are projected (*The Death of the Enemy,* 1928–1933, and *Pacific End,* 1791–1884). Presumably, the novels unpublished and unwritten will extend forward and backward the ramifications of the fortunes of the Gant and Pentland families.

Look Homeward, Angel and the present volume are essentially two parts of an autobiography; the pretense of fiction is so thin and slovenly that Mr. Wolfe in referring to the hero writes indifferently "Eugene Gant" or "I" and "me." There may be many modifications, omissions, and additions in character and event, but the impulse and material are fundamentally personal. The story begins in *Look Homeward, Angel* in the latter part of the nineteenth century with the arrival of Gant, the father of the hero, in Altamont, in the state of Catawba, which is Asheville, North Carolina. It continues with the marriage to Eliza Pentland, the birth of the various children, the debaucheries and repentances of old Gant, the growth of the village into a flourishing resort, the profitable real-estate speculations of Eliza, her boarding house, the education of Eugene Gant in Altamont and at the State University, the collapse of old Gant's health, and the departure of Eugene for Harvard. *Of Time and the River* resumes on the station platform as Eugene leaves for Harvard, sees him through three years there in the drama school under "Professor Thatcher," presents in full horror of detail the death of old Gant from cancer of the prostate, treats the period in New York when Eugene teaches the Jews in a college there, and takes the hero to Europe, where he reads, writes, and dissipates tremendously. He is left at the point of embarking for America. During this time he is serving his apprenticeship as a writer and trying to come to terms with his own spirit and with America. So much for the bare materials of the two books.

The root of Mr. Wolfe's talent is his ability at portraiture. The figures of Eliza Gant and old Gant, of Ben and Helen, in *Look Homeward, Angel,* are permanent properties of the reader's imagination. Mr. Wolfe has managed to convey the great central vitality of the old man, for whom fires would roar up the chimney and plants would grow, who stormed into his house in the evening laden with food, and whose quality is perpetually heroic, mythical, and symbolic. It is the same with Eliza, with her flair for business; her almost animal stupidity; her great, but sometimes aimless, energies; her almost sardonic and defensive love for her son, whom she does not understand; her avarice and her sporadic squandering of money.

These two figures dominate both books; even after old Gant is dead the force of his personality, or rather the force of the symbol into which that personality has been elevated, is an active agent, and a point of reference for interpretation.

These two characters, and Ben and Helen in a lesser degree, are triumphs of poetic conception. The uncle in *Of Time and the River,* Bascom Pentland, shares some of their qualities. He exhibits the family lineaments, the family vitality, and something of the symbolic aspect of the other characters; but the method of presentation is more conventional and straightforward, and the result more static and anecdotal.

Mr. Wolfe's method in presenting these characters, and the special kind of symbolism he manages to derive from them, is subject to certain special limitations. Obviously it would not serve as a routine process for the treatment of character, at least not on the scale on which it is here rendered. The reader of a novel demands something more realistic, less lyrical; he demands an interplay of characters on another and more specific level, a method less dependent on the direct intrusion of the novelist's personal sensibility. As I have said, the figures of the Gant family are powerful and overwhelming as symbols, as an emotional focus for the novel, and as a point of reference. But the method collapses completely when applied to Starwick, a character of equal importance in Mr. Wolfe's scheme.

We amass a great fund of information concerning Francis Starwick. He was born in a town in the Middle West and early rebelled against the crudities and ugliness of his background. At Harvard he assists Professor Thatcher in the drama school and leads the life of a mannered and affected aesthete, foppish in dress, artificial in speech, oversensitive, and sometimes cruel. At Harvard, he becomes Eugene's best friend. Later he appears in Europe in company with two young women of Boston families, somewhat older then he, who are in love with him and who are willing to pay, with their reputations and their purses, for the pleasure of his conversation. With these three Eugene enters a period of debauchery in Paris. Finally he discovers that Starwick is homosexual, and in his undefinable resentment beats him into unconsciousness.

But this body of information is not all that the writer intends. F. Scott Fitzgerald and Ernest Hemingway have been able to use effectively such characters as Starwick and to extract their meaning, because as novelists they were willing to work strictly in terms of character. But in *Of Time and the River* the writer is forever straining to convince the reader of some value in Starwick that is not perceptible, that the writer himself cannot define; he tries, since he is writing an autobiography, to make Starwick a symbol, a kind of alter ego, for a certain period of his own experience. The strain is tremendous; and without conviction. The writing about Starwick, as the climax of the relationship approaches, sinks into a slush of poetical bathos. And here is the end of the long scene of parting:

"You are my mortal enemy. Goodbye."

"Goodbye, Eugene," said Starwick sadly. "But let me tell you this before I go. Whatever it was I took from you, it was something that I did not want or wish to take. And I would give it back again if I could."

"Oh, fortunate and favored Starwick," the other jeered. "To be so rich—to have such gifts and not to know he has them—to be forever victorious, and to be so meek and mild."

"And I will tell you this as well," Starwick continued. "Whatever anguish and suffering this mad hunger, this impossible desire, has caused you, however fortunate or favored you may think I am, I would give my whole life if I could change places with you for an hour—know for an hour an atom of your anguish and your hunger and your hope. . . . Oh, to feel so, suffer so, and live so!—however mistaken you may be! . . . To have come lusty, young, and living into this world. . . . not to have come like me, stillborn from your mother's womb—never to know the dead heart and the passionless passion—the cold brain and the cold hopelessness of hope—to be wild, mad, furious, and tormented—but to have belief, to live in anguish, but to live—and not to die." . . . He turned and opened the door. "I would give all I have and all you think I have, for just one hour of it. You call me fortunate and happy. *You* are the most fortunate and happy man I ever knew. Goodbye, Eugene."

"Goodbye, Frank. Goodbye, my enemy."

"And goodbye, my friend," said Starwick. He went out, and the door closed behind him.

The dialogue, the very rhythms of the sentences, and the scene itself, scream the unreality.

The potency of the figures from the family and the failure with Starwick may derive from the autobiographical nature of Mr. Wolfe's work. Eliza and old Gant come from a more primary level of experience, figures of motherhood and fatherhood that gradually, as the book progresses, assume a wider significance and become at the same time a reference for the hero's personal experience. And the author, knowing them first on that level, has a way of knowing them more intimately and profoundly as people than he ever knows Starwick. Starwick is more artificial, because he is at the same time a social symbol and a symbol for a purely private confusion of which the roots are never clear.

Most of the other characters are treated directly. Mr. Wolfe has an appetite for people and occasionally a faculty of very acute perception. The portrait of Abe Jones, the Jewish student at the college in New York, and those of the people at the Coulson household in Oxford, are evidence enough of this capacity. But his method or, rather, methods of presentation are various and not unvaryingly successful. There are long stretches of stenographic dialogue that has little focus, or no focus whatsoever; for instance, the first part of the conversation of the businessmen in the Pullman in Book I, of the residents of the hotel in Book IV, of the artistic hangers-on at the Cambridge tea parties, or even of Eugene and his companions in the Paris cafés. Some of this reporting is very scrupulous, and good as reporting, but in its mass, its formlessness, and its lack of direction it is frequently dull; the momentary interest of recognition is not enough to sustain it, and it bears no precise relation to the intention of the novel. It is conversation for conversation's sake, a loquacity and documentation that testify to the author's talent but not to his intelligence as an artist. Generally this type of presentation is imitative of Sinclair Lewis's realistic dialogue, but it lacks the meticulous, cautious, and selective quality of the best of Lewis, the controlled malice; it is too random, and in an incidental sense, too heavily pointed.

Further, there are tremendous masses of description and characters. Mr. Wolfe has the habit of developing his own clichés for description of character, and of then exhibiting them at irregular intervals. It is as if he realized the bulk of the novel and the difficulty a reader might experience in recognizing a character on reappearance, and so determined to prevent this, if possible, by repetition and insistence. For instance, Starwick and Ann, one of the young women from Boston who is in love with Starwick, have a complete set of tags and labels that are affixed to them time after time during the novel. Mr. Wolfe underrates the memory of the reader; or this may be but another instance of the lack of control that impairs his work.

Only in the section dealing with the Coulson episode does Mr. Wolfe seem to have all his resources for character presentation under control. The men who room in the house, the jaunty Captain Nicholl with his blasted arm and the other two young men from the motorcar factory—these with the Coulsons themselves are very precise to the imagination, and are sketched in with an economy usually foreign to Mr. Wolfe. The Coulson girl, accepting the mysterious ruin that presides over the household, is best drawn and dominates the group. Here Mr. Wolfe has managed to convey an atmosphere and to convince the reader of the reality of his characters without any of his habitual exaggerations of method and style. This section, with slight alternations, originally appeared as a short story; it possesses what is rare enough in *Of Time and the River,* a constant focus.

I have remarked that some of Mr. Wolfe's material is not subordinated to the intention of the book. What is his intention? On what is the mass of material focused? What is to give it form? His novels are obviously autobiographical. This means that the binding factor should be, at least in part, the personality of the narrator, or, since Mr. Wolfe adopts a disguise, of the hero, Eugene Gant. The two books are, in short, an account of the development of a sensibility; obviously something more is intended than the looseness and irresponsibility of pure memoirs or observations. The work demands comparison with such works as Joyce's *Portrait of the Artist as a Young Man* or Lawrence's *Sons and Lovers;* it may even demand comparison with proper autobiographies, such as Rousseau's *Confessions* or *The Education of Henry Adams.* But the comparison with these books is not to the advantage of Mr. Wolfe's performance. It has not the artistry of the first two, the constant and dramatic relation of incident to a developing consciousness of the world, nor has it the historical importance of the third, or the philosophical and intellectual interest of the last.

The hero of *Look Homeward, Angel,* though a child and adolescent, is essentially more interesting than the Eugene of *Of Time and the River*. He is more comprehensible, because there is a real (and necessarily conventional) pattern to his developing awareness of the world around him. Further, the life of the Gant household, and even of the community, is patterned with a certain amount of strictness in relation to Eugene: the impress of the vast vitality of old Gant, the lack of understanding on the part of the mother and the perpetual emotional drag of resentment and affection she exerts on her son, the quarrels with Steve, the confusion and pathos of the sexual experiences, the profound attachment between Ben and Eugene, and the climactic and daring scene with Ben's spirit. There is a progress toward maturity, a fairly precise psychological interest. The novel contains much pure baggage and much material that is out of tone, usually in the form of an ironic commentary that violates the point of view; but the book is more of a unit, and is, for that reason perhaps, more exciting and forceful.

In *Of Time and the River,* as Eugene in his Pullman rides at night across Virginia, going "northward, worldward, towards the secret borders of Virginia, towards the great world cities of his hope, the fable of his childhood legendry," the following passage is interpolated:

> Who has seen fury riding in the mountains? Who has known fury striding in the storm? Who has been mad with fury in his youth, given no rest or peace or certitude by fury, driven on across the earth by fury, until the great vine of his heart was broke, the sinews wrenched, the little tenement of bone, blood, marrow, brain, and feeling in which great fury raged, was twisted, wrung, depleted, worn out, and exhausted by the fury which it could not lose or put away? Who has known fury, how it came?
>
> How have we breathed him, drunk him, eaten fury to the core, until we have him in us now and cannot lose him anywhere we go? It is a strange and subtle worm that will . . .

The furious Eugene is scarcely made comprehensible. The reader amasses a large body of facts about him, as about Starwick, but with something of the same result. He knows that Eugene is big; that he is a creature of enormous appetites of which he is rather proud; that he has the habit of walking much at night; that he is fascinated by the health and urbanity of his friend Joel and by the personality of

Starwick; that he ceases to like Shelley after spending an afternoon in a jail cell; that he reads twenty thousand books in ten years; that he is obsessed by the idea of devouring all of life. Then, the reader knows the facts of Eugene's comings and goings, and knows the people he meets and what they say. But the Eugene susceptible of such definition is not the hero of the book, or at least does not function adequately as such. The hero is really that nameless fury that drives Eugene. The book is an effort to name that fury, and perhaps by naming it, to tame it. But the fury goes unnamed and untamed. Since the book is formless otherwise, only a proper emotional reference to such a center could give it form. Instead, at the center there is this chaos that steams and bubbles in rhetoric and apocalyptic apostrophe, sometimes grand and sometimes febrile and empty; the center is a maelstrom, perhaps artificially generated at times; and the other, tangible items are the flotsam and jetsam and dead wood spewed up, iridescent or soggy, as the case may be.

It may be objected that other works of literary art, and very great ones at that, have heroes who defy definition and who are merely centers of "fury." For instance, there is Hamlet, or Lear. But a difference may be observed. Those characters may defy the attempt at central definition, but the play hangs together in each case as a structure without such definition; that is, there has been no confusion between the sensibility that produced a play, as an object of art, and the sensibility of a hero in a play. (And the mere fact that *Hamlet* and *Lear* employ verse as a vehicle adds further to the impression of discipline, focus, and control.)

There are two other factors in the character of Eugene that may deserve mention. The hero feels a sense of destiny and direction, the sense of being "chosen" in the midst of a world of defeated, aimless, snobbish, vulgar, depleted, or suicidal people. (This is, apparently, the source of much of the interpolated irony in both books, an irony almost regularly derivative and mechanical.) In real life this conviction of a high calling may be enough to make a "hero" feel that life does have form and meaning; but the mere fact that a hero in a novel professes the high calling and is contrasted in his social contacts with an inferior breed does not, in itself, give the novel form and meaning. The transference of the matter from the actuality of life to the actuality of art cannot be accomplished so easily. Second, at the very end of the novel, Eugene, about to embark for America, sees a woman who, according to the somewhat extended lyrical epilogue, makes him "lose" self and so be "found":

> After all the blind, tormented wanderings of youth, that woman would become his heart's centre and the target of his life, the image of immortal one-ness that again collected him to one, and hurled the whole collected passion, power, and might of his one life into the blazing certitude, the immortal governance and unity, of love.

Certainly this is what we call fine writing; it may or may not be good writing. And probably, falling in love may make a man "find himself"; but this epilogue scarcely makes the novel find itself.

It is possible sometimes that a novel possessing no structure in the ordinary sense of the word, or not properly dominated by its hero's personality or fortunes, may be given a focus by the concrete incorporation of an idea, or related ideas. Now, *Of Time and the River* has such a leading idea, but an idea insufficient in its operation. The leading symbol of the father, old Gant, gradually assumes another aspect, not purely personal; he becomes, in other words, a kind of symbol of the fatherland, the source, the land of violence, drunkenness, fecundity, beauty, and vigor, on which the hero occasionally reflects during his wanderings and to which in the end he returns. But this symbol is not the total expression of the idea, which is worked out more explicitly and at length. There are long series of cinematic flashes of "phases of American life": locomotive drivers, gangsters, pioneers, little towns with the squares deserted at night, evangelists, housewives, rich and suicidal young men, whores on subways, drunk college boys. Or there are more lyrical passages, less effective in pictorial detail, such as the following:

> It was the wild, sweet, casual, savage, and incredibly lovely earth of America, and of the wilderness, and it haunted them like legends, and pierced them like a sword, and filled them with a wild and swelling prescience of joy that was like sorrow and delight.

This kind of material alternates with the more sedate or realistic progress of the chronicle, a kind of running commentary of patriotic mysticism on the more tangible events and perceptions. For Mr. Wolfe has the mysticism of the American idea that we find in Whitman, Sandburg, Masters, Crane, and Benét. He pants for the

Word, the union that will clarify all the disparate and confused elements which he enumerates and many of which fill him with revulsion and disgust. He, apparently, has experienced the visionary moment he proclaims, but, like other mystics, he suffers some difficulty when he attempts to prepare it for consumption by the ordinary citizens of the Republic. He must wreak some indignity on the chastity of the vision. This indignity is speech; but he burns, perversely, to speak.

The other promulgators of the American vision have been poets. Mr. Wolfe, in addition to being a poet in instinct, is, as well, the owner on a large scale of many of the gifts of the novelist. He attempts to bolster, or as it were, to prove, the mystical and poetic vision by fusing it with a body of everyday experience of which the novelist ordinarily treats. But there is scarcely a fusion or a correlation; rather, an oscillation. On the tangible side, the hero flees from America, where his somewhat quivering sensibilities are frequently tortured, and goes to Europe; in the end, worn out by drinking and late hours, disgusted with his friends, unacquainted with the English or the French, and suffering homesickness, he returns to America. But Mr. Wolfe, more than most novelists, is concerned with the intangible; not so much with the psychological process and interrelation as with the visionary "truth."

The other poets, at least Whitman and Crane, have a certain advantage over the poet in Mr. Wolfe. They overtly consented to be poets; Mr. Wolfe has not consented. Therefore their vision is purer, the illusion of communication (*illusion,* for it is doubtful that they have really communicated the central vision) is more readily palatable, because they never made a serious pretense of proving it autobiographically or otherwise; they were content with the hortatory moment, the fleeting symbol, and the affirmation. (Benét, of course, did attempt in *John Brown's Body* such a validation, but with a degree of success that does not demand comment here.) It may simply be that the poets were content to be lyric poets, and therefore could more readily attempt the discipline of selection and concentration; in those respects, even Whitman shows more of an instinct for form than does Mr. Wolfe. Mr. Wolfe is astonishingly diffuse, astonishingly loose in his rhetoric—qualities that, for the moment, may provoke more praise than blame. That rhetoric is sometimes grand, but probably more often tedious and tinged with hysteria. Because he is officially writing prose and not poetry, he has no caution of the clichés of phrase or rhythm, and no compunction about pilfering from other poets.

His vocabulary itself is worth comment. If the reader will inspect the few passages quoted in the course of this essay he will observe a constant quality of strain, a fancy for the violent word or phrase (but often conventionally poetic as well as violent): "wild, sweet, casual, savage . . . ," "haunted them like legends," "no rest or peace or certitude of fury," "target of his life," "blazing certitude, the immortal governance and unity, of love." Mr. Wolfe often shows very powerfully the poetic instinct, and the praise given by a number of critics to his "sensuousness" and "gusto" is not without justification in the fact; but even more often his prose simply shows the poetic instinct unbuckled on a kind of weekend debauch. He sometimes wants it both ways: the structural irresponsibility of prose and the emotional intensity of poetry. He may overlook the fact that the intensity is rarely to be achieved without a certain rigor in selection and structure.

Further, Mr. Wolfe, we understand from blurbs and reviewers, is attempting a kind of prose epic. American literature has produced one, *Moby Dick*. There is much in common between *Moby Dick* and *Of Time and the River,* but there is one major difference. Melville had a powerful fable, a myth of human destiny, which saved his work from the centrifugal impulses of his genius, and which gave it structure and climax. Its dignity is inherent in the fable itself. No such dignity is inherent in Mr. Wolfe's scheme, if it can properly be termed a scheme. The nearest approach to it is in the character of old Gant, but that is scarcely adequate. And Mr. Wolfe has not been able to compensate for the lack of a fable by all his well-directed and misdirected attempts to endow his subject with a proper dignity, by all his rhetorical insistence, all the clarity and justice of his incidental poetic perceptions, all the hysteria or magnificent hypnosis.

Probably all of these defects, or most of them, are inherent in fiction which derives so innocently from the autobiographical impulse. In the first place, all the impurities and baggage in the novel must strike the author as of peculiar and necessary value because they were observed or actually occurred. But he is not writing a strict autobiography in which all observations or experiences, however vague, might conceivably find a justification. He is trying, and this in the second place, to erect the autobiographical material into an epical and symbolic importance, to make of it a fable, a "Legend of Man's Hunger in His Youth." This much is declared by the subtitle.

Mr. Wolfe promises to write some historical novels, and they may well be crucial in the definition of his genius, because he may be required to reorder the use of his powers. What, thus far, he has produced is fine fragments, several brilliant pieces of portraiture, and many sharp observations on men and nature; in other words, these books are really voluminous notes from which a fine novel, or several fine novels, might be written. If he never writes these novels, it may yet be that his books will retain a value as documents of some historical importance and as confused records of an unusual personality. Meanwhile, despite his admirable energies and his powerful literary endowments, his work illustrates once more the limitations, perhaps the necessary limitations, of an attempt to exploit directly and naïvely the personal experience and the self-defined personality in art.

And meanwhile it may be well to recollect that Shakespeare merely wrote *Hamlet;* he was *not* Hamlet.

Irving Halperin

17. Wolfe's *Of Time and the River*

THE TRAIN EPISODE in the opening section of *Of Time and the River* appears, at first glance, like a series of disjointed fragments. Now covering some eighty pages, it originally was, according to Wolfe's own admission in "The Story of a Novel," many times that length. Here I intend to show how this episode is organized into an artistic whole through (1) the use of characters representing certain ideational values, and (2) the pattern of the protagonist's discoveries.

The episode begins aboard a New York-bound train. As he is being carried further away from the hills of Altamont, Eugene Gant ponders on the unreality of things. The faces and voices of friends and kinsmen back home seem "far and strange as dreams." Gradually, the continuous rhythm of the train's movement through space stimulates him to muse on the mystery of time, which is compared to the South of his boyhood. Both are "buried," "silent," "dark." Thus at this point in the episode, the hero, having escaped from home, from the circumstances which were frustrating his development, feels "lost," lacking in identity and purpose.

Escaping from these disquieting thoughts, Eugene leaves his seat to seek human companionship. In the smoking compartment he finds some Altamont business men; their myopic, greedy temperaments repel him. In the course of conversation, these men evoke the name of Ben Gant. They speak respectfully of him because he had been a hard worker, because he had kept his "nose clean." But for Eugene the memory of his dead brother has more significant associations. For example, in presenting him with a watch on his twelfth birthday, Ben had asked, "Do you know what a watch is for?" "To keep time with," he had answered. Then Ben had warned that he "keep it better than the rest of us. Better than Mama or the old man—better than me! God help you if you don't!" Now the connection between this remembrance and the men in the smoking car is clarified: first, Eugene avows he will not only keep time better than his family, but also better than the townspeople of Altamont; secondly, he recognizes the narrowness of the latter in contrast to Ben, who was "a flame, a light, a glory."

Eugene's identification with his brother is implicit in his remembrance of Ben as one who "lived here a stranger . . . trying to recall the great forgotten language, the lost faces, the stone, the leaf, the door." The former also thinks of himself as a stranger, a "misunderstood" one in a world of transiency. Until he finds a door (the ordering of flux in the present through the creative process), Eugene will be haunted by the "dream of time"; he will feel unreal, "like a creature held captive by an evil spell." Once having discovered a door, he will achieve the real and permanent (a stone); that is, he will rescue experience from the flow (a leaf) of time and give it lasting meaning.

In the next scene of the episode there is a transition from the smoking car to the frenzied drinking party staged by Eugene and two young companions. Liquor, like the train (the symbol of enormous man-made energy), gives a "rhyme to madness, a tongue to hunger and desire, a certitude to all the savage, drunken, and exultant fury that keeps mounting, rising, swelling in them all the time!" Compared to the "eternal silent waiting earth" over which the train passes, the young men are "three atoms," "three ciphers," "three nameless grains of life." Yet they have about them a kind of heroic aura, for they have left their roots and are going forth to do battle with the cities of the North. Hence the three youths, like Ben, represent for Eugene the nobility of "little" man adventuring courageously in an impersonal universe.

There remains Part V of the train episode—Eugene's awakening in his pullman berth the morning after the drinking party. The "old brown earth" that he sees through a window is related to the recurring hill image of the novels. The earth, like the hills, symbolizes permanence and purpose. To Eugene, this plot of earth is more familiar than his mother's face with its associations of endurance and "fixity." While looking out of the window and listening to the steady, stroking rhythm of the train, he perceives an image of "eternity forever—in moveless movement, unsilent silence, spaceless flight." In the suspended moment, he feels that there is permanence in change and that he, like the earth, will prevail through the continuing growth of the self.

In sum, it may be seen that the shape of the train episode consists of a three-part pattern: in the first part, Eugene feels "lost," because in escaping from home he loses a sense of identity; in the second, he returns to his "roots" in the past by recalling the significance of Ben's life; and in the third, he attempts to adjust to his present circumstances by becoming aware of his peculiar strength—the capacity for growth. Thus the pattern formed by the hero's experiences and recognitions during the train trip both unifies the various sections of the episode and relates to the controlling idea of the novel—the quest of the hero to achieve order and maturity in his life and art through growth.

Paschal Reeves

18. Esther Jack as Muse

THE PUBLICATION of *The Web and the Rock* (New York, 1939), which gave the world the George Webber-Esther Jack love story, fulfilled a long-standing desire of Thomas Wolfe to render his great romance into fiction. He began writing this story for "The October Fair" in 1930 and worked on it sporadically for the remaining eight years of his life. Although its appearance was finally shaped by Edward Aswell as Wolfe's posthumous editor, it nonetheless is Wolfe's fictionalized account of the most important relationship of his adult life.

This famous romance, one of the most celebrated in American literature, is unique in that the reading public possesses fictional accounts of the tortured affair by both the participants. It was the woman's side which first appeared in print; Aline Bernstein published her novel *The Journey Down* in 1938. Her account illuminates Wolfe's version in many ways in spite of its different emphases.

Esther Jack is not only one of Wolfe's greatest character creations but she is undoubtedly one of the most versatile heroines in literature. Seldom in the annals of amour have greater demands been made on mortal woman or have been more willingly and fully met by her. When Wolfe wrote in exultation of Esther "in all the world there was no one like her" (p. 369), his romantic praise embodies a literal truth that would be difficult to dispute. Surely the ghosts of many women from Helen of Troy to Jennie Gerhardt must have curtsied to Esther Jack. For Esther the lover is cast in the hexamerous role of mistress, cook, mentor, patron, mother, and muse, all of which combine into a tripartite ministration to the heart, body, and spirit of George Webber. While each of these roles is important to the lonely, frustrated young man in the million-footed city, to George Webber the aspiring author that of muse is a paramount one. To Webber, however, even a muse has a dual function: she is both a source of inspiration and a fountainhead of information. Esther readily fills this dichotomous office.

Esther's vitality and enthusiasm provide a powerful stimulus to George's smoldering literary aspirations, and her own artistic temperament proves to be a catalytic agent to his latent powers. Certainly Esther functioned in her other capacities also to make possible the literary upsurge in George Webber and to direct it to fruition. She brought to the wild young man, who was about to be engulfed by the city, the love and certitude that he desperately needed. Her firm belief in a Carlylean doctrine of work aided her in bringing order to the chaos of George's life and setting him upon a regular schedule of work that would in time yield results. And spiritual succor was augmented by financial subsidization. But all of this important aid would have been ineffectual had not the creative fire in Webber been fanned to a consuming flame. Whether this artistic impetus was accomplished largely by her own competent craftsmanship, her deep understanding of and sympathy for the whole artistic process, or her loyal and oft articulated belief in George's ability is not revealed. It may have been a combination of these and other factors, but the important thing is that under Esther's aegis Webber did conceive and execute his novel *Home to Our Mountains*. In the primary function of muse Esther played no small part.

Likewise the secondary function of muse was equally well performed by Esther. In Webber's ardent quest for fictive material he found in her a rich source, and he mined the lode with the relentlessness of a forty-niner who discovered gold. This drawing on Esther for literary material is overtly described in *The Web and the Rock*:

> As Mrs. Jack talked about herself and her life, and told in her vivid and glowing manner of her daily little discoveries in the streets, Monk began to get a vision of the city's life that was as different from the swarming horror of his own Faustine vision as anything could be. . . . In these stories to which her vivid and visual mind reduced experience, and in which her childhood and youth appeared so often, a picture of the old New York, and the old America,

was already expanding and being given order and perspective in Monk's mind. (pp. 380–81)

His method is that of a hostile lawyer cross-examining a witness: "He would go for her with ceaseless questions until she was bewildered and worn out; then he would come pounding back at her again" (p. 406).[1] The example given of this method, following the above statement, indeed reads like a transcript of a trial; Webber is pressing for information about Mock's, a restaurant frequented by Esther's father. This technique, however, produced the desired results: "In that way he kept after her, prying, probing, questioning about everything she told him, until at last he got from her the picture of her lost and vanished years" (p. 407). If Esther became an exhausted muse, it is not surprising, because of Webber's efforts to squeeze her dry of literary material.

There is, moreover, yet another important service which Esther rendered in her role of muse. A fiction writer may write upon one or more of three ascending levels of experience. The first level is that of the experience of the author himself, the material which his own life provides him. The second level is the experience of others, that which the author learns through observation and investigation. The third level, and the one generally conceded to be the highest, is that of pure creation, the working of the author's imagination. Almost all novelists—it would probably not be amiss to say *every* novelist—write at times on the first level. Melville in *Moby Dick,* Dickens in *David Copperfield,* Hawthorne in *The Blithedale Romance,* Charlotte Brontë in *Villette,* Mark Twain in *Huckleberry Finn,* Hemingway in *A Farewell to Arms* certainly show instances of writing on the first level. The great masters, however, are not confined to the first level. Dickens employs all three in *David Copperfield,* and in *Huckleberry Finn* Mark Twain plays up and down the scale at will. Hemingway treads heavily on the second level in *The Sun Also Rises,* just as does Melville in *White Jacket.* Few novels hold to the third level with the pristine purity of *The Scarlet Letter,* but *Wuthering Heights* and *The Sound and the Fury* must be cited as classical examples.

Writing on the first level, an author runs the risk of producing autobiography rather than fiction. Since Webber wrote *Home to*

Our Mountains on the first level, that is the very trap into which he fell.[2] This is not to maintain that fictionalized autobiography is inartistic per se; it may be artistry of a high quality as is exemplified by the works of Proust and D. H. Lawrence. But until autobiographical fiction becomes a recognized and accepted genre, Webber will of course be deprecated by some critics for his persistence in writing *Home to Our Mountains* largely on the first level. However, Webber was not doomed to continue writing mostly on the first level, because Esther added a tertiary function to the role of muse. Not only did she provide Webber with fresh literary material but her zest for it enabled him to use the material with confidence and to break through his self-limiting barrier. Thus she aided him in progressing from the first to the second level, thereby greatly extending his range as a writer and adding a new dimension to his work.

Esther Jack's contributions to George Webber's literary achievements indeed are many. But in supplying a source of inspiration, furnishing fictive material, and assisting him to rise to the second level of fiction writing, she was in a very real sense George Webber's muse.

But what of Thomas Wolfe?

The temptation is always strong to make a hundred per cent carry-over from Wolfe's fiction to his own life, and to read into his fiction a literalness that he did not intend and indeed is, in many instances, just *not* present. This distinction—the difference between actuality and the fictional treatment of actuality—is one of the difficult problems confronting serious Wolfe scholarship, and the problem arises from the fact that in some instances there is practically no distinction at all while in others it is very great.

In the relationship between Thomas Wolfe and Aline Bernstein there are many obvious parallels to the George Webber-Esther Jack story. When Wolfe met Mrs. Bernstein in 1925, he was a frustrated playwright still trying to peddle his plays. If he had possessed the playwriting ability he at that time thought he had, she could have been a very great asset to him because her knowledge of the theater was truly extensive. But his attempt to write plays was, as he was later to say in his Purdue Speech, "not only wrong—it was as fantastically wrong as anything could be." [3] While all of the reasons

for his shift from drama to fiction writing are not entirely clear, it
is true that this shift was made during the period of his closest
association with Mrs. Bernstein and she encouraged him fully in it.
Mrs. Bernstein's great faith in Wolfe's talents was unwavering and her
trust was undergirded with financial support that enabled him to
devote his full time to writing for long periods. It is undeniable that
during her tenure *Look Homeward, Angel* was conceived, written,
and published.

Wolfe was fascinated with the anecdotes Mrs. Bernstein told him
of her girlhood in New York and he intended to write the story of
her early years. During his Guggenheim year abroad he worked a
good deal on this story, which he thought of at times as a part of
"The October Fair" but more frequently as a separate book to which
he gave the title "The Good Child's River." In the summer of 1930
he compiled long outlines for "The Good Child's River," which follow the actual events in Mrs. Bernstein's life rather closely, and he
later wrote up a number of episodes. The first episode that he brought
to a finished state is entitled "In the Park." It was rejected by
Scribner's Magazine but was later published in *Harper's Bazaar* and
is included in *From Death to Morning* (New York, 1935). This
sketch is particularly interesting in that it contains a reference to
Mock's (pp. 170–71), the subject of George Webber's sample interrogation of Esther Jack. Wolfe never completed "The Good Child's
River," but some of the material was worked into "Penelope's Web,"
Chapter 26 of *The Web and the Rock,* and other parts are scattered
elsewhere in his posthumous books. Wolfe did not rely solely on his
memory of conversations, however, but asked Mrs. Bernstein to write
out her story for him, which she gladly did, even supplying him information long after their final estrangement. Later she used some
of this material for her own account of her girlhood, *An Actor's
Daughter* (New York, 1941).

In the years following the completion of *Look Homeward, Angel*
Wolfe made several false starts which he either abandoned or later
reshaped. His long struggle to produce his second novel is well known.
While this delay is due to a number of factors, apparently one of
those factors was his initial lack of readiness to progress from the first
to the second level of fiction writing. Thus his attempt to write "The

River People" came to naught because his familiarity with the world
of Olin Dows was insufficient to sustain a novel written in the same
way he had composed *Look Homeward, Angel* (even though it
would later provide the Joel Pierce episode in *Of Time and the
River*). Therefore, when Wolfe was groping for fictive material that
would enable him to produce a novel without resorting to his own
experience, he turned to the account Mrs. Bernstein had so vividly
given him of her girlhood. Although he did not bring this work to
final completion, he could write about her life with greater confidence
than any other outside of his own family, and his success in using
some of her material helped to expand his scope—and at the very
time when he needed to do so.

Though Wolfe returned time and time again to his own life to
structure his work, actually he did some of his best writing using
other people's experiences as fictive material. "Chicamauga," one of
his best stories, is based on the experiences of his great-uncle, John
Westall, who was ninety-five when he related them to Wolfe in the
spring of 1937. His Joycean gem, "The Web of Earth," is based on
his mother's reminiscences. His unfinished novel *The Hills Beyond*
is replete with similar examples. During the last three years of his
life Wolfe wrote much more frequently on the second level and his
work profited accordingly.[4]

From 1925 to 1930 the greatest single influence on the life of
Thomas Wolfe was Aline Bernstein. After his return from Europe in
1931 the romance was virtually over; there were painful confronta-
tions and a few brief reconciliations after that, but the period of great
intimacy had passed. Even though Wolfe burrowed into Brooklyn
to escape her, he could never banish her completely from his mind;
the powerful memories were stirred anew when he wrote or reworked
the love story. Hence Aline Bernstein not only fulfilled a multi-role
function in the life of Wolfe during a crucial period but she continued to hover over his literary material in spirit after their estrangement. It is no wonder, therefore, that when he developed the character Esther Jack he portrayed Esther, among other things, as George
Webber's muse. Perhaps this is another of those instances in Wolfe's
writing where a distinction between actuality and its fictional treatment does not exist, or if it does exist, that distinction is minimal.

Notes

1. Mrs. Bernstein in her novel pictures the interrogation as much more gentle and expresses her delight at having the opportunity to reveal this information: "he would ask her what New York was like when she was a little girl; she would tell him all the things he loved to hear, about her aunts and her father and the actors and the theater, things she had always wanted to talk about but no one else ever cared to hear." *The Journey Down* (New York: Alfred A. Knopf, Inc., 1938), p. 47.

2. "George had called his novel, *Home to Our Mountains,* and in it he had packed everything he knew about his home town in Old Catawba and the people there. He had distilled every line of it out of his own experience of life." *You Can't Go Home Again* (New York: Harper and Brothers, 1940), p. 19.

3. William Braswell and Leslie A. Field, eds., *Thomas Wolfe's Purdue Speech: "Writing and Living,"* (Lafayette, Ind.: Purdue University Studies, 1964), p. 46.

4. Certain passages of his work show that he also rose on occasion to the third level. However, in all his published work prior to *The Hills Beyond,* with the exception of such isolated instances as the consummate final chapter of *Look Homeward, Angel* and the stultified "Fame and the Poet," there is little evidence that he attempted sustained writing on the third level. His unpublished work, on the other hand, gives abundant evidence of writing on the third level.

Clyde C. Clements, Jr.

19. Symbolic Patterns in You Can't Go Home Again

IN *You Can't Go Home Again* Thomas Wolfe rendered his lifetime experience and reflection into a meaningful art form, a message made more universal by certain symbolic patterns in the novel. It is hoped that definition and explication of these symbolic patterns will assist in a re-evaluation of Wolfe as a literary artist. All too often Wolfe has been pictured by scholars and even by sympathetic commentators as a Protean writer of great energies whose later work revealed little form and artistry except that which his editors imposed upon it. Indeed, the problem has its basis not in the incoherence of Wolfe's imagination but in his extreme frankness and naïveté in laying before the public his literary as well as personal problems.

Richard S. Kennedy in his scholarly work *The Window of Memory: The Literary Career of Thomas Wolfe* does little to dispel this general impression of formlessness in his thoroughgoing account of the gestation process of Wolfe's works, saying "although all Wolfe's books since *Look Homeward, Angel* lack cohesiveness, *You Can't Go Home Again* seems more choppy than any others." [1] This is curious in light of his earlier assertion that Edward Aswell neatly edited the book "like George Kaufman's doctoring of a faulty script for the stage." [2] Certainly, Kennedy's book is invaluable for a detailed history of the writing of the manuscript that became *You Can't Go Home Again* and an account of the editorial relationship, but it still leaves the reader wondering about the most important question: is there a total and significant meaning to the work itself beyond that of a skillful fictional biography?

My contention is that partly because Wolfe was working steadily on one elaborate manuscript in his later life (from 1931–1934 with a large section taken out for *Of Time and the River* and from 1936–1937 in a later stretch) [3] he created symbolic patterns which inform and structure his work. This patternation of the artistic endeavor, best known to artists themselves, is pointed out by D. H. Lawrence when he says, "Symbols are the artist's means of creating patterns of thought and emotion which did not previously exist and of communicating what had previously been ineffable." [4] And E. K. Brown has said in his stimulating article, "Thomas Wolfe: Realist and Symbolist," that Wolfe "joined with the perceptive and devouring eye of the master realist, the imaginative symbolist's regard for relationships, occult and profound." [5]

Plainly Wolfe meant *You Can't Go Home Again* to embody a symbolic complex of meaning, but these patterns, which inform the meaning, are not readily apparent from the seven book divisions set up by Edward Aswell or by the explication in the bridge between the 44th and 45th chapters:

> *The phrase had many implications for him. You can't go back home to your family, back home to your childhood, back home to romantic love, back home to a young man's dreams of glory and of fame, back home to exile, to escape to Europe and some foreign land, back home to lyricism, to singing just for singing's sake, back home to aestheticism, to one's youthful idea of "the artist" and the all-sufficiency of "art" and beauty and love, back home to the ivory tower, back home to places in the country, to the cottage in Bermuda, away from all the strife and conflict of the world, back home to the father you have lost and have been looking for, back home to someone who can help you, save you, ease the burden for you, back home to the old forms and systems of things which once seemed everlasting, but which are changing all the time—back home to the escapes of Time and Memory.*[6]

Rather the line of development of the novel must be scrutinized to find "patterns of thought and emotion" that structure the symbolic complex of "you can't go home again." For example, while in Europe Webber meets Lloyd McHarg, a portrayal of a world-renowned American writer, modeled after Sinclair Lewis; for Webber he is clearly symbolic, abstract fame embodied. *"For when Mr. Lloyd McHarg swept like a cyclone through his life, George knew that he was having his first encounter in the flesh with that fair Medusa, Fame herself"* (p. 510).

Moreover, the idea of fame is inextricably linked with Webber's own notion of finding recognition in exile, just as many famous American writers are first tapped with the wand of importance abroad, James, Eliot, Frost, to name a few; and with Webber's triumphant reception in Germany in 1936, where he is hailed as "the great American epic writer." His attraction to the idea of fame as all-sufficient, then subsequent disillusionment with Lloyd McHarg, and with his own "fame" in a Germany taken over by Nazi excesses, suggest the whole symbolic pattern of "Fame in Exile." The symbolic pattern, described briefly here, follows the usual sequence: attraction, enlightenment, and severance.

The rejection of "Fame in Exile" points toward the real concern of the novel, the development of the protagonist, George Webber, who is a conscientious artist struggling with his life material to find a philosophic purpose, that is, where he can go spiritually with his allegiances. The process of rejecting personal and social illusions as he matures is essential to the ultimate veracity of his vision. Thus Wolfe's book lies in a literary tradition with the short stories of Hawthorne and James, which trace the development of the artistic credo.

These syndromes in the artist-philosopher's search are structured by symbolic patterns,[7] in each case Webber feels attraction, undergoes enlightenment and then forces severance of an illusion which he had held to be all-sufficient. The symbolic patterns fall into three groupings, Reminiscence, Progression, and Projection, reflecting stages in his search. I have identified the following symbolic patterns in *You Can't Go Home Again:*

> *Symbolic Patterns of Reminiscence*
>   The Pattern of the Family
>   The Pattern of the Hometown
> *Symbolic Patterns of Progression*
>   The Pattern of the Business Ethic
>   The Pattern of Love and Art
> *Symbolic Patterns of Projection*
>   The Pattern of Fame in Exile
>   The Pattern of the Father

Pattern of the Family

Although the novel starts out with George Webber in the city, the first significant action occurs when he is summoned home for the funeral of Aunt Maw. Webber feels the pull of a powerful sense of family ties: "Ever since his mother had died when he was only eight years old, Aunt Maw had been the most solid and permanent fixture in his boy's universe" (p. 45). "As far back as he could remember, Aunt Maw had seemed to him an ageless crone, as old as God" (p. 46).

Thus Aunt Maw had become a symbol of his blood ties with the mountain clan. From her fantastic memory she had told stories of their family history, demonstrating their psychic and enduring powers, instilling in the young boy's impressionable consciousness an idea of mythical qualities in the Joyners. In the cemetery Webber encounters Delia Flood, an old friend of the family, who reminds him: " 'Your Aunt Maw always hoped you'd come home again. And you *will!*' she said. 'There's no better or more beautiful place on earth than in these mountains—and some day you'll come home again to stay' " (p. 108).

But the young writer rejects the entreaty to return to the family, for George Webber is *not* Eugene Gant, nor is Aunt Maw an eternal mother symbol like Eliza Gant whom the son will always feel drawn back to. When Wolfe changed the history of his protagonist, he replaced the fecund Eliza with Aunt Maw, a virgin who regards any interest in the flesh with suspicion, and substituted John Webber, a shadowy figure who ran away from his responsibilities as a father, for the monumental W. O. Gant. With his foster mother dead and his father gone, Webber painfully realizes that there can be no lasting relationship between an educated writer who moved in fashionable New York society and his half-mad mountain kin. Thus the illusion of the family which seemed to represent security, understanding, and everlasting ties is not sufficient, and Webber has experienced attraction, enlightenment, and severance in this symbolic pattern.

Pattern of the Hometown

If Webber feels a lost security in his family, he anticipates in the familiar rural landmarks of his hometown, a symbol of permanence in a life of mutability, "But why had he always felt so strongly the magnetic pull of home . . . if this little town, and the immortal hills around it, was not the only home he had on earth?" (p. 89). Yet no sooner does he board the train for Libya Hill than Webber hears talk of burgeoning real-estate developments, of remaking his hometown into something bigger and better. Wolfe has drawn portraits in the social satire mold of Sinclair Lewis of the corrupt townsmen who relate the "progress" in Libya Hill—Jarvis Riggs, who runs the fastest growing bank in the state by manipulating the funds of the town, with the assistance of the amiable Mayor Baxtor Kennedy and the politician "Parson" Flack. However, the changes in his hometown are scored upon Webber's consciousness by his encounter with three symbolic characters: Nebraska Crane, J. Timothy Wagner, and Judge Rumford Bland.

Nebraska Crane, a character of pure invention, the Cherokee Indian who was a boyhood friend of Webber, has become a famous baseball star, wealthy and able to retire wherever he wants. On the train, when Wolfe asks him if he will be bored by life back on a farm in Zebulon, he reveals an attitude directly opposite to the corrupt town leaders. Crane is the only one of Webber's hometown acquaintances who conceives of land as a place to live and work on.

Still another meaning is evident in J. Timothy Wagner, "the high priest and prophet of this insanity of waste" (p. 118), a symbol of the complete derangement of values of the town; for an understanding of the changed values of the town is gained by seeing their new attitude toward J. Timothy Wagner. Webber recalls from his childhood memories a picture of Wagner as a local Bacchus, an extravagant young man who had run through two fortunes before he was twenty-five, turned into a drunk, and was regarded by the town with disgust. Since the start of the real-estate speculation, J. Timothy Wagner had been apotheosized: "Tim Wagner had now become the supreme embodiment of the town's extravagant folly . . . so the people of the town now listened prayerfully to every word Tim Wagner uttered. They sought his opinion in all their speculations, and acted instantly on his suggestions" (p. 118). Even Wagner's habit of sleeping in a discarded hearse has morbid overtones for the town in which forty people committed suicide when their god of speculation failed.

If the townspeople flung paper fortunes away on the whim of a false prophet, they failed to heed another local prophet, Judge Rumford Bland. In a short number of pages, Wolfe has created a symbolic figure of the proportions of the Gant family. Bland is a mixture of good and evil, "a fallen angel" who has tasted the fruits of forbidden knowledge. Blind now, an unmistakable parallel to Tiresias, he had started with all the advantages of a distinguished family, a lawyer's education, and a good record in the Southern community. Yet for some reason Bland's reputation soon became stained; his marriage ended in a quick divorce, and he gave up law for the practice of usury on hapless Negroes. He was as callous in his dealings with his debtors as he was with the prostitutes who gave him syphilis. Wolfe writes, "he was stained with evil. There was something genuinely old and corrupt at the sources of his life and spirit. It had got into his blood, his bone, his flesh" (p. 77).

Yet this same Bland exposes the corruptness of the local politicians on the train within Webber's hearing. They are "afraid of him because his blind eyes saw straight through them" (p. 84). Like the Greek prophet, Bland brings the truth no one wants to hear, " 'Do I remember now the broken fragments of a town that waits and fears and schemes to put off the day of its impending ruin?' " (p. 87). Reminding them that he will *see* them again, the full twist of irony comes when it is Bland who first discovers the dead mayor's body in the public washroom. It is also Bland who asks the nervous Webber the question that structures his future work, " 'I mean, do you think you can really go *home* again?' " (p. 83).

Sensing the inner honesty of the man, Webber thought that the terrible and cynical release of Bland's abilities had occurred because "there had once been a warmth and an energy that had sought for an enhancement of the town's cold values, and for a joy and a beauty that were not there, but that lived in himself alone" (p. 145). The tragedy of Judge Bland, a potentially great man who had ruined himself, was symbolic of the basically honest and rural Libya Hill, a town that had ruined itself. Webber has learned that the hometown of his spirit has changed radically in form and values, and he cannot go back to any certainty there.

Pattern of the Business Ethic

Disappointed in his philosophic search in reminiscence, Webber, an activist, turns to the present for answers—to the values of the new

"American way" of the 1920's, the business ethic. The symbolic pattern of the business ethic goes beyond "the city" as a stronghold of dishonest privilege, being a folly of all America from Libya Hill to New York City, eventually bringing economic and moral collapse.

Webber perceives in the company man, Randy Shepperton, a new kind of evil masking as "sound business." For Randy the Federal Weight, Scales, and Computing Company, a nationwide organization of salesmen, is "the Company," a plainly marked symbol of the way to success. The Company President had swept away the old business ethic based on fulfilling need and substituted a creed of creating a desire for his product (p. 133). Represented by Merritt, a suggestively named, glad-handing boss, The Company seems paternalistic until business declines and Webber overhears him threatening to dismiss the faithful employee, Shepperton (p. 138). Thus the company ethic is based on the naturalistic principle, survival of the fittest. Webber recalls a picture of slave labor building the pyramids, the only reward a lashing, as an image of the company structure (p. 140). Shepperton is unable to comprehend his own dismissal because he has become a disciple of the magic of salesmanship, "that commercial brand of special pleading—that devoted servant of self-interest—that sworn enemy of truth" (pp. 395–96). Meanwhile, in Libya Hill the financial and moral terror that followed the closing of the municipal bank and the mayor's suicide was the last legacy of land speculation.

In New York City Webber feels the same attraction to the world of society, supported by the business ethic, before he senses enlightenment about its values and forces severance. The wealthy Mr. Jack and his friends delight in the animal-like struggle of laissez faire, convinced that their professional hardness and amorality selects them for privilege: "When they looked about them and saw everywhere nothing but the myriad shapes of privilege, dishonesty, and self-interest, they were convinced that this was inevitably 'the way things are'" (p. 191).

Wolfe uses the party at Jack's, which ends in a climactic fire, as a symbolic device to represent both the privilege and the disintegration of society based on the business ethic. He juxtaposes the events at the party just one week before the stock market crash, which ushered in the depression. The figures from the world of finance, the theatrical, literary and international set are superficial, jaded with power, or perverse. Their phony liberalism is exposed by such business practices as child labor and strike-breaking.

The eventual failure of the business ethic is foreshadowed by the accidental fire in the apartment building, which reveals the impotence of their wealth, and the leveling of social classes in the depression, as all types and classes seek refuge and mingle in the sidewalk below. Ironically, and to the point, the only persons killed in the fire are two working men, Enborg and Anderson. Corrosion of moral values becomes more apparent in the attitude of the management, concerned only with protecting their wealthy tenants from unpleasant news.

After the party Webber rejects the world of the business ethic, noting the sordid conditions of tramps in the depression year, 1932. He concludes that the predicament in America has come about because of "catch phrases like 'prosperity' and 'rugged individualism' and 'the American way'" (p. 393). America would not be able to go home again to any easy way of success, for the future "would not be built on business as we know it" (p. 396).

Pattern of Love and Art

Love and art function closely as a single symbolic pattern in *You Can't Go Home Again*. Webber has a selfish and self-justifying attitude toward love, and toward art for the sake of art; these are tied up with his sexual relationship to Mrs. Jack. He is the young provincial who comes to the city to find fulfillment: "From his early childhood, when he was living like an orphan with his Joyner relatives back in Libya Hill, he had dreamed that one day he would go to New York and there find love and fame and fortune" (p. 15).

As the novel opens, Webber returns to New York, finding Esther Jack and feeling again their tremendous pull of love. (Although their tumultuous affair had been the primary development of *The Web and the Rock,* Webber still believes that love can be the one fulfilling life action, if the lovers will use reason in their demands on each other.) "April had come back again" (p. 11) for them.

As symbolic device, the party at Jack's functions to show him that personal bonds of love are wrong because they bind him to a world with twisted values about life and art. The characters at the party treat love as an experiment or as a purchasable commodity. The beautiful Lily Mandell's aversion toward the wealthy Mr. Hirsch is calculated to raise the price of her eventual seduction. Even the extravagant critical acclaim given to Piggy Logan's circus cannot blunt the inanity of this tedious spectacle. The *pièce de résistance* of Logan's circus, an act in which he persists in pressing a pin down the doll's throat until the stuffed entrails spill out, suggests the hollowness of the society approving this spectacle. Piggy Logan's circus, which has been held up as the ultimate measure of sensibility and culture, is a symbol of the inner emptiness of Esther's society. Since the illusion of love means condoning the twisted values of Esther Jack's society, Wolfe writes, "The fire was over" (p. 312), ambiguously suggesting the extinguishment of Webber's love as well as the apartment conflagration.

After his break with Esther Jack, Webber is free to reevaluate his artistic credo—his pained reaction to hometown disapproval has been to assume the role of the artist, sensitive and misunderstood: "George began to talk now about 'the artist,' . . . a kind of fabulous, rare, and special creature who lived on 'beauty' and 'truth' and had thoughts so subtle that the average man could comprehend them no more than a mongrel could understand the moon he bayed at" (p. 383). Under Randy Shepperton's questioning he begins to realize that his arrogant posture may have marred his art, " 'The failure comes from the false personal. There's the guilt. That's where the young genius business gets in—the young artist business, what you called a while ago the wounded faun business. It gets in and it twists the vision' " (p. 385).

From now on, Webber resolves to be as objective about himself as he would be about any material for fiction. In rejecting the illusions of the young provincial, he finds he "can't go home again" to art for the sake of art, or to love for the sake of love. The rejection of these values within this symbolic pattern helps to prepare Webber for a broader vision.

Pattern of Fame in Exile

Failing to find a purpose in reminiscence or progression, Webber seeks in a projection, the idea of fame in exile, an answer to his quest. Since the main outline of this symbolic pattern is given in the introduction, a few corroborative details will be presented. Bound for Europe, Webber seeks renewal in a search for fame: *"And by his side was that stern friend, the only one to whom he spoke what*

in his secret heart he most desired. To Loneliness he whispered,
'Fame!'" (p. 398). His projection assumes grandiose proportions,
Milton and Goethe are cited as authority, and even the American
Dream becomes the chance for anyone to achieve fame.

But his trip through the English countryside with the embodiment of fame, McHarg, is a fiasco, compared to the Walpurgis Night
of *Faust,* and Webber perceives fame has given his idol no security
or peace. Nevertheless, he cannot resist fame in Germany where he
receives adulation and praise for his work, although he becomes
uneasy at the Olympic games of 1936, which seem to be chosen as
"a symbol of the new collective might" (p. 626). The fear, suspicion,
and tyranny of the Nazis are concretized in the abduction of the
Jewish banker on Webber's train. His fellow passengers felt, "they
were saying farewell, not to a man, but to humanity" (p. 699). Wolfe
seems to use traditional Christian symbolism to emphasize the inner
torment Webber experiences as he conceals the money the banker
had given him to hide: "Turning half away, he thrust his hands
into his pockets—and drew them out as though his fingers had been
burned. The man's money—he still had it! . . . felt the five two-
mark pieces. The coins seemed greasy, as if they were covered with
sweat" (p. 697). There can be no return to the illusory place that
promised identity and purpose for the writer.

Pattern of the Father

When Webber leaves Germany, one illusion still binds him to a
pattern of return: that of the symbolic father. In *The Story of a*
Novel Wolfe makes the following assertion: ". . . the deepest search
in life, it seemed to me, the thing that in one way or another was
central to all living was man's search to find a father . . . the image
of strength and wisdom external to his need and superior to his
hunger, to which the belief and power of his own life could be
united." [8] In *You Can't Go Home Again* Webber's editor, Foxhall
Edwards, assumes this role. "Little by little it seemed to George
that he had found in Fox the father he had lost and had long been
looking for. And so it was that Fox became a second father to him—
the father of his spirit" (p. 27). Wolfe also provides a suitable fictional background by giving Webber a most indistinct father and
making Edwards a father without a son.

But after this attraction, the emotional Webber begins to tire of Edwards' rationalistic fatalism. Edwards' intelligence is described in animal imagery usually reserved for unsympathetic characters like Piggy Logan (p. 439). The temperamental differences between the two are illustrated by their attitudes toward C. Green, an unidentified middle-aged American who jumped to his death out of the Admiral Drake Hotel. To Edwards this C. Green is a statistic of the American death rate, a cipher in an industrial society, a poor contrast to Admiral Drake. However, Webber refuses to admit Green's suicide was meaningless. Instead he considers Green's death as his distinguishing act from conformity, a symbolic redemption of his type, for the blood of C. Green brings his salvation (pp. 481–82).

In his letter of resignation to Edwards' publishing house, Webber rejects the editor's fatalistic attitude, which he equates with Ecclesiasticus, for a philosophy of activism: "You and the Preacher may be right for all eternity, but we Men-Alive, dear Fox, are right for Now. And it is for Now, and for us the living, that we must speak, and speak the truth, as much of it as we can see and know" (p. 738). Webber realizes that the search for the symbolic father is over; there exists no magical "someone who can help you, save you, ease the burden for you." Again Webber's reaction to the father figure has been in the customary form: attraction, enlightenment, and severance.

The meaning of the final symbolic statement of "you can't go home again" is found in the summation of the individual symbol patterns of reminiscence, progression, and projection. By the process of attraction, enlightenment, and severance Webber has suggested six major illusions that may prevent a meaningful vision for the artist. Divested of his false personal and social symbols, he is liberated to concern himself with the problems of his fellow man. And just as for him there is no going back, there can be no return of America to old ways and solutions. Only if society is ever ready "to look into the face of fear itself, to probe behind it, to see what caused it, and then to speak the truth about it" (p. 730), will the recurring "single selfishness and compulsive greed" (p. 742) be overcome, in short, be willing to discard its own illusions.

Where can Webber find the purpose he so earnestly desires? The answer lies where the quest began, in America—in the promise and true discovery of the American Dream. Finally, Webber stands as the artist firmly within his society, not alienated from it.

Notes

1. Chapel Hill: Univ. of North Carolina Press, 1962, p. 410.

2. Kennedy, pp. 405–406.

3. Kennedy, pp. 299–322; pp. 334–414.

4. D. H. Lawrence, "The Dragon of the Apocalypse," *Selected Literary Criticism,* ed. Anthony Beal (London: William Heinemann, Ltd., 1955); reprinted in Maurice Beebe, ed., *Literary Symbolism* (San Francisco: Wadsworth, 1960), pp. 31–32.

5. E. K. Brown, "Thomas Wolfe: Realist and Symbolist," *University of Toronto Quarterly,* X (January, 1941); reprinted in Richard Walser, ed., *The Enigma of Thomas Wolfe* (Cambridge, Mass.: Harvard Univ. Press, 1953), p. 209.

6. Thomas Wolfe, *You Can't Go Home Again* (New York: Harper and Brothers, 1941), p. 706. All subsequent references indicated by parentheses in the text will be to this edition.

7. Possibly, these symbolic patterns may be applied to a major part of Wolfe's work. A longer explication of symbolic patterns in *You Can't Go Home Again* is to be found in Thesis No. 761 (Bowling Green State University, August, 1961), by Clyde C. Clements, Jr.

8. Thomas Wolfe, *The Story of a Novel* (New York: Charles Scribner's Sons, 1936), p. 39.

Leslie A. Field

20. The Hills Beyond: A Folk Novel of America

FOR MOST STUDENTS of Thomas Wolfe, *The Hills Beyond*[1] is a postscript to his total work. Ironically, the plan for this book appears first as an *actual* postcript to a letter which Wolfe wrote his mother in 1934. In the postscript Wolfe asks his mother to "jot down" a brief history of her family. He would like, he says,

> to get a list of the twenty children or more that your grandfather had by his two marriages and what happened to them and where they settled and what parts of the country they moved to, and so forth. . . .
>
> I'm asking you to do this because some day after I get through with these books I'm working on now, I may wind the whole thing up with a book that will try to tell through the hundreds of members of one family the whole story of America.[2]

Wolfe did go on with his plan, but he died leaving behind only ten chapters of his fragmentary novel—a novel which has thus far received little critical attention. Although incomplete, *The Hills Beyond* is a significant sample of Wolfe's writing in that it does an extraordinary job of fusing autobiographical fiction, objectivity, and American folklore. It may very well be that in this novel Wolfe had departed completely from his *Look Homeward, Angel* approach to writing and was now pointing in an entirely new direction. Surprisingly, most Wolfe critics, including the folklorists, have failed to examine this new direction.

This study, therefore, will attempt to show that in *The Hills Beyond* Wolfe did draw heavily on folklore material for the purpose of writing his fictional history of America. Moreover, Wolfe's fictional America will be seen emerging from two strong folklore strains: the frontiersman and the Yankee. We have, of course, Constance Rourke's *American Humor* to thank for its pioneering success in detailing and demonstrating a fusion of these traditions in American culture. But Wolfe adds a third dimension: the American utilitarian scholar. Perhaps it would be more in keeping with Wolfe's actual use of this third dimension to label it simply "practical book learning."

By and large Wolfe's critics do agree that Wolfe is steeped in a native American tradition. But they hasten to add that Wolfe's work is flavored by non-American myths. Furthermore, most students of Wolfe recognize his heavy dependence upon autobiography in his fiction. His work, to be sure, is deeply personal. As a result of this last element in his work, Wolfe has been praised by a few and damned by many.

Again, most agree that Wolfe was tending towards more objective, less autobiographical writing as he returned to his native tradition. That *The Hills Beyond* is the culmination of this movement cannot be easily refuted. Perhaps then it may be rewarding to see what it is that Wolfe has taken from his native tradition for use in *The Hills Beyond* and how the folk material acted as a controlling image for his "great new plan."

Wolfe's tentative plan we already have in his letter to his mother. But in its more complete form it goes as follows: [3] Now that he has written four large "novels," the last two published posthumously, dealing with his own family history from about the turn of the century, he wants to backtrack to trace his ancestry as it relates to the American pioneer. William (Bear) Joyner, who lived about 1800, is to be the father of America—an American Moses.

In ten chapters of *The Hills Beyond* Wolfe traces the careers of Bear and those of eight of his children. The children are the off-spring of Bear's two marriages. Wolfe does not get around to dealing with the twenty or so children and hundreds of grandchildren and great-grandchildren that his original plan calls for. The children he does develop, in their various occupations—lawyer, politician, teacher, businessman—represent the occupational face of America. They stand as prototypes of myriad rural and urban occupations. In the chapter entitled "The Great Schism," as a matter of fact, Bear's huge family does split up, some staying on the farm and others going to the city. In effect, these people are the beginnings of the American heritage as Wolfe sees it in his projected novel.

But just what is their source? What makes their heritage American rather than, say, Pakistanian? Their source is the grand old man who fathers this new race of fictional Americans. He is none other than William (Bear) Joyner, the man who fuses the two most powerful strains of American folk tradition, the frontiersman and the Yankee, and the third strain which Wolfe saw as a necessary addition. This last strain is the American practical or utilitarian scholar, the new American who learns to read so that he can rise above his fellow man, so that he can add to the Crockett-Bunyan type of hero another dimension—book learning. Not only does the content of Wolfe's tales bear a striking resemblance to general American folk tales, but the manner in which they are told is often far too similar to admit coincidence.

It is doubtful that Wolfe drew upon purely regional North Carolina folklore. In *North Carolina Folklore* by Frank C. Brown and the Hendrick's collection of "tar heel tales," for example, little resemblance seems to appear between North Carolina lore and Wolfe's material. More probable sources, however, are Professor Frederick Koch's and Paul Green's works in the folklore area. Wolfe and Green were fellow students in Koch's folk-play class at Chapel Hill. Furthermore, Wolfe wrote two folk plays, *The Return of Buck Gavin* and *Third Night*. He also acted in several folk plays at the University. Thus in his undergraduate years Wolfe could not escape the influence of American folklore as interpreted by Professor Koch. Still another source for Wolfe's folklore material derives quite naturally from oral transmission filtered through his own immediate family. Wolfe's family, a family of irrepressible talkers, loved to "tell tales." Wolfe's mother, for instance, could, in folklore jargon, be termed a fairly good "informant," as demonstrated in Hayden Norwood's *The Marble Man's Wife*.

Again we may ask this question, how specifically does Bear Joyner, our American Moses, relate to folklore? Thanks to the monumental fieldwork done by an army of folklorists, we are able to compare actual folklore tales with the portrait Wolfe paints of Bear Joyner.

Wolfe tells the following of Bear's fighting prowess:

> The stories of his great physical strength, for example, were prodigious, and yet apparently were founded in substantial fact.
> He was said to have been, particularly in his earlier years, a man of hot temper, who liked a fight. There is a story of his fight with a big blacksmith: a quarrel having broken out between them over the shoeing of a horse, the blacksmith brained him with an iron shoe and knocked him flat. As William started to get up again, bleeding and half conscious, the blacksmith came at him again, and Joyner hit him while still resting on one knee. The blow broke the blacksmith's ribs and caved in his side as one would crack a shell. (pp. 213–14)

Bear's powers in and relish for hand-to-hand combat calls to mind another fighter—Mike Fink. Fink's love of fighting and excellence as a fighter are legendary, of course. In Emerson Bennett's version of Mike Fink, the hero roars:

> I can lick five times my own weight in wildcats. I can use Injens by the cord. I can swallow niggers whole, raw or cooked. I can out-run, out-dance, out-jump, out-dive, out-holler, and out-lick any white things in the shape o' human that's ever put foot within two thousand miles of the big Missassip. . . . Oh, for a fight!. . . O for a fight, boys, to stretch these here limbs, and get the jints to working easy! [4]

A. B. Longstreet has a spectator report the aftermath of a frontier Georgia fight in this way:

> I looked, and saw that Bob had entirely lost his left ear and a large piece from his left cheek. His right eye was a little discolored, and the blood flowed profusely from his wounds. . . . Bill presented a hideous spectacle. About a third of his nose, at the lower extremity, was bit off, and his face was so swelled and bruised that it was difficult to discover in it anything of the human visage. . . . [5]

And in Paulding's *The Lion of the West,* Nimrod Wildfire says, "My father can whip the best man in old Kaintuck, and I can whip my father" (Lynn, p. 176). The depiction of Bear Joyner as a strong man, a fighter, the gory details of hand-to-hand combat, and the actual "frame" in which the Bear Joyner story is told all point to more than coincidental parallels with the stock fighting characters and their stories in American folklore.

One of the most important folklore episodes concerning William (Bear) Joyner is the one in which he acquired his nickname.

He was known in his own day to be a mighty hunter; and old men who remembered him used to tell of the time he "chased the dogs the whole way over into Tennessee, and was gone four days and nights, and never knowed how fer from home he was."

There is also the story of his fight with a grizzly bear: the bear charged him at close quarters and there was nothing left for him to do but fight. A searching party found him two days later, more dead than living—as they told it, "all chawed up," but with the carcass of the bear: "and in the fight he had bit the nose off that big b'ar and chawed off both his years, and that b'ar was so tored up hit was a caution." (p. 214)

Professor Dorson comments about the frontier folk: "Legion were the stories that described fierce brushes, grapples, and encounters between a woodsman and a bear." [6] In "A Bear Hunt in Vermont," for instance, there is the following account of a Vermonter's hand-to-hand encounter with a bear:

"There he was, rolling round on the ground grappling with the fierce animal which was at least four times his weight, and not a weapon about him. . . . Presently he got one hand in the bear's mouth and grappled his tongue. The bear writhed like a serpent, and chawed away on his arm as if it had been a stick. . . . There he was floundering in the mud with a great bear and nothing but his hands to help him." Then the hunter almost effortlessly drowns the bear in a slough of mud and emerges victorious, but "winding his handkerchief round his arm which was horribly mangled . . ." (Dorson, pp. 116–17)

In a similar vein—hand-to-antler combat—Mike Fink subdues a monstrous moose (Blair, pp. 210–11).

Note that in all three fights—Vermont bear hunt, Mike Fink and the moose, and Bear Joyner's encounter—the hunters were attacked at close quarters and could make use of no weapons, or for some reason their weapons failed to function so that they had to proceed with the fight in a primitive fashion. This approach to telling the story in each case adds a spark of folk realism.

Perhaps one of the most famous frontier stories concerning a bear fight appears at the end of Thorpe's "The Big Bear of Arkansas." This bear hunt differs from Joyner's, of course, in that our Arkansas hero felled his game with a rifle (Lynn, pp. 122-37).

Paul Bunyan's superhuman hunting prowess is more closely allied to Joyner's, however:

> There are three [Bunyan] hunting stories; in one, Paul grabs the Timber Wolf by the ears, hollers, and the wolf dies of fright. In another, Paul confronts a Polar Bear; having no railroad spikes for his gun, he rams it full of icicles and kills the bear with them. In the third, he grabs one mountain lion by the tail, and used it to club two others to death.[7]

Still another story is told of Bear Joyner in which he outwitted one of his own kin, won a bet, and as a reward "walked off with enough leather on his back to shoe a regiment." After a wager, Bear Joyner's relative, a storekeeper, kept his part of the bargain:

> He pointed to the pile of leather in his store and told William he could take as much as he could carry. Joyner stood there while his companions heaped the leather on, and finally staggered out the door with eight hundred pounds of it on his shoulders. (pp. 214-15)

And Professor Dorson comments on strong men:

> Fact and legend blended in tales of pioneer strong men. Home-making in the wilderness had stimulated physical performances that more tender generations recalled with awe and retold with relish. Most of these feats had to do with lifting great weights. Benjamin Tarr of Rockfort, Massachusetts, lifted an anchor weighing 800 pounds. (pp. 122-23)

Dorson goes on to cite a number of other strong-men folk tales, one being of a man who effortlessly carries sixteen hundred pounds of boom chains on his back. It should be noted that in all three strong man tales depicted above we have the use of a seemingly magic weight, eight hunderd pounds, or some multiple thereof.[8]

Throughout *The Hills Beyond* we have samples of the other folklore strain in Bear Joyner's makeup. He was the shrewd trader, the keen Yankee wit (even though he is a Southerner), the teller of tall tales, and the Yankee with a wry sense of humor.

His ability to drive a hard bargain, acquire property, and then multiply his holdings until the final accumulation of wealth from the deal completely overshadowed his initial gain, would do justice to a nineteenth-century Robber Baron.

Nor did Bear's offspring lack their parent's talents. One of Bear Joyner's sons offered to sell a man some land for two hundred dollars. The man refused, but later bemoans his folly: "And I was such a fool I didn't take it! If I had, I'd have been a rich man today. You couldn't buy it now for a million dollars" (p. 242). And Wolfe adds:

> By the time the Civil War broke out the Joyners were accounted wealthy folk. It was "the big family" of the whole community. Even long before that their position was so generally acknowledged throughout the western mountains that when the boys began to "make their mark," it occasioned no surprise. (p. 243)

The traditional tales told of the Yankee often emphasized this very thriftiness, shrewdness, and parsimony which made Bear Joyner's people "wealthy folk." But the Yankee was more. He was a conglomeration, often depicted "as a sly and scheming knave . . . regional in projection and design [but a type that] . . . did not differ fundamentally from backward and backwater types throughout the land." [9]

Even though Bear Joyner could hold his own in the realm of the tall tale and keen wit, it was really his son Zack Joyner who was "noted for his ready wit, his coarse humor, and his gift of repartee. People would come into the store 'just to hear Zack Joyner talk'" (p. 247). The townspeople were proud of the "tincture of charlatanism and smooth dealing" in Zack. They told tales of his "superior adroitness and cunning, and men would wag their heads and laugh with envious approval, as though they wished they could do such things themselves, but knew, being merely average men, they could not make the grade" (p. 248).

As Dorson illustrates, the Yankee was a spinner of yarns. He told land stories, sea stories, fight stories, hunting and fishing stories, almost any kind of story—all tall tales. His repertoire, however, is inexhaustible (p. 102). Not only did his story-telling display the Yankee's versatility and shrewdness, but his trickster nature also confirmed it. More often than not the trickster quirk in the Yankee was turned to profit. In short, Dorson continues, we have a practical joker who delighted in duping the country bumpkin (pp. 78–79), who twinkled as he passed off his glue-factory candidates for good, solid plow horses (pp. 82–85), and who luxuriated in the warm aura of his own yarn spinning (p. 102).

In one respect we can contrast an army of unlettered folk heroes with Bear and Zack Joyner because Wolfe did add the third dimension. And he emphasized this dimension. "It is important, then, to know, [Wolfe points out] that William Joyner 'chawed the b'ar.' But it is even more important to know that William Joyner was a man who learned to read a book" (p. 218). And in the next few pages "learned to read a book" almost becomes a refrain. No unlettered Moses he, Wolfe insists. Our clan must be of the people, close to the land, but it must rise above the land through learning.

> At a time when it was the convention for all men in the wilderness to be illiterate, in a place where the knowledge contained in books was of no earthly use, nothing would suit old Bear Joyner but that he must learn to read. . . .
>
> For no one ever really knew where his father came from. And it did not matter. Old Bear Joyner came from the same place, and was of the same kind, as all the other people in the mountains. But he was a man who learned to read. And there is the core of the whole mystery. (p. 221)

If Bear Joyner was the Moses, the beginning of Wolfe's fictional tribe, both his first and second wife shared part of the glory with him. And the second wife especially, who effortlessly bore and reared some fourteen of Bear's twenty children, has some of the frontier tall tale rub off on her. Zack, for instance, has spoken of "the physical sharpness of her sense of smell, which really was amazing, and which all of her children inherited (she is said one time to have 'smelled burning leaves five miles away upon the mountain, long before any-one else knowed there was a fire'). . ." (p. 232).

And just as our American Moses had a more striking wife than was Zipporah of the traditional biblical patriarch, so did he have in his son Zachariah a man more marked than Gershom. Zack Joyner, one of the oldest sons, is an extension of old Bear himself. Zack becomes a lawyer-politician, a forerunner of the Willie Stark-Huey Long Southern demagogue.

To the people of Catawba, Zack was

> not only their native Lincoln—their backwoods son who marched to glory by the log-rail route—he was their Crockett and Paul Bunyan rolled in one. He was not alone their hero; he was their legend and their myth. He was and has remained so to this day, a kind of living prophecy of all that they themselves might wish to be; a native divinity, shaped out of their own clay, and breathing their own air; a tongue that spoke the words, a voice that understood and spoke the language, they would have him speak. (p. 223)

Almost as if Wolfe were explaining the evolution of a folk tale or a myth, he goes on to discuss Zack:

> They tell a thousand stories about him today. What does it matter if many of the things which they describe never happened? They are true because they are the kind of things he would have said, the kind of things that would have happened to him. Thus, to what degree, and in what complex ways, he was created so in their imaginations, no one can say. How much the man shaped the myth, how much the myth shaped the man, how much Zack Joyner created his own folk, or how much his people created him—no one can know, and it does not matter. (pp. 223–24)

And as Wolfe continues to describe Zack Joyner, the folk hero of the people, we hear more echoes of the academic folklorist.

> In examining the history of that great man, we have collected more than eight hundred stories, anecdotes, and jokes that are told of him, and of this number at least six hundred have the unmistakeable ring—or *smack*—of truth. If they did not happen—they *should* have! They belong to him: they fit him like an old shoe. (p. 224)

Shades of Professor Koch's Chapel Hill folklore class!

> . . . "Did they happen?" . . . We are not wholly unprepared for these objections. . . . We have actually verified three hundred as authentic beyond the shadow of a doubt, and are ready to cite them by the book—place, time, occasion, evidence—to anyone who may inquire. In these stories there is a strength, a humor, a coarseness, and a native originality that belonged to the man and marked

his every utterance. They come straight out of his own earth.
(p. 224)

But back to the father, the American Moses himself. Is he merely
Wolfe's transplant of the Bunyan-Crockett hero? Indeed not. Bear
Joyner is at first very much the traditional American hero. He has
no background, no parents, no tyrannical father; he overthrows no
throne, is no prince in disguise; no one has cursed his birth or set
him in the water. Thus he is no Oedipus, Heracles, Apollo, Zeus,
Watu, Gunung, Nychang, Sigurd, or Arthur—at first. But from an
almost one-dimensional American hero he is changed. The hero-
bachelor takes a wife. And the wife begets children. And they beget.
And so on.[10]

So we have the patriarch who starts a clan. Perhaps we may say
that we have in Bear Joyner a semitraditional American hero. Bear
does not disappear after a series of picaresque-like superhuman
episodes. He stays and becomes the patriarch—the Moses of the
American family.

That Wolfe was conscious of his use of folklore in *The Hills
Beyond* becomes a pedestrian statement in the light of the above
evidence. How much "pure" folklore he would have brought to a
complete version of *The Hills Beyond* is a matter for conjecture
only. But there can remain very little doubt concerning Wolfe's
overall literary plan, his controlling image. His four huge novels, as
has already been mentioned, were autobiographical. In part, *The
Hills Beyond* is also autobiographical. Wolfe's ancestry is so closely
knit with the hill folk he discusses in *The Hills Beyond* that Wolfe
becomes folk and folk becomes Wolfe. But his use of the various
strains of folklore tradition does help him to objectify the personal
elements in his characterizations.

Wolfe's novels document a pilgrimage—a pilgrimage which
begins in the hills of North Carolina, moves to cosmopolitan New
York and then Europe, and finally returns to old Catawba—the hills
beyond—old North Carolina.[11] Furthermore, the journey documents
under various names the Joyner-Gant (Westall-Wolfe) life cycle.
To be sure, the four novels, the vehicle for the "story," consisted of
autobiography, myth, and folklore of a much more imaginative vein

than we find in *The Hills Beyond*. But in this fragmentary novel, Wolfe was moving away from the first two elements and was attempting a story steeped in the last element—folklore.

The Hills Beyond may have provided an excellent folkloristic ancestry for the Wolfe tribe he had already depicted in his novels. *Look Homeward, Angel* and the other books, however, are complete. *The Hills Beyond* is a fragment. As such it must be judged. It has power, life, and color extracted from Wolfe's knowledge of the hills of North Carolina and of folklore in general—but it is shaped (albeit imperfectly) by Wolfe's own large imagination. As it stands, the story is rough, partmolded, incomplete. As a counterpoint it may be enough to conclude that *The Hills Beyond* encompasses far more than the traditional Bunyan-Crockett episode. But it may be even more important to end with this conjecture: Wolfe's fragmentary novel shows that he was approaching a most significant corner in his artistry. Had he lived long enough to turn the corner successfully, perhaps we would now have his "whole story of America" in addition to his "whole story" of Eugene Gant-George Webber.

Notes

1. Thomas Wolfe, *The Hills Beyond* (New York: Harper and Brothers, 1941). In this essay this title refers only to the ten chapters of the fragment called "The Hills Beyond," and not to any of the ten short stories usually bound together with the fragmentary novel. Note also that numbers in parentheses in this essay with no designation are always page references to *The Hills Beyond*.

2. Thomas Wolfe, *Thomas Wolfe's Letters to His Mother* (New York: Charles Scribner's Sons, 1951), pp. 292–93.

3. See also Edward C. Aswell, "A Note on Thomas Wolfe," *The Hills Beyond* (New York: Harper and Brothers, 1941), pp. 351–86.

4. Walter Blair and Franklin J. Meine, *Half Horse Half Alligator* (Chicago: Univ. of Chicago Press, 1956), pp. 170–71.

5. Kenneth S. Lynn, ed., *The Comic Tradition in America* (New York: Doubleday-Anchor, 1958), p. 78.

6. Richard M. Dorson,, *Jonathan Draws the Long Bow* (Cambridge, Mass.: Harvard Univ. Press, 1946), p. 116.

7. Daniel G. Hoffman, *Paul Bunyan: Last of the Frontier Demigods* (Philadelphia: Univ. of Pennsylvania Press, 1952), p. 84. See also Vance Randolph, *We Always Lie to Strangers* (New York: Columbia Univ. Press, 1951), pp. 95–130, 168.

8. See also Lynn, pp. 169–70, and Hoffman, pp. 28–31.

9. Dorson, p. 69. For more folk parallels of the shrewd trader see Hoffman, "Paul's Cleverality," pp. 43–48; Lynn, Longstreet's "The Horseswap," pp. 81ff.

10. Frazer's *The Golden Bough*, Raglan's *The Hero*, Rank's *The Myth of the Birth of the Hero*, Campbell's *The Hero With a Thousand Faces* taken collectively, categorize the European hero of mythology. Rourke, Hoffman, Blair, and Dorson do likewise for the American folklore hero.

11. See J. M. Maclachlan, "Folk Concepts in the Novels of Thomas Wolfe," *Southern Folklore Quarterly*, IX (Dec., 1945), 175–86. Maclachlan convincingly points out that Wolfe "was a man bound to interpret the culture of an epoch and do it from the vantage-point of his origin in an indigenous and integrated social structure" (p. 177). He further says that when Wolfe returns to his heritage, he recognizes value and identity only in his own roots—the hill folk of North Carolina.

Part IV   *The Short Stories*

Wallace Stegner

21. Analysis of "The Lost Boy"

THE WRITINGS of Thomas Wolfe, whatever their other virtues, are not usually notable for the strictness of their form. At any length Wolfe was large and loose; his talents were antipathetic to the concentration and control by which the short story has always been marked. But "The Lost Boy" is something of an exception. It is large enough and loose enough, but it does have an unmistakable form, which arises immediately and inevitably out of the intention and is inseparable from it.

"The Lost Boy" has within it most of what Thomas Wolfe made his total message. It has the haunting evocation of the past, the preoccupation with Time, the irreparable loneliness of the individual, the constant solipsistic attempt to convert the remembered into the real. The characteristic search for the father is apparently not here, but the search for the brother which is the subject of this story is so closely related as to seem a part of Wolfe's extraordinary longing to project himself backward toward someone loved and respected and envied and lost. And the style and manner are Wolfe's typical manner; the form the story takes does not hinder his incantatory flow of words.

Wolfe was a magician, a witch doctor, drawing upon the same profundities of awe and ecstasy and fear which primitive religions and magic and superstition draw upon. His writing impulse was very often directed toward the laying of ghosts, the evoking of spirits, the making of medicine to confound restricting Time, the exorcism of evil, the ritual expiation of sin. It is entirely appropriate that the form of this story should be very close to that of a primitive or superstitious ritual. The story is as surely an act of healing as a Navajo Yehbetzai, as much a superstitious rite as the calling up of a spirit at a séance. It has the same compulsive, ritualistic, gradual accretion of excitement toward the point of the ghost's appearance. It observes rules older than literary criticism and taboos embedded in the subconscious of the race. This is a very subsurface story; it comes close to being pure necromancy. Story and ritual are one; the form is utterly compulsive, though perhaps largely unconscious.

It does not begin like an exercise in voodoo, but like one of Wolfe's hymns to Time. In the beginning Wolfe evokes the Square in all its concreteness, from the dry whisking of the tails of the fire-horses to the catalogue of implements in the hardware store window. Here is Grover, the lost boy, before he was lost; here is Grover "caught upon a point of Time." Grover is real in a real place, but the Square is more than a square, Grover is a child who is more than a child. There is a quality of trance: the returning plume of the fountain, the returning winds of April, the streetcars that go and come, the chanting of the strong repetitious rhetoric and the sonority of recurrent sounds put a magic on this Square even at its most real. Grover's birthmark is a mark of difference and perhaps of doom. And we cannot miss the heightening of everything, from Grover's gravity to old Gant's Old-Testament potency as the Father. Gant is all but God. It is not accidental that he works at an altarlike bench among half-formed shapes of angels and that he strikes awe into Grover. Neither is it accident that Grover prays to him and that Gant in a godlike rage seizes him by the hand and goes to enforce justice upon old twisted Crocker. The father leaves an absence in the story because after the first section he is not mentioned again. His absence is like the absence of Grover. He duplicates and parallels that tantalizing ghost.

There are magic words in this story with magic powers to evoke. "St. Louis" and "the Fair" are two of them. It will be observed that the story follows a course from the Square where Grover's real life was, through Indiana to St. Louis, to the street called King's High-way, to the house where the family lived during the summer of the Fair, and finally to the room where Grover died. There is a progression from the more general to the more particular, a constant working closer to the point of mystery. But at the same time there is progression of another kind. This story fades and sharpens, comes and goes, like the fountain plume and the streetcars, and like the memory that recreates the past and sees it fade again, but it always works closer and closer toward the mystery of Grover, the mystery of Time, the thing which is being summoned and the thing which has been lost. As it comes closer it grows in tension; its climax, surely, will be the dramatic appearance of this ghost, the dramatic revelation of mystery.

But the spell moves slowly. The lost boy must be built up bit by bit. First his mother and then his sister bear testimony about him, recreating him in quality and feature. Their testimony is like that of mourners at a funeral of one much loved: they have fixed the dead in their minds so that he cannot entirely disappear or be entirely lost. Through the mother, as the family travels down through Indiana to St. Louis and the Fair, we see Grover from one side. Through the sister, less sentimental, more touched with questionings, more moved by irrecoverable loss, we see him from another, and we follow him through the St. Louis summer to his death.

For the sister the Past is dead, the things they were and dreamed as children are dead, there is a kind of horror in thinking of how sad and lonely is the gap between Then and Now, and a sharper compulsion to cling to it and linger over it and understand it. Through the sister's part of the story we have come closer to the place of magic, and we have come much closer to Grover, for at the heart of her recollection is the photograph. There is his veritable face; there are the faces of all of them as they were—caught and petrified unchanged, but strange, almost unbelievable. Wolfe makes the same use of the photograph that a medicine man might make of nail parings or hair cuttings or gathered-up footprints in the mud: the possession of this picture gives us a power, by associative magic, over Grover's spirit.

And in both these witnesses note the hypnotic mumbling of the spell—the words and images that will roll Time back and restore the lost, or seem to for a moment:

. . . you remember how it was, and see again those two funny, frightened, skinny little kids with their noses pressed against the dirty window of that lunchroom thirty years ago. You remember the way it felt, the way it smelled, even the strange smell in the old pantry in that house we lived in then. And the steps before the house, the way the rooms looked. And those two little boys in sailor suits who used to ride up and down before the house on tricycles . . . And the birthmark on Grover's neck . . . The Inside Inn . . . St. Louis, and the Fair.

Over and over the images are recalled, the words of magic repeated. In section four the story begins to tighten toward its climactic moment. It has here the same trancelike repetitions, the same bewitched enslavement to memory, and it insists more upon the supernatural. In Eugene's childhood King's Highway had been "a kind of road that wound from magic out of some dim and haunted land," but he finds it now a common street, and his compulsive return toward the core of the mystery is delayed and made irritable by the contrasts between what he remembers and what really is. Finding the street, the house, the steps, he pauses and looks back "as if the street were Time," and waits "for a word, for a door to open, for the child to come."

But neither the dead nor the child that he himself once was can be recalled so easily. He knows he is close to them. He feels how it is all the same "except for absence, the stained light of absence in the afternoon, and the child who had once sat there, waiting on the stairs." It is as tantalizing as a séance where the ghost is coy. Eugene is near to making contact, but the thing fades and weakens, and he strengthens and deepens the incantation, running over and over the images that come from the past, trying by their repetition to enforce them upon the present. He is at a threshold, and he gives us the contrasted images of the hot backyard and the cool cellar which is the Past, the lost place in Time that he wants now to return to. Now, as then, the thought of the dark cellar fills him "with a kind of numb excitement, a kind of visceral expectancy."

It sharpens and fades for him. He feels that if he could only sit on the stairs as he had long ago "he would be able to get it back again. Then he would be able to remember all that he had seen and been, the brief sum of himself."

He moves closer, inside the house, up to the very door of the room where Grover has died. Now comes Mrs. Bell's occult knowledge that Grover died in that room. Without being told, she knows. The presence is between them, somehow. They feel him.

And suddenly he is evoked and present and palpable. The witch doctor has made the Past real by naming its every particle, chanting and cataloging the memories it is made of. Now he brings up the ghost by the same "name" magic. "Say *Grover!*" the ghost is saying. "No—not Gova—*Grover!* Say it!"

Among many primitive tribes the name is a secret revealed to none, for fear strength and life will be exposed with it. Among organizations as various as street gangs and Catholic sisterhoods the spiritual or special self has its special name. Among the ancient Irish it was a capital crime to put a man by name into a poem, for both poem and name were potent with magic and power could be got over anyone so be-spelled. It is the name that reveals Grover briefly and brings him up from the dark cellar of Time. It is as if, if only the child Eugene could say the name right, Grover might now literally appear. But this attempt to cross between Forever and Now is never more than half successful. The closest we get to Grover's quiet ghost is his little brother's lisping "Gova."

But this is enough. Wolfe's magic, like Eugene's, invokes the ghost briefly and holds him a moment before he fades. The ghost that troubled Eugene, the rival that he loved and half envied, is laid and quieted. The man sick with Time is healed, the voodoo spell is finished, the spirit has spoken its cryptic word and departed. "And out of the enchanted wood, that thicket of man's memory . . . the dark eye and the quiet face of his friend and brother—poor child, life's stranger and life's exile, lost like all of us, a cipher in blind mazes, long ago—the lost boy was gone forever and would not return."

When the ghost has been summoned and held briefly and allowed to fade, the story is over. Ritual and story are one, with one shape. What suspense the story has is the suspense of the growing, circling, nearing incantation. Its climax is the moment of confrontation. Its peculiar emotional power comes from the chanting, the repetition, the ceremonial performances, the magical tampering with Time, the sure touching of symbols that lie deep among the sources of all superstition and all religion, above all by the anguished invocation of the dead. No one who has lived at all with his dead can be left entirely unmoved by this.

Not a line of this story, not a trick in it, could have been learned from any generalization about the shaping of fiction. The shape this story takes it takes by a process of transplantation, associated images and ideas being moved from one category of thought to another. A formal ritual becomes a formal fiction by what William James calls "similar association." Material and form are so nearly one that they can never be effectively separated.

Lois Hartley

22. Theme in Thomas Wolfe's "The Lost Boy" and "God's Lonely Man"

IN Thomas Wolfe's story "The Lost Boy" three related themes are eventually absorbed into what became perhaps the major theme of Wolfe's writing and of his life. The first of these is the theme of change, of the loss of illusions through change, and it is so closely related to the second, the loss of innocence through experience, that the two can only be examined together. The third is the theme of loneliness, and it is with the implications of this theme that I wish ultimately to deal.

One is aware of time, of change, from the first paragraphs of the story when the boy Grover is conscious of the light that "came and went and came again" in the square of Altamont, of the strokes of the town clock booming across the town, of the streetcars on their quarter-hourly schedule. Yet to Grover this is a sort of change without significance, and he is unaware of any more significant kind of change, for he is not yet "the lost boy": "It seemed to him that the Square, itself the accidental masonry of many years, the chance agglomeration of time and of disrupted strivings, was the center of the universe. It was for him, in his soul's picture, the earth's pivot, the granite core of changelessness, the eternal place where all things came and passed, and yet abode forever and would never change."

In the central episode of part one of "The Lost Boy," Grover goes into the candy store of the Crockers to buy candy with stamps given him for running errands. He buys fifteen-cents' worth of candy, but accidentally pays with eighteen-cents' worth of stamps. Crocker refuses to return the three cents in stamps. He and his wife imply that Grover stole the stamps, and put Grover out of the shop. Now "something had gone out of day. He felt the overwhelming, soul-sickening guilt that all the children, all the good men of the earth, have felt since Time began. And even anger had died down, had been drowned out, in this swelling tide of guilt, and 'This is the Square'—thought Grover as before—'This is Now. There is my father's shop. And all of it is as it has always been—save I.' " Through time and experience Grover has changed. He is now the lost boy. He has learned something about separateness, about isolation, about inhumanity; and perhaps Grover's feeling of guilt is a symptom of this failure in fellowship.

The lost boy moves across the square to his father's stonecutter's shop; it may be significant that he passes the "angel with strong marble hands of love." Grover intends to maintain deliberately a sort of separation from his father, for he fears that his father will hear of the Crockers' accusation. Then suddenly he finds himself blurting, "Papa, I never stole the stamps." Gant's nearly immediate action is to take Grover to Crocker's shop and to demand repayment. Then Grover is alone again in the square: "And light came and went and came again —but now not quite the same as it had done before. The boy saw the pattern of familiar shapes and knew that they were just the same as they had always been. But something had gone out of day, and something had come in again. Out of the vision of those quiet eyes some brightness had gone, and into their vision had come some deeper color. He could not say, he did not know through what transforming shadows life had passed within that quarter hour. He only knew that something had been lost—something forever gained." Grover has lost something of innocence; he has gained in experience and knowledge.

If this first episode of the story says something tentatively about time and change, it says something more about isolation, about loneliness. In the autobiographical essay "God's Lonely Man," which appeared with "The Lost Boy" in the volume *The Hills Beyond* (1941) but which was begun perhaps seven years previously, Wolfe said:

> The whole conviction of my life now rests upon the belief that loneliness, far from being a rare and curious phenomenon, peculiar to myself and to a few other solitary men, is the central and inevitable fact of human existence. When we examine the moments, acts, and statements of all kinds of people—not only the grief and ecstasy of the greatest poets, but also the huge unhappiness of the

average soul, as evidenced by the innumerable strident words of abuse, hatred, contempt, mistrust, and scorn that forever grate upon our ears as the manswarm passes us in the streets—we find, I think, that they are all suffering from the same thing. The final cause of their complaint is loneliness.

Grover, the "dark-eyed and grave," the "too quiet and too listening" boy, is like Wolfe himself in that "there are times when anything, everything, all or nothing, the most trivial incidents, the most casual words" can strip him of defenses, can plunge him into despair, can take from him hope and joy and truth. They can show him his separateness and yet send him searchingly to his father, who also has lonely eyes and who is immediately responsive to his son, but whose indignation surely has an element of failure in it as he lashes at Crocker: "You never knew the feelings of a father, or understood the feelings of a child; and that is why you acted as you did. But a judgment is upon you. God has cursed you. He has afflicted you. He has made you lame and childless as you are—and lame and childless, miserable as you are, you will go to your grave and be forgotten!" There is a loneliness too in the light that came and went, in the strokes of the town clock, even in the "His Master's Voice" dog, in the music-store window, listening to the silent horn, listening for the unspeaking voice.

In parts two and three of "The Lost Boy," the mother, Eliza Gant, and the sister remember Grover, but they reveal also their nostalgia regarding time and change and disillusionment. The tone for these sections is partially set by the poetic refrain playing variations on the final line of part one: "Just then a buggy curved out through the Square, and fastened to the rear end was a poster, and it said 'St. Louis' and 'Excursion' and 'The Fair.'"

Years after the family went to the St. Louis Fair, the Exposition of 1904, the mother remembers "all of you the way you looked that morning, when we went down down through Indiana, going to the Fair." Her children have all grown up and gone away, and she says she is proud of them all, but she adores in memory grave and earnest, curious and intelligent Grover. He is for her, paradoxically, the symbol of all that has changed, of all who have either died or gone away, and yet of the changeless, because he is fixed forever in memory as he was "that morning when we went down through Indiana, by the river, to the Fair." The mother has known change and loss, and even in the words of her refrain there is a loneliness.

In part three Wolfe emphasizes the sister's disillusionment and her bewilderment in the face of time and change. She too remembers Grover and the summer of the Fair, the summer when Grover died of typhoid; she remembers also her lost ambitions—to be a famous pianist, to be an opera star:

> All my hopes and dreams and big ambitions have come to nothing, and it's all so long ago, as if it happened in another world. . . . Sometimes I lie awake at night and think of all the people who have come and gone, and how everything is different from the way we thought that it would be. Then I go out on the street next day and see the faces of the people that I pass. . . . Don't you see something funny in people's eyes, as if all of them were puzzled about something? As if they were wondering what had happened to them since they were kids? Wondering what it is that they have lost?

She feels the separateness and yet the likeness of people, who all lose something, who all reach points other than those of their dreams. And again there is a loss of innocence, a nostalgia regarding time and change, and a loneliness comprehending them both.

The fourth and final section of the story describes the brother Eugene's return to St. Louis, many years later, in search of the magic of the past and particularly in search of the "lost boy." Here change through time and loss of innocence are strongly dramatized. Eugene finds the house of that summer of the Fair very much the same, but the feeling is different and he himself is different, and different too is the magic street, the King's Highway, which "had not been a street in those days but a kind of road that wound from magic out of some dim and haunted land, and that along the way . . . got mixed in with Tom the Piper's son, with hot cross buns, with all the light that came and went, and with coming down through Indiana in the morning, and the smell of engine smoke, the Union Station, and most of all with voices lost and far and long ago that said 'King's Highway.'" In the change in the King's Highway, which is now just a street, in the absence of Grover, in the absence of the child he himself used to be, in the fact that "as a child he had sat there feeling things were *Some-*

where—and now he *knew*," Eugene is aware of time and change and the effect of experience.

And above all there is the mood of loneliness, of remembered loneliness and present loneliness. He remembers how, as a boy, he felt "a kind of absence in the afternoon" after the streetcar had passed, "a sense of absence and vague sadness" in the afternoons when he sat alone in the house, on the hall steps, and listened to the silence; he remembers how he waited in loneliness for the return of Grover and the family from the Fair. But his present loneliness is more inclusive and more sophisticated. He knows the summer desolation of the great American cities; he knows the desolation, the separateness

> that one feels at the end of a hot day in a great city in America— when one's home is far away, across the continent, and he thinks of all that distance, all that heat, and feels, "Oh God! but it's a big country!" And he feels nothing but absence, absence, and the desolation of America, the loneliness and sadness of the high, hot skies, and evening coming on across the Middle West, across the sweltering and heat-sunken land, across all the lonely little towns, the farms, the fields.

He feels that he should not have come and must not come again, that lost magic is forever lost, that his brother was "life's stranger, and life's exile, lost like all of us, a cipher in blind mazes." And he himself seems "drowned in desolation and in no belief."

If the prevailing mood of "The Lost Boy" is loneliness, then the story should be examined in the light of "God's Lonely Man," Wolfe's tragic and definitive statement on his own loneliness. First, we should be aware that he sees loneliness as "the central and inevitable fact of human existence" and that he knows that it is sometimes evidenced in such ways as the mistrust and meanness of Crocker and the shrill words of scorn of Gant. He knows that men are both cursed and blessed by separateness, for he has learned that upon the doubt and despair of loneliness may be built the triumph and joy of creativity.

In "God's Lonely Man" Wolfe has much to say about the Old Testament as the chronicle of loneliness and the New Testament as an answer to loneliness through love, but although he says that "the way and meaning of Christ's life is a far, far better way and meaning than my own," he repudiates it as his own way: "For I have found the constant everlasting weather of man's life to be, not love, but loneliness. Love itself is not the weather of our lives. It is the rare, the precious flower. Sometimes it is the flower that gives us life. . . . But sometimes love is the flower that brings us death." In "The Lost Boy" love is present—the love of Eugene, particularly, for life; the love of all the family for Grover, although this feeling sometimes appears to be better described as pride than love. But love is not presented as a solution and is not pervasive. It must not be emphasized as a theme in the story nor inferred as a solution to the loneliness, the separateness. No solution is given.

In "The Lost Boy" Eugene seems "drowned in desolation and in no belief," and in "God's Lonely Man" Wolfe, himself a lonely man, "is united to no image save that which he creates himself, . . . is bolstered by no other knowledge save that which he can gather for himself with the vision of his own eyes and brain. He is sustained and cheered and aided by no party, he is given comfort by no creed, he has no faith in him except his own." It is in this sense that "God's Lonely Man" is a tragic statement, for although such independence may be heroic and Promethean, such denial of dependence implies a tragedy of misunderstanding. And even when Wolfe asserts that "suddenly, one day, for no apparent reason, his faith and his belief in life will come back to [the lonely man] in a tidal flood," we wish that it would come back for an apparent reason, that it might be the result of the re-ascendancy of reason and judgment, or of the healthful wedding of judgment and feeling.

Yet his faith in life does come back, and he is compelled to speak whatever truth he knows, in his renewed confidence; and among the truths which Wolfe speaks, out of his loneliness, is that "the lonely man, who is also the tragic man, is invariably the man who loves life dearly—which is to say, the joyful man." Like Eugene in "The Lost Boy," he knows loneliness, death, time, change: "Out of this pain of loss, this bitter ecstasy of brief having, this fatal glory of the single moment, the tragic writer will therefore make a song for joy. . . . And his song is full of grief, because he knows that joy is fleeting, gone the instant that we have it, and that is why it is so precious, gaining its full glory from the very things that limit and destroy it." These lines from "God's Lonely Man" may be taken as a description of "The Lost Boy," for surely this story describes the pain of loss, the bitter ecstasy of brief having, and it is a song for joy at the same time that it is a cry of grief.

Wolfe's treatment of the theme of loneliness is detailed and thoughtful. And since this theme appears to be highly characteristic of modern American literature and thought, Wolfe's statement is meaningful for us all.

Edward A. Bloom

23. Critical Commentary on "Only the Dead Know Brooklyn"

UNTIL THE concluding paragraphs, the story has what might be taken for a clear enough literal meaning. That is, we read a rather amusing account of an experience in Brooklyn, a well-tried subject. But the literal, we discover, does not carry us very far. What does simple paraphrase reveal? A stranger in Brooklyn looking for a location asks some natives for directions. None can agree on the location or a way of getting there, and they quarrel among themselves. Ironically, although they have lived in Brooklyn all their lives and pride themselves on their familiarity with the city, they do not have this particular information.

It is then that the truculent first-person narrator takes over, tries to guide the stranger and fails. But at the same time he has the irrepressible curiosity of the legendary Brooklynite, and pumps the stranger to discover his motives. The narrator learns—to his intense surprise—that the unnamed stranger habitually wanders around Brooklyn with a map, looking for places that have pleasant-sounding names. Suddenly, without forewarning, the stranger asks the narrator (also unnamed) whether he can swim, and whether he has ever seen a drowning. The story ends on this puzzling note and the narrator, with justification, considers the incident one of some lunacy. For such peculiar things simply do not happen in Brooklyn.

Before we consider the actual meaning, point, or significance of the story, let us look at the fundamental details of technique.

MOOD. Although we may choose to identify Wolfe with the stranger, the author at no time exposes his private personality. Rather, he permits two unidentified characters to carry the entire emotional and intellectual burden. The feeling of the story thus becomes fairly complex, even ambivalent. The stranger evokes a mood of wistfulness and sympathy. We can appreciate the esthetic hunger which drives him. Simultaneously, though we respect his yearning, we wonder whether the discovery is ever as rich as the anticipation. These are emotional details implied in the dialogue between protagonist and antagonist. The antithesis of the stranger is the narrator—commonplace, literal, irascible, and yet kindly. He intensifies a feeling of futility because of his banal repudiation of the search for beauty. The mood, then, combines sadness and frustration with provincial humor and unresolved optimism for the stranger's success.

TONE. By subtle means the author is able to assert his attitude toward the reader. First he warns us in the title that only the dead know Brooklyn. Then he draws attention to normal impatience with idealistic, impractical quests such as the stranger's. Consequently, Wolfe implies the confusion and crudity of the vast area in which the search takes place. Toward this end he relies upon the aimless arguments of the anonymous speakers, who are like disembodied voices representative of ordinary mankind. Contrasting with this disorder is the map to which the stranger refers throughout the story. Presumably a symbol of order and stability, this manmade device is hopelessly misleading. Wolfe appears to say that the individual really has nothing material to guide him in his groping for values; only innate desire can direct him toward knowledge and beauty, which cannot be charted on a map: note the random (if esthetically motivated) manner in which the stranger selects the places he will visit.

Looking for an ultimate truth which he cannot readily isolate, he nevertheless persists. Each new place that he visits may provide him with the insight he seeks, so he must continue to roam about. Indeed, to cease striving, to endure the atrophy of the sense of wonder and inquiry—as the narrator has done—is to perish. Once the stranger hits upon the notion of drowning, it becomes a disturbing metaphor to connote human failure. The word "drowning" offers a significant clue to the tone of the story, because as a form of suffocation, drowning can be incorporeal as well as physical. The literal-minded narrator responds to the stranger as though he were talking about physical death. But the latter is not concerned here with physical death, only with that other death, the wasting away of the spirit. Although the stranger's attitude must be inferred, the inference follows logically from his consistent inattention to mundane matters. While the narrator returns to his world of actuality, the stranger pursues his ineffable search. In Brooklyn, where physical drowning is an impractical feat, the stranger consults his map and contemplates another kind of smothering. From his depiction of these men at cross-purposes, Wolfe has established tone in a twofold way: 1) to show us the aimlessness and inner bankruptcy of ordinary life; 2) to admonish and warn us against surrendering to spiritual and esthetic indifference.

Tone and mood are closely bound in with theme. The search for order, beauty, and individuality, it is suggested, may indeed be fruitless but must never be abandoned. Striving for positive values, one must also contend with ugliness and ignorance, for the good and the bad coexist. Yet that there can be no guarantee of success is implied in the ironical title. The dead are those who, like the narrator, have physically survived the material confusion and stifling effects of existence. Their survival, however, has depended upon an unquestioning attitude, one that is antithetical to the ultimate truth sought by the stranger. If people like the narrator are alive physically, the stranger's questions appear to disclose, they are dead spiritually. They know Brooklyn—which is life—only on the confused surface, and fragmentarily at that. The stranger, therefore, is left with a riddle of the disparity between material appearance and its hidden meaning. His own resolution of the riddle is left unstated, but we may assume that he will continue his search for answers.

Against the very real backdrop of Brooklyn, the atmosphere is paradoxically hazy and unrealistic. It emerges as a pervasive feeling of futility and impersonality—possibly an overwhelming challenge to individualism. Wolfe withholds names from his characters, who—as in allegory—are representative of society, of everyman. The conflict is not between flesh-and-blood people but between concepts: the restless individual search for the bluebird and the passivity of acceptance. The struggle is one between a broad idea of absorptive materialism and threatened ideals. The surface humor of the dialect turns to bitter realization through our awareness of the complete absence of humor in the situation. There is, indeed, a sense of tragedy, enlarged by the blindness of the narrator to his own loss of individuality.

Except for superficial details, everything in this story is implicit. Wolfe does not tell us through any direct means the exact nature of the problem with which he is concerned. Nor does he develop his characters explicitly. Everything must come out through dialogue or through the rational process of the narrator's puzzlement. Only by inference do we discover Wolfe's allegorical intention of representing Brooklyn as modern confused society which suffocates individuality. By inference also we recognize that for most people this state of suffocation is acceptable, while those who resist are stigmatized as outsiders and eccentrics.

Maurice Beebe
and Leslie A. Field

Criticism of Thomas Wolfe:
A Selected Checklist

NOTE: Because the fiction of Thomas Wolfe is most frequently seen as one continuous story, we have not attempted to provide an index to studies of individual works. Instead, we have made a single alphabetical list of the more important biographical, critical, and scholarly studies. Titles of major books on Wolfe are capitalized. Books and essays by the same writer are listed in chronological order. We have omitted foreign criticism, unpublished theses or dissertations, transient reviews, and routine discussions in encyclopedias, handbooks, and histories of literature. Our list covers materials through 1965; a more complete list of pre-1959 materials on Wolfe may be found in the bibliography by Elmer D. Johnson cited below. Essays and excerpts which appear in this present collection are noted by an asterisk.

Adams, Agatha Boyd. "Thomas Wolfe at Chapel Hill," *Carolina Quarterly,* II (Dec., 1949), 21–29.
———. "Thomas Wolfe: The Friendliness of a Lonely Man," *Carolina Quarterly,* II (May, 1950), 16–22.
———. THOMAS WOLFE: CAROLINA STUDENT/A BRIEF BIOGRAPHY. Chapel Hill: University of North Carolina Library, 1950.
Albrecht, W. P. "Time as Unity in the Novels of Thomas Wolfe," *New Mexico Quarterly Review,* XIX (Autumn, 1949), 320–29. Reprinted as "Time as Unity in Thomas Wolfe" in Walser, ed., *The Enigma of Thomas Wolfe,* pp. 239–48.

———. "The Title of 'Look Homeward, Angel,'" *Modern Language Quarterly*, XI (March, 1950), 50–57.

Angoff, Charles. "Thomas Wolfe and the Opulent Manner," *Southwest Review*, XLVIII (Winter, 1963), 81–84.

Anonymous. "Literary Estate," *New Yorker*, XXXII (Feb. 9, 1957), 24–26.

———. "The Colossus of Asheville," *Times Literary Supplement*, No. 2952 (Sept. 26, 1958), p. 544.

Armstrong, Anne W. "As I Saw Thomas Wolfe," *Arizona Quarterly*, II (Spring, 1946), 5–14.

Aswell, Edward C. "Thomas Wolfe's Unpublished Works," *Carolina Magazine*, XLVIII (Oct., 1938), 19–20.

*———. "A Note on Thomas Wolfe," in Wolfe's *The Hills Beyond*. New York: Harper and Brothers, 1941. Pp. 349–86. Partly reprinted as Introduction to Wolfe's *You Can't Go Home Again* (Harper's Modern Classics, 1949) and in Holman, ed., *The World of Thomas Wolfe*, pp. 45–48.

———. "En Route to a Legend," *Saturday Review*, XXI (Nov. 27, 1948), 7, 34–36. Also published as Introduction to Wolfe's *The Adventures of Young Gant* (New York: New American Library, 1948) and reprinted in Walser, ed., *The Enigma of Thomas Wolfe*, pp. 103–108.

———. "Thomas Wolfe Did Not Kill Maxwell Perkins," *Saturday Review*, XXXIV (Oct. 6, 1951), 16–17, 44–46.

———. "Note on a Western Journey," in Wolfe's *A Western Journal*. University of Pittsburgh Press, 1951. Pp. v–vi.

———. "Thomas Wolfe: The Playwright Who Discovered He Wasn't," in Ketti Frings's *Look Homeward, Angel: A Play Based on the Novel by Thomas Wolfe*. New York: Scribner's, 1958. Pp. [3–5].

Baker, Carlos. "Thomas Wolfe's Apprenticeship," *Delphian Quarterly*, XXIII (Jan., 1940), 20–25.

Barber, Philip W. "Tom Wolfe Writes a Play," *Harper's Magazine*, CCXVI (May, 1958), 71–76.

Basso, Hamilton. "Thomas Wolfe," in Malcolm Cowley, ed., *After the Genteel Tradition: American Writers Since 1910*. New York: W. W. Norton & Company, Inc., 1937. Pp. 202–12.

Bates, Ernest S. "Thomas Wolfe," *English Journal*, XXVI (Sept., 1937), 519–27.

———. "Thomas Wolfe," *Modern Quarterly*, XI (Fall, 1938), 86–88.

Beach, Joseph Warren. *American Fiction, 1920–1940.* New York:
The Macmillan Company, 1941. Pp. 173–215. Partly reprinted in
Holman, ed., *The World of Thomas Wolfe,* pp. 96–100.

Beja, Morris. "Why You Can't Go Home Again: Thomas Wolfe and
'The Escapes of Time and Memory,'" *Modern Fiction Studies,* XI
(Autumn, 1965), 297–314.

Bell, Alladine. "T. Wolfe of 10 Montague Terrace," *Antioch Review,*
XX (Fall, 1960), 315–30.

Benét, Stephen Vincent. "Thomas Wolfe's Torrent of Recollection,"
Saturday Review, XXI (Sept. 21, 1940), 5. Reprinted as "A Torrent
of Recollection" in Walser, ed., *The Enigma of Thomas Wolfe,*
pp. 154–57.

Bentinck-Smith, William. "The Legend of Thomas Wolfe," *Harvard
Alumni Bulletin,* L (Nov. 22, 1947), 210–14.

Bernstein, Aline. "Eugene," in her *Three Blue Suits.* New York:
Equinox Cooperative Press, 1933. Pp. 49–74. [A short story based
on her relationship with Wolfe.]

———. *The Journey Down.* New York: Alfred A. Knopf, Inc., 1938.
[A novel.]

———. *An Actor's Daughter.* New York: Alfred A. Knopf, Inc., 1941.

Bishop, Donald E. "Thomas Wolfe," *The New Carolina Magazine*
(March, 1942), pp. 28–29, 35, 47–48. Reprinted as "Tom Wolfe as
Student" in Walser, ed., *The Enigma of Thomas Wolfe,* pp. 8–17.

Bishop, John Peale. "The Myth and Modern Literature," *Saturday
Review,* XX (July 22, 1939), 3–4, 14. Reprinted in *The Collected
Essays of John Peale Bishop,* ed. Edmund Wilson (New York:
Charles Scribner's Sons, 1948), pp. 127–28.

———. "The Sorrows of Thomas Wolfe," *Kenyon Review,* I (Winter,
1939), 7–17. Reprinted in his *Collected Essays,* pp. 129–37; John
Crowe Ransom, ed., *The Kenyon Critics* (Cleveland: The World
Publishing Company, 1951), pp. 3–12; John W. Aldridge, ed.,
Critiques and Essays on Modern Fiction (New York: The Ronald
Press Company, 1952), pp. 362–69; Philip Rahv, ed., *Literature in
America* (New York: World Publishing Co. [Meridian Books],
1958), pp. 391–99; A. Walton Litz, ed., *Modern American Fiction:
Essays in Criticism* (New York: Oxford University Press Inc.,
1963), pp. 256–64. Partly reprinted in Holman, ed., *The World
of Thomas Wolfe,* pp. 92–95.

Blackmur, R. P. "Notes on the Novel," *Southern Review,* I (Spring,
1936), 898–99. Reprinted in his *Expense of Greatness* (New York:
Arrow Editions, 1940).

*Bloom, Edward. "Critical Commentary on 'Only the Dead Know Brooklyn,'" in his *The Order of Fiction: An Introduction*. New York: The Odyssey Press, Inc., 1964. Pp. 143–46.

Blythe, LeGette. "The Thomas Wolfe I Knew," *Saturday Review*, XXXVIII (Aug. 25, 1945), 18–19.

Bowden, Edwin T. *The Dungeon of the Heart: Human Isolation and the American Novel*. New York: The Macmillan Company, 1961. Pp. 66–71.

Boyle, Thomas E. "Thomas Wolfe: Theme Through Imagery," *Modern Fiction Studies*, XI (Autumn, 1965), 259–68.

Boynton, Percy H. *America in Contemporary Fiction*. University of Chicago Press, 1940. Pp. 204–24.

Bradbury, John M. *Renaissance in the South: A Critical History of the Literature, 1920–1960*. Chapel Hill: University of North Carolina Press, 1963. Pp. 92–94.

Braham, Lionel. "Wolfean Baby Talk," *American Speech*, XXXI (Dec., 1956), 302–03.

Braswell, William. "Thomas Wolfe Lectures and Takes a Holiday," *College English*, I (Oct., 1939), 11–22. Reprinted in Braswell and Field, eds., *Thomas Wolfe's Purdue Speech . . .* , pp. 117–29, and in Walser, ed., *The Enigma of Thomas Wolfe*, pp. 64–76.

———. "Introduction," *The Web and the Rock*. (New York: Harper's Modern Classics, 1958), pp. ix–xix.

*———, and Field, Leslie A. (eds.). THOMAS WOLFE'S PURDUE SPEECH: "WRITING AND LIVING," Lafayette, Indiana: Purdue University Studies, 1964.

Bridgers, Emily. "Thomas Wolfe," in her *The South in Fiction*. Chapel Hill: University of North Carolina Press, 1948. Pp. 42–44.

Brodin, Pierre. *Thomas Wolfe*, translated by Imogene Riddick with Introduction by Richard Walser. Asheville, North Carolina: The Stephens Press, 1949.

Brown, E. K. "Thomas Wolfe: Realist and Symbolist," *University of Toronto Quarterly*, X (Jan., 1941), 153–66. Reprinted in Walser, ed., *The Enigma of Thomas Wolfe*, pp. 206–21.

Brown, John Mason. "Thomas Wolfe as a Dramatist," in his *Broadway in Review*, New York: W. W. Norton & Company, Inc., 1940. Pp. 282–86.

———. *Still Seeing Things*, New York: McGraw-Hill, Inc., 1950. Pp. 39–40, 43–45, 285.

Buchanan, Kenneth C. "Thomas Wolfe," *Bluets*, XX (1947), 10–12.

Budd, Louis J. "The Grotesques of Anderson and Wolfe," *Modern Fiction Studies,* V (Winter, 1959–1960), 304–10.

Burger, Nash K. "A Story To Tell: Agee, Wolfe, Faulkner," *South Atlantic Quarterly,* LXIII (Winter, 1964), 32–43.

Burgum, Edwin Berry. "Thomas Wolfe's Discovery of America," *Virginia Quarterly,* XXII (Summer, 1946), 421–37. Reprinted in his *The Novel and the World's Dilemma* (New York: Oxford University Press, 1947), pp. 302–21; and Walser, ed., *The Enigma of Thomas Wolfe,* pp. 179–94. Partly reprinted in Holman, ed., *The World of Thomas Wolfe,* pp. 115–19.

Burlingame, Roger. *Of Making Many Books.* New York: Scribner's, 1946. Pp. 40–42, 169–90, 324–26.

Burt, Struthers. "Catalyst for Genius: Maxwell Perkins," *Saturday Review,* XXXIV (June 9, 1951), 6–8, 36–39.

———. "Wolfe and Perkins," *Saturday Review,* XXXIV (Aug. 11, 1951), 22–25.

Cameron, May. "An Interview with Thomas Wolfe," *New York Post* (March 14, 1936). Reprinted in *Press Time* (1936), pp. 247–52.

Canby, Henry Seidel. "The River of Youth," in his *Seven Years' Harvest.* New York: Farrar and Rinehart, 1936. Pp. 163–70. Reprinted in Walser, ed., *The Enigma of Thomas Wolfe,* pp. 133–39.

———. "Literary Gymnastics," in his *American Memoir.* Boston: Houghton Mifflin Company, 1947. Pp. 330–38.

*Cargill, Oscar. "Gargantua Fills His Skin," *University of Kansas City Review,* XVI (Autumn, 1949), 20–30.

———. "Introduction," Thomas Clark Pollock and Oscar Cargill, *Thomas Wolfe at Washington Square.* New York: New York University Press, 1954. Pp. 3–84.

———, and Pollock, Thomas Clark (eds.). THE CORRESPONDENCE OF THOMAS WOLFE AND HOMER ANDREW WATT. New York: New York University Press, 1954.

Carpenter, Frederic I. "Thomas Wolfe: The Autobiography of an Idea," *University of Kansas City Review,* XII (Spring, 1946), 179–87. Reprinted in his *American Literature and the Dream* (New York: Philosophical Library, 1955), pp. 155–66.

Cassill, R. V. "The Wolfe Revival," *Western Review,* XVI (Summer, 1952), 337.

Chamberlain, John. *"Look Homeward, Angel," Bookman,* LXX (Dec., 1929), 449–50. Reprinted in Louis D. Rubin, Jr. and John Rees Moore, eds., *The Idea of an American Novel* (New York: Crowell, 1961), pp. 344–46.

Chase, Richard. "Introduction," *The Web and the Rock* (New York: Dell Books, 1960), pp. 7–19. Reprinted in Dell edition of *You Can't Go Home Again,* 1960.

Chittick, V. L. O. "Thomas Wolfe's Farthest West," *Southwest Review,* XLVIII (Spring, 1963), 93–110.

*Church, Margaret. "Thomas Wolfe: Dark Time (and Proust)," *PMLA,* LXIV (Sept., 1949), 629–38. Reprinted in her *Time and Reality: Studies in Contemporary Fiction* (Chapel Hill: University of North Carolina Press, 1963), pp. 207–26; and as "Dark Time" in Walser, ed., *The Enigma of Thomas Wolfe,* pp. 249–62.

*Clements, Clyde C. "Symbolic Patterns in *You Can't Go Home Again,*" *Modern Fiction Studies,* XI (Autumn, 1965), 286–96.

Collins, Thomas Lyle. "Thomas Wolfe," *Sewanee Review,* L (Oct., 1942), 487–504. Reprinted as "Wolfe's Genius vs. His Critics" in Walser, ed., *The Enigma of Thomas Wolfe,* pp. 161–78.

Colton, Gerald B. "Talking About Reading Thomas Wolfe," *The Assistant Librarian,* XLVIII (Aug., 1955), 135–38.

Commager, Henry Steele. *The American Mind.* New Haven: Yale University Press, 1950. Pp. 267–68. Reprinted in Holman, ed., *The World of Thomas Wolfe,* pp. 139–140.

Coughlan, Robert. "Tom Wolfe's Surge to Greatness," *Life,* XLI (Sept. 17, 1956), 178–96.

———. "Grand Vision: A Final Tragedy," *Life,* XLI (Sept. 24, 1956), 168–84.

Cowley, Malcolm. "Thomas Wolfe's Legacy," *New Republic,* XCIX (July 19, 1939), 311–12.

———. "Wolfe and the Lost People," *New Republic,* CV (Nov. 3, 1941), 592–94.

———. "Maxwell Perkins," *New Yorker,* XX (April 8, 1944), 30–43.

———. "Twenty-Five Years After—The Lost Generation Today," *Saturday Review,* XXXIV (June 2, 1951), 6–7, 33–34.

———. "The Life and Death of Thomas Wolfe," *New Republic,* CXXXV (Nov. 19, 1956), 17–21.

———. "Thomas Wolfe," *Atlantic,* CC (Nov., 1957), 202–12. Reprinted in Holman, ed., *The World of Thomas Wolfe,* pp. 167–74.

———. "Miserly Millionaire of Words," *Reporter,* XVI (Feb. 7, 1957), 38–40.

———. "Sherwood Anderson's Epiphanies," *London Magazine,* VII (July, 1960), 61–66.

Cross, Neal, "Thomas Wolfe: If I Am Not Better," *Pacific Spectator,* IV (Autumn, 1950), 488–96.

Culver, John W. "Thomas Wolfe," *Andean Quarterly* (Summer, 1945), pp. 61–66.

Curley, Thomas F. "Thomas Wolfe: Novelist of the Normal," *Commonweal,* LXV (Nov. 23, 1956), 209–11.

Daniels, Jonathan. "Poet of the Boom," in his *Tar Heels.* New York: Dodd, Mead & Company, 1941. Pp. 218–35. Reprinted in Walser, ed., *The Enigma of Thomas Wolfe,* pp. 77–90.

————. *Thomas Wolfe: October Recollections.* Columbia, South Carolina: Bostwick and Thornley, 1961. [Pamphlet.]

Davenport, Basil. "C'est Maitre François," *Saturday Review,* VI (Dec. 21, 1929), 584. Reprinted in Holman, ed., *The World of Thomas Wolfe,* pp. 54–56.

Delakas, Daniel. "Thomas Wolfe and Anatole France: A Study of Some Unpublished Fragments," *Comparative Literature,* IX (Winter, 1957), 33–50.

*DeVoto, Bernard. "Genius Is Not Enough," *Saturday Review,* XIII (April 25, 1936), 3–4, 14–15. Reprinted in his *Forays and Rebuttals* (Boston: Little, Brown and Company, 1936); Holman, ed., *The World of Thomas Wolfe,* pp. 86–90; and Walser, ed., *The Enigma of Thomas Wolfe,* pp. 140–48.

————. "English '37," *Saturday Review,* XVI (Aug. 7, 1937), 8, 14.

————. "American Novels, 1939," *Atlantic,* CLXV (Jan., 1940), 69–71.

————. *The World of Fiction.* Boston: Houghton Mifflin Company, 1950. Pp. 85, 161, 260–64. Partly reprinted in Holman, ed., *The World of Thomas Wolfe,* pp. 72–74, 91.

Dodd, Martha. *Through Embassy Eyes.* New York: Harcourt, Brace, 1939. Pp. 89–95.

Dow, Robert. "And Gladly Teche . . . ," in Pollock and Cargill, *Thomas Wolfe at Washington Square,* pp. 104–107.

Downing, Susan. "Thomas Wolfe: Point of View in Autobiographical Fiction," *Lit,* No. 6 (Spring, 1965), 50–55.

Doyle, A. Gerald. "Drunk with Words," in Pollock and Cargill, *Thomas Wolfe at Washington Square,* pp. 87–89.

Dykeman, Wilma. "The Chateau and the Boarding House," in her *The French Broad.* New York: Holt, Rinehart and Winston, Inc., 1955. Pp. 210–27.

Eaton, Clement. "Student Days with Thomas Wolfe," *Georgia Review,* XVII (Summer, 1963), 146–55.

Evans, Robert O. "Wolfe's Use of *Iliad,* I, 49," *Modern Language Notes,* LXX (Dec., 1955), 594–96.

Fadiman, Clifton. *"The Web and the Rock,"* New Yorker, XV (June 24, 1939), 82–84. Reprinted in Walser, ed., *The Enigma of Thomas Wolfe,* pp. 149–53.

——. "The Wolfe at the Door," in his *Party of One.* New York: The World Publishing Company, 1955. Pp. 455–60. Reprinted in Holman, ed., *The World of Thomas Wolfe,* pp. 37–39, and as "Of Nothing and the Wolfe" in Robert P. Falk, ed., *The Antic Muse: American Literature in Parody* (New York: Grove Press, 1955), pp. 266–70.

Fagin, N. Bryllion. "In Search of an American *Cherry Orchard,"* Texas Quarterly, I (Summer-Autumn, 1958), 132–44.

Falk, Robert. "Thomas Wolfe and the Critics," *College English,* V (Jan., 1944), 186–92.

Field, Leslie A. "Wolfe's Use of Folklore," *New York Folklore Quarterly,* XVI (Autumn, 1960), 203–15.

*——. *"The Hills Beyond:* A Folk Novel of America." [Revision of above for this collection.]

Fisher, Vardis. "My Experiences with Thomas Wolfe," *Tomorrow,* X (April, 1951), 24–30. Reprinted in Pollock and Cargill, *Thomas Wolfe at Washington Square,* pp. 127–45, and as "Thomas Wolfe as I Knew Him" in his *Thomas Wolfe as I Knew Him and Other Essays* (Denver: Alan Swallow, 1963), pp. 24–41.

——. "Thomas Wolfe and Maxwell Perkins," *Tomorrow,* X (July, 1951), 20–25. Reprinted in his *Thomas Wolfe as I Knew Him and Other Essays,* pp. 42–55.

Forrey, Robert. "Whitman to Wolfe," *Mainstream,* XIII (1960), 19–27.

Foster, Ruel E. "Fabulous Tom Wolfe," *University of Kansas City Review,* XXIII (June, 1957), 260–64.

Frenz, Horst. "A German Home for *Mannerhouse,"* Theatre Arts, XL (August, 1956), 62–63, 95.

Frere, A. S. "My Friend Thomas Wolfe," *Books and Bookmen* (Sept., 1958), p. 15.

Frings, Ketti. "O Lost! At Midnight!" *Theatre Arts,* XLII (Feb., 1958), 30–31, 91.

Frohock, W. M. "Thomas Wolfe: Of Time and Neurosis," *Southwest Review,* XXXIII (Autumn, 1948), 349–60. Reprinted as "Thomas Wolfe: Time and the National Neurosis" in his *The Novel of Violence in America,* Second Edition (Dallas: Southern Methodist University Press, 1957), pp. 52–68, and as "Of Time and Neurosis" in Walser, ed., *The Enigma of Thomas Wolfe,* pp. 222–38.

Geismar, Maxwell. "Thomas Wolfe: The Unfound Door," in his *Writers in Crisis: The American Novel Between Two Wars*. Boston: Houghton Mifflin Company, 1942. Pp. 187–235. Partly reprinted as "Diary of a Provincial" in Walser, ed., *The Enigma of Thomas Wolfe*, pp. 109–19.

————. "Thomas Wolfe: The Hillman and the Furies," *Yale Review*, XXXV (Summer, 1946), 649–65.

————. "A Cycle of Fiction," in Robert E. Spiller and others, eds., *Literary History of the United States*. New York: The Macmillan Company, 1948. Vol. II, pp. 1309–11. Reprinted in Holman, ed., *The World of Thomas Wolfe*, pp. 133–35.

————. "Thomas Wolfe," in his *American Moderns: From Rebellion to Conformity*. New York: Hill and Wang, 1958. Pp. 119–44.

———— (ed.). *The Portable Thomas Wolfe*. New York: The Viking Press, Inc., 1946. Geismar's Introduction is included in his *American Moderns*, pp. 119–39.

Gelfant, Blanche Housman. *The American City Novel*. Norman: University of Oklahoma Press, 1954. Pp. 119–32. Partly reprinted in Holman, ed., *The World of Thomas Wolfe*, pp. 153–56.

George, Daniel (ed.). *Selected Letters*, by Thomas Wolfe. Introduction by Elizabeth Nowell. London: William Heinemann Ltd. 1958.

Golden, Harry. "Thomas Wolfe," *Carolina Israelite*, XIV (Sept.-Oct., 1956), 3.

Gossett, Louise Y. *Violence in Recent Southern Fiction*. Durham, North Carolina: Duke University Press, 1965. Pp. 5–16.

Gray, James. "Forever Panting and Forever Young," in his *On Second Thought*. Minneapolis: University of Minnesota Press, 1946. Pp. 98–110.

Greenblatt, William. "Thomas Wolfe: An Appreciation," *City College Monthly* (May, 1939), pp. 5–8, 24–25.

Gurko, Leo. *The Angry Decade*. New York: Dodd, Mead & Company, 1947. Pp. 28–32, 148–70.

Halperin, Irving. "Faith as Dilemma in Thomas Wolfe," *Prairie Schooner*, XXVII (Summer, 1953), 213–17.

————. " 'Torrential Production': Thomas Wolfe's Writing Practices," *Arizona Quarterly*, XIV (Spring, 1958), 29–34.

*————. "Wolfe's *Of Time and the River*," *Explicator*, XVIII (Nov., 1959), Item 9.

————. "Hunger for Life: Thomas Wolfe, a Young Faust," *American-German Review*, XXX (Aug.-Sept., 1964), 12–14, 31.

Hamblen, Abigail Ann. "Ruth Suckow and Thomas Wolfe: A Study in Similarity," *Forum* (Houston), III (Winter, 1961), 27–31.

Harris, Arthur S., Jr. "The House on Spruce Street," *Antioch Review*, XVI (Winter, 1956–1957), 506–11.

*Hartley, Lois. "Theme in Thomas Wolfe's 'The Lost Boy' and 'God's Lonely Man,'" *Georgia Review*, XV (Summer, 1961), 230–35.

Hawthorne, Mark D. "Thomas Wolfe's Use of the Poetic Fragment," *Modern Fiction Studies*, XI (Autumn, 1965), 234–44.

Heath, John R. *The Strange Case of Thomas Wolfe.* Chicago Literary Club, 1949.

Heiderstadt, Dorothy. "Studying Under Thomas Wolfe," *Mark Twain Quarterly*, VIII (Winter, 1950), 7–8.

Henderson, Archibald. "Thomas Wolfe, Playmaker: An Unanswered Query," *Carolina Playbook*, XVI (March-June, 1943), 27–33.

Hicks, Granville. "Our Novelists' Shifting Reputations," *English Journal*, XL (Jan., 1951), 1–7.

Hilfer, Anthony Channell. "Wolfe's Altamont: The Mimesis of Being," *Georgia Review*, XVIII (Winter, 1964), 451–56.

Hill, John S. "Eugene Gant and the Ghost of Ben," *Modern Fiction Studies*, XI (Autumn, 1965), 245–49.

Hindus, Milton. "American Writer," *Commentary*, XXII (Dec., 1956), 585–88.

Hoffman, Frederick J. *The Modern Novel in America, 1900–1950.* Chicago: Henry Regnery Company, 1951. Pp. 164–70, 178, 190.

Holman, C. Hugh. "The Loneliness at the Core," *New Republic*, CXXXIII (Oct. 10, 1955), 16–17. Reprinted in Louis D. Rubin, Jr. and John Rees Moore, eds., *The Idea of an American Novel* (New York: Crowell, 1961), pp. 348–51, and partly reprinted in Holman, ed., *The World of Thomas Wolfe*, pp. 57–59.

———. "Thomas Wolfe: A Bibliographical Study," *Texas Studies in Literature and Language*, I (Autumn, 1959), 427–45.

———. *Thomas Wolfe.* University of Minnesota Pamphlets on American Writers. Minneapolis: University of Minnesota Press, 1960. Reprinted in William Van O'Connor, ed., *Seven Modern American Novelists: An Introduction* (Minneapolis: University of Minnesota Press, 1964), pp. 189–225, and partly reprinted in Holman, ed., *The World of Thomas Wolfe*, pp. 175–78.

*———. "'The Dark, Ruined Helen of His Blood': Thomas Wolfe and the South," in Louis D. Rubin, Jr. and Robert Jacobs, eds. *South: Modern Southern Literature in Its Cultural Setting.* Garden City, New York: Doubleday-Dolphin Books, 1961. Pp. 177–97.

————. "Thomas Wolfe and the Stigma of Autobiography," *Virginia Quarterly*, XL (Autumn, 1964), 614–25.

———— (ed.). *The Short Novels of Thomas Wolfe*. New York: Charles Scribner's Sons, 1961. ["Introduction," pp. *vii–xx*, and head-notes to each selection.]

———— (ed.). THE WORLD OF THOMAS WOLFE. New York: Charles Scribner's Sons, 1962.

———— (ed.). *The Thomas Wolfe Reader*. New York: Charles Scribner's Sons, 1964. ["Introduction," pp. 1–10.]

Huff, William H. "Thomas Clayton Wolfe," *Wilson Library Bulletin*, XXV (Sept., 1950), 72–74.

Hutsell, James K. "Thomas Wolfe and 'Altamont,'" *Southern Packet*, IV (April, 1948), 1–8.

Jelliffe, Belinda. "More on Tom Wolfe," *American Mercury*, LXV (July, 1947), 125–26.

Johnson, Edgar. "Thomas Wolfe and the American Dream," in his *A Treasury of Satire*. New York: Charles Scribner's Sons, 1945. Pp. 741–45. Reprinted in Holman, ed., *The World of Thomas Wolfe*, pp. 112–14.

Johnson, Elmer D. "Thomas Wolfe Abroad," *Louisiana Library Association Bulletin*, XVIII (1955), 9–11.

————. "On Translating Thomas Wolfe," *American Speech*, XXXII (May, 1957), 95–101.

————. OF TIME AND THOMAS WOLFE: A BIBLIOGRAPHY WITH A CHARACTER INDEX OF HIS WORKS. New York: Scarecrow Press, 1959. [For additions and corrections, see the review by Alexander D. Wainwright in *Papers of the Bibliographical Society of America*, LV (1961), 258–63.]

Johnson, Pamela Hansford. THOMAS WOLFE: A CRITICAL STUDY. London: William Heinemann Ltd., 1947. Published in America as HUNGRY GULLIVER: AN ENGLISH CRITICAL APPRAISAL OF THOMAS WOLFE (New York: Charles Scribner's Sons, 1948) and reprinted with new Preface in Scribner Library Edition as THE ART OF THOMAS WOLFE (New York: Charles Scribner's Sons, 1963).

————. "Thomas Wolfe and the Kicking Season," *Encounter*, XII (April, 1959), 77–80. Partly reprinted in Holman, ed., *The World of Thomas Wolfe*, pp. 60–62.

Johnson, Stewart. "Mrs. Julia Wolfe," *New Yorker*, XXXIV (April 12, 1958), 39–44.

Katz, Joseph. "Balzac and Wolfe: A Study of Self-Productive Over-productivity," *Psychoanalysis,* V (Summer, 1957), 3–19.

Kauffman, Bernice. "Bibliography of Periodical Articles on Thomas Wolfe," *Bulletin of Bibliography,* XVII (May and Aug., 1942), 162–65, 172–90.

Kazin, Alfred. *On Native Grounds: An Interpretation of Modern American Prose Literature.* New York: Harcourt, Brace & World, Inc., 1942. Pp. 466–84.

———. "Chile Takin' Notes," *New Republic,* CVIII (May 3, 1943), 607–09.

———. "The Writer's Friend," *New Yorker* (Feb. 17, 1951), 88–92. Reprinted in his *The Inmost Leaf: A Selection of Essays* (New York: Harcourt, Brace & World, Inc., 1955), pp. 185–90.

Kearns, Frank (ed.). "Tom Wolfe on the Drama," *Carolina Quarterly,* XI (Spring, 1960), 5–10.

Keever, T. W. "The Legend of a Lost Man," *Bluets,* XVIII (Jan., 1945), 43–48.

Kennedy, Richard S. "Thomas Wolfe at Harvard, 1920–1923," *Harvard Library Bulletin,* IV (Spring and Autumn, 1950), 172–90, 304–19. Adapted as "Wolfe's Harvard Years" in Walser, ed., *The Enigma of Thomas Wolfe,* pp. 18–32.

———. "Thomas Wolfe's Don Quixote," *College English,* XXIII (Dec., 1961), 185–91.

———. THE WINDOW OF MEMORY: THE LITERARY CAREER OF THOMAS WOLFE. Chapel Hill: University of North Carolina Press, 1962.

*———. "Wolfe's *Look Homeward, Angel* as a Novel of Development," *South Atlantic Quarterly,* LXIII (Spring, 1964), 218–26.

———. "Thomas Wolfe and the American Experience," *Modern Fiction Studies,* XI (Autumn, 1965), 219–32.

Kennedy, William F. "Economic Ideas in Contemporary Literature: The Novels of Thomas Wolfe," *Southern Economic Journal,* XX (July, 1953), 35–50. Partly reprinted in Holman, ed., *The World of Thomas Wolfe,* pp. 149–52.

———. "Are Our Novelists Hostile to the American Economic System?" *Dalhousie Review,* XXV (1955), 32–44.

Kilgore, Carl J. "Thomas Wolfe: A Flash of Genius," *Aurora* (Spring, 1949), pp. 8–10, 22–24.

Kinne, Wisner P. "Enter Tom Wolfe," *Harvard Alumni Bulletin,* LVII (Oct. 23, 1954), 101–102, 122–23. Adapted and expanded in his *George Pierce Baker and the American Theatre* (Cambridge: Harvard University Press, 1954), pp. 228–39.

Koch, Frederick H. "Thomas Wolfe, Playmaker," *Carolina Playbook* (June, 1935), pp. 65–69.

―――. "A Young Man of Promise," *Theatre Arts*, XXIII (Feb., 1939), 150.

―――. "Introduction to 'The Third Night,'" *Carolina Folk-Plays: First, Second, and Third Series*. New York: Henry Holt, 1941. Pp. 127–31.

Kofsky, Bernard. "Overloaded Black Briefcase," in Pollock and Cargill, *Thomas Wolfe at Washington Square*, pp. 90–92.

Kohler, Dayton. "All Fury Spent: A Note on Thomas Wolfe," *Southern Literary Messenger*, I (Aug. 1, 1939), 560–64.

―――. "Thomas Wolfe: Prodigal and Lost," *College English*, I (Oct., 1939), 1–10. Also in *English Journal*, XXVIII (Oct., 1939), 609–18.

Krauss, Russell. "Replacing Thomas Wolfe," in Pollock and Cargill, *Thomas Wolfe at Washington Square*, pp. 146–52.

Krim, Seymour. "Wolfe, the Critics, and the People," *Commonweal*, LVIII (Sept. 4, 1953), 540–42.

Kronenberger, Louis. "The Autobiography of Thomas Wolfe," in his *The Republic of Letters*. New York: Alfred A. Knopf, Inc., 1955. Pp. 257–60.

Kussy, Bella. "The Vitalist Trend in Thomas Wolfe," *Sewanee Review*, L (Summer, 1942), 306–24. Reprinted in Holman, ed., *The World of Thomas Wolfe*, pp. 101–11.

Ledig-Rowohlt, H. M. "Thomas Wolfe in Berlin," *American Scholar*, XXII (Spring, 1953), 185–201.

Little, Thomas. "The Thomas Wolfe Collection of William B. Wisdom," *Harvard Library Bulletin*, I (Autumn, 1947), 280–87.

Loggins, Vernon. "Dominant Primordial," in his *I Hear America: Literature in the United States Since 1900*. New York: Crowell, 1937. Pp. 113–41.

Luccock, Halford E. *American Mirror*. New York: The Macmillan Company, 1941. Pp. 39, 60, 105–108.

McCole, C. J. "Thomas Wolfe Embraces Life," *Catholic World*, CXLIII (April, 1936), 42–48. Reprinted in his *Lucifer at Large* (New York: Longmans, Green and Co., Ltd., 1937), pp. 231–54.

McCormick, John. *Catastrophe and Imagination: A Reinterpretation of the Recent English and American Novel*. London: Longmans, Green and Co., Ltd., 1957. Pp. 193–97, 249–54, 261–67.

McCoy, George W. "Asheville and Thomas Wolfe," *North Carolina Historical Review*, XXX (April, 1953), 200–17.

McDowell, David. "The Renaissance of Thomas Wolfe," *Sewanee Review*, LVI (Summer, 1948), 536–44.

McElderry, Bruce R., Jr. "The Autobiographical Problem in Thomas Wolfe's Early Novels," *Arizona Quarterly*, IV (Winter, 1948), 315–24.

*———. "The Durable Humor of *Look Homeward, Angel*," *Arizona Quarterly*, XI (Summer, 1955), 123–28.

———. "Wolfe and Emerson on 'Flow,' " *Modern Fiction Studies*, II (May, 1956), 77–78.

———. "Thomas Wolfe: Dramatist," *Modern Drama*, VI (May, 1963), 1–11.

———. THOMAS WOLFE. Twayne's United States Authors Series. New York: Twayne, 1964.

McGovern, Hugh. "A Note on Thomas Wolfe," *New Mexico Quarterly*, XVII (Summer, 1947), 198–200.

Maclachlan, John M. "Folk Concepts in the Novels of Thomas Wolfe," *Southern Folklore Quarterly*, IX (Dec., 1945), 175–86.

Malcolmson, David. "Prodigal's Return," in his *Ten Heroes*. New York: Duell, Sloan and Pearce, 1941. Pp. 126–30.

*Maloney, Martin. "A Study of Semantic States: Thomas Wolfe and the Faustian Sickness," *General Semantics Bulletin*, Nos. 16–17 (1955), 15–25.

Mandel, James. "Thomas Wolfe: A Reminiscence," in Pollock and Cargill, *Thomas Wolfe at Washington Square*, pp. 93–103.

Martin, F. David. "The Artist, Autobiography, and Thomas Wolfe," *Bucknell Review*, V (March, 1955), 15–28.

Meder, Thomas. "Notes on Wolfe and the American Spirit," *Carolina Magazine*, XLVIII (Oct., 1938), 22–24.

Meyerhoff, Hans. "Death of a Genius: The Last Days of Thomas Wolfe," *Commentary*, XIII (Jan., 1952), 44–51.

———. *Time in Literature*. Berkeley: University of California Press, 1955. Pp. 16, 26, 41, 44, 81.

Middlebrook, L. Ruth. "Reminiscences of Tom Wolfe," *American Mercury*, LXIII (Nov., 1946), 544–49.

———. "Further Memories of Tom Wolfe," *American Mercury*, LXIV (April, 1947), 413–20.

Morgan, H. Wayne. "Thomas Wolfe: The Web of Memory," in his *Writers in Transition: Seven Americans*. New York: Hill and Wang, 1963. Pp. 127–51.

Morris, Wright. "The Function of Appetite: Thomas Wolfe," in his *The Territory Ahead*. New York: Harcourt, Brace & World, Inc., 1958. Pp. 147–55.

Moser, Thomas C. "Thomas Wolfe: *Look Homeward, Angel*," in Wallace Stegner, ed., *The American Novel: From James Fenimore Cooper to William Faulkner*. New York: Basic Books, Inc., 1965. Pp. 206–18.

Muller, Herbert J. *Modern Fiction: A Study of Values*. New York: Funk and Wagnalls, 1937. Pp. 407–18.

——. THOMAS WOLFE. Makers of Modern Literature Series. Norfolk: New Directions, 1947. Extracts in Holman, ed., *The World of Thomas Wolfe*, pp. 120–29.

Natanson, M. A. "Privileged Moment: A Study in the Rhetoric of Thomas Wolfe," *Quarterly Journal of Speech*, XLIII (April, 1957), 143–50. Reprinted in Holman, *The World of Thomas Wolfe*, pp. 78–84.

Norman, James. "The Gargantuan Gusto of Thomas Wolfe," *Scholastic*, XXVII (Nov. 2, 1935), 5, 12.

Norwood, Hayden. "Julia Wolfe: Web of Memory," *Virginia Quarterly*, XX (April, 1944), 236–50.

——. THE MARBLE MAN'S WIFE: THOMAS WOLFE'S MOTHER. New York: Charles Scribner's Sons, 1947.

Nowell, Elizabeth. THOMAS WOLFE: A BIOGRAPHY. Garden City, New York: Doubleday & Company, Inc., 1960.

—— (ed.). THE LETTERS OF THOMAS WOLFE. New York: Charles Scribner's Sons, 1956.

Perkins, Maxwell. "Scribner's and Thomas Wolfe," *Carolina Magazine*, XLVIII (Oct., 1938), 15–17. Reprinted in Walser, ed., *The Enigma of Thomas Wolfe*, pp. 57–63.

——. "Thomas Wolfe," *Scribner's Magazine*, CV (May, 1939), 5.

*——. "Thomas Wolfe," *Harvard Library Bulletin*, I (Autumn, 1947), 269–77. Adapted as "Introduction" to Modern Standard Authors edition of *Look Homeward, Angel* (New York: Charles Scribner's Sons, 1952) and partly reprinted in Holman, ed., *The World of Thomas Wolfe*, pp. 42–44.

——. *Editor to Author: The Letters of Maxwell E. Perkins*, ed. John Hall Wheelock. New York: Charles Scribner's Sons, 1950. *Passim*.

Phillips, Gene. "Milton and Wolfe," *Saturday Review*, XL (Dec. 21, 1957), 26.

Phillipson, John S. "Thomas Wolfe: The Appeal to Youth," *Catholic Library World*, XXXII (November, 1960), 101–02.

Polk, William. "Thomas Wolfe," *Carolina Magazine*, LXVIII (Oct., 1938), 4–5.

Pollock, Thomas Clark, and Cargill, Oscar. THOMAS WOLFE AT WASHINGTON SQUARE. New York: New York University Press, 1954.

Powell, Desmond. "Wolfe's Farewells," *Accent* (Winter, 1941), 114–18.

———. "Of Thomas Wolfe," *Arizona Quarterly*, I (Spring, 1945), 28–36.

Preston, George R., Jr. THOMAS WOLFE: A BIBLIOGRAPHY. New York: Charles S. Boesen, 1943.

Priestley, J. B. "Introduction," *The Web and the Rock*. London: William Heinemann Ltd., 1947. Pp. *ix–xii*.

———. *Literature and Western Man*. New York: Harper and Row, Publishers, 1960. Pp. 438–40. Reprinted in Holman, ed., *The World of Thomas Wolfe*, pp. 179–80.

Pritchett, V. S. "Self-portrait of a Mastodon," *New Statesman and Nation*, LVI (Sept. 27, 1958), 423–24.

Pugh, C. E. "Of Thomas Wolfe," *Mark Twain Quarterly*, VII (Summer-Fall, 1945), 13–14.

Pusey, W. W., III. "The Germanic Vogue of Thomas Wolfe," *Germanic Review*, XXIII (April, 1948), 131–48.

Raynolds, Robert. *Thomas Wolfe: Memoir of a Friendship*. Austin: University of Texas Press, 1965.

*Reaver, J. Russell and Strozier, Robert I. "Thomas Wolfe and Death," *Georgia Review*, XVI (Fall, 1962), 330–50.

Reeves, George, Jr. "A Note on the Life and Letters of Thomas Wolfe," *South Atlantic Quarterly*, LVII (Spring, 1958), 216–21.

Reeves, Paschal. "The Humor of Thomas Wolfe," *Southern Folklore Quarterly*, XXIV (Dec., 1960), 109–20.

———. "Thomas Wolfe and His Scottish Heritage," *Southern Folklore Quarterly*, XXVIII (1964), 134–41.

———. "Thomas Wolfe on Publishers: Reaction to Rejection," *South Atlantic Quarterly*, LXIV (Summer, 1965), 385–89.

*———. "Thomas Wolfe: Notes on Three Characters," *Modern Fiction Studies*, XI (Autumn, 1965), 275–85.

Ribalow, Harold U. "Of Jews and Thomas Wolfe," *Chicago Jewish Forum*, XIII (Winter, 1954–1955), 89–99.

Robertson, Michael. "Giant from Asheville," *Cosmopolitan*, CXLV (Aug., 1958), 46–51.

Rothman, Nathan L. "Thomas Wolfe and James Joyce: A Study in Literary Influence," in Allen Tate, ed., *A Southern Vanguard*. New York: Prentice-Hall, 1947. Pp. 52–77, Reprinted in Walser, ed., *The Enigma of Thomas Wolfe*, pp. 263–89.

Rubin, Larry. "Thomas Wolfe and the Lost Paradise," *Modern Fiction Studies,* XI (Autumn, 1965), 250–58.

Rubin, Louis D., Jr. "Thomas Wolfe in Time and Place," *Hopkins Review,* VI (Winter, 1953), 117–32. Reprinted in Louis D. Rubin, Jr. and Robert D. Jacobs, eds., *Southern Renascence: The Literature of the Modern South.* Baltimore: Johns Hopkins Press, 1953. Pp. 117–32.

————. THOMAS WOLFE: THE WEATHER OF HIS YOUTH. Baton Rouge: Louisiana State University Press, 1955. Extract appears in Holman, ed., *The World of Thomas Wolfe,* pp. 157–63.

*————. "Thomas Wolfe: Time and the South," in his *The Faraway Country: Writers of the Modern South.* Seattle: University of Washington Press, 1963. Pp. 72–104.

————. "The Self Recaptured," *Kenyon Review,* XXV (Summer, 1963), 393–415.

Russell, Phillips. "The Meaning of Thomas Wolfe," *Carolina Magazine,* LXVIII (Oct., 1938), 3.

Scherman, David E. *Literary America.* New York: Dodd, Mead & Company, 1952. Pp. 158–61.

Schoenberner, Franz. "My Discovery of Thomas Wolfe," in his *The Inside Story of an Outsider.* New York: The Macmillan Company, 1949. Reprinted in Walser, ed., *The Enigma of Thomas Wolfe,* pp. 290–97.

Schorer, Mark. "Technique as Discovery," *Hudson Review,* I (Spring, 1948), 67–87. [On Wolfe, pp. 80–81.] First reprinted in William Van O'Connor, ed., *Forms of Modern Fiction.* Minneapolis: University of Minnesota Press, 1948. Pp. 9–29.

Schramm, Wilbur L. "Careers at Crossroads," *Virginia Quarterly,* XV (Oct., 1939), 627–32.

Simpson, Claude M., Jr. "Thomas Wolfe: A Chapter in His Biography," *Southwest Review,* XXV (April, 1940), 308–21.

Skipp, Francis E. "The Editing of *Look Homeward, Angel,*" *Papers of the Bibliographical Society of America,* LVII (First Quarter, 1963), 1–13.

*Slack, Robert C. "Thomas Wolfe: The Second Cycle," in Arthur T. Broes and others, *Lectures on Modern Novelists.* Carnegie Series in English, No. 7. Pittsburgh: Carnegie Institute of Technology, 1963. Pp. 41–53.

Slochower, Harry. "Cosmic Exile," in his *No Voice Is Wholly Lost.* New York: Creative Age Press, 1945. Pp. 93–103.

Sloyan, Gerald S. "Thomas Wolfe: A Legend of a Man's Youth in His Hunger," in Harold C. Gardiner, ed., *Fifty Years of the*

American Novel: A Christian Appraisal. New York: Charles Scribner's Sons, 1952. Pp. 197–215.

Smith, Chard P. "Perkins and the Elect," *Antioch Review,* XXII (Spring, 1962), 85–102.

Smith, Harrison. "Midwife to Literature," *Saturday Review,* XXX (July 12, 1947), 15–16.

Snell, George. "The Education of Thomas Wolfe," in his *Shapers of American Fiction, 1798–1947.* New York: E. P. Dutton & Co., Inc., 1947. Pp. 173–87.

Snelling, Paula. "Thomas Wolfe: The Story of a Marvel," *Pseudopodia* (Spring, 1936), pp. 1, 8–12.

Solon, S. L. "The Ordeal of Thomas Wolfe," *Modern Quarterly,* XI (Winter, 1939), 45–53.

Southern Packet, IV (April, 1948)—Thomas Wolfe Memorial Number.

Spearman, Walter. *North Carolina Writers.* Chapel Hill: University of North Carolina Press, 1949. Pp. 18–20.

Spiller, Robert E. *The Cycle of American Literature: An Essay in Historical Criticism.* New York: The Macmillan Company, 1955. Pp. 263–70. Partly reprinted in Holman, ed., *The World of Thomas Wolfe,* pp. 164–66.

Spitz, Leon. "Was Wolfe an Anti-Semite?" *American Hebrew,* CLVIII (Nov. 19, 1948), 5.

Starrett, Agnes Lynch. "Notes on 'A Western Journal,'" in *A Western Journal,* by Thomas Wolfe. University of Pittsburgh Press, 1951. Pp. *vii–ix.*

Stearns, Monroe M. "The Metaphysics of Thomas Wolfe," *College English,* VI (Jan., 1945), 193–99. Reprinted in Walser, ed., *The Enigma of Thomas Wolfe,* pp. 195–205.

*Stegner, Wallace. "Analysis of 'The Lost Boy,'" in Wallace Stegner, Richard Scowcroft, and Boris Ilyin, eds., *The Writer's Art: A Collection of Short Stories.* Boston: D. C. Heath and Company, 1950. Pp. 178–83.

Stevens, Virginia. "Thomas Wolfe's America," *Mainstream,* IX (Jan., 1958), 1–24.

Stokley, James. "Perkins and Wolfe," *Saturday Review,* XXXIV (July 7, 1951), 22.

Stone, Edward. "A Rose for Thomas Wolfe," *Ohio University Review,* V (1963), 17–24.

Stone, Geoffrey. "Thomas Wolfe: Romantic Atavism," *The Examiner,* I (Fall, 1938), 385–93.

Stovall, Floyd. *American Idealism*. Norman: University of Oklahoma Press, 1943. Pp. 154–58, 163–64.

Sutton, Horace. "Look Homeward, Asheville," *Saturday Review*, XXXVII (Nov. 6, 1954), 45–48.

Talmey, Allene. "Wolfe and the Angel," *Vogue*, CXXXI (March 1, 1958), 142–43, 180–81, 183.

Taylor, Walter Fuller. "Thomas Wolfe and the Middle-Class Tradition," *South Atlantic Quarterly*, LII (Oct., 1953), 543–54. Reprinted in Holman, ed., *The World of Thomas Wolfe*, pp. 141–48.

Tedd, Eugene. "House of Hell and Anguish," *Prairie Schooner*, XXIX (Summer, 1955), 95–108.

Terry, John Skally. "En Route to a Legend," *Saturday Review*, XXXI (Nov. 27, 1948), 7–9. Reprinted as "Wolfe and Perkins" in Walser, ed., *The Enigma of Thomas Wolfe*, pp. 51–56.

—— (ed.). THOMAS WOLFE'S LETTERS TO HIS MOTHER. New York: Charles Scribner's Sons, 1943. ["Introduction," pp. *vii–xxii*.]

Thompson, Betty. "Thomas Wolfe: Two Decades of Criticism," *South Atlantic Quarterly*, XLIX (July, 1950), 378–92. Reprinted in Walser, ed., *The Enigma of Thomas Wolfe*, pp. 298–313.

Thornton, Mary Lindsay. " 'Dear Mabel': Letters of Thomas Wolfe to His Sister, Mabel Wolfe Wheaton," *South Atlantic Quarterly*, LX (Autumn, 1961), 469–83.

Trilling, Lionel. "Contemporary American Literature in Its Relation to Ideas," in Margaret Denny and William H. Gilman, eds., *The American Writer and the European Tradition*. Minneapolis: University of Minnesota Press, 1950. Pp. 144–49.

Untermeyer, Louis. "Foreword," *A Stone, a Leaf, a Door: Poems by Thomas Wolfe*, selected and arranged in verse by John S. Barnes. New York: Charles Scribner's Sons, 1945. Pp. *v–vi*.

——. "Thomas Wolfe," in his *Makers of the Modern World*. New York: Simon and Schuster, Inc., 1955. Pp. 726–35.

Van Doren, Carl. *The American Novel, 1789–1939*. New York: The Macmillan Company, 1940. Pp. 343–48.

Van Gelder, Robert. *Writers and Writing*. New York: Charles Scribner's Sons, 1946. Pp. 114–19.

Vining, Lou Myrtis. "I Cover a Writer's Conference," *Writer's Digest*, XV (Sept., 1935), 30–32.

Volkening, H. T. "Tom Wolfe: Penance No More," *Virginia Quarterly*, XV (Spring, 1939), 196–215. Reprinted in Pollock and Cargill, *Thomas Wolfe at Washington Square*, pp. 108–26, and Walser, ed., *The Enigma of Thomas Wolfe*, pp. 33–50.

Wade, John Donald. "Prodigal: An Essay on Thomas Wolfe," *Southern Review*, I (July, 1935), 192–98.

Walser, Richard. "Some Notes on Wolfe's Reputation Abroad," *Carolina Quarterly*, I (March, 1949), 37–41.

*———. THOMAS WOLFE: AN INTRODUCTION AND INTERPRETATION. American Authors and Critic Series. New York: Barnes and Noble Inc., 1961. (Reissued by Holt, Rinehart and Winston, Inc., same series, 1961.)

———. "An Early Wolfe Essay—and the Downfall of a Hero," *Modern Fiction Studies*, XI (Autumn, 1965), 269–74.

——— (ed.). THE ENIGMA OF THOMAS WOLFE: BIOGRAPHICAL AND CRITICAL SELECTIONS. Cambridge, Mass.: Harvard University Press, 1953.

Walter, Felix. "Thomas Wolfe," *Canadian Forum*, XI (Oct., 1930), 25–26.

*Warren, Robert Penn. "A Note on the Hamlet of Thomas Wolfe," *American Review*, V (May, 1935), 191–208. Reprinted in his *Selected Essays* (New York: Random House, Inc., 1958), pp. 170–83, and as "The Hamlet of Thomas Wolfe" in Walser, ed., *The Enigma of Thomas Wolfe*, pp. 120–32.

Watkins, Floyd C. "Thomas Wolfe and the Southern Mountaineer," *South Atlantic Quarterly*, L (Jan., 1951), 58–71.

———. "Thomas Wolfe and the Nashville Agrarians," *Georgia Review*, VII (Winter, 1953), 410–23.

———. "Thomas Wolfe's High Sinfulness of Poetry," *Modern Fiction Studies*, II (Dec., 1956), 197–206.

———. THOMAS WOLFE'S CHARACTERS: PORTRAITS FROM LIFE. Norman: University of Oklahoma Press, 1957.

*———. "Rhetoric in Southern Writing: Wolfe," *Georgia Review*, XII (Spring, 1958), 79–82.

Watts, Georgia. "An Afternoon with Thomas Wolfe," *Writer's Digest* (Feb., 1959), 30–34.

Wheaton, Mabel Wolfe, and LeGette Blythe. THOMAS WOLFE AND HIS FAMILY. Garden City, New York: Doubleday and Company, Inc., 1961.

Wheelock, John Hall. "Introduction," *The Face of a Nation: Poetical Passages from the Writings of Thomas Wolfe*. New York: Charles Scribner's Sons, 1939. Pp. *v–vi*.

Williams, Cecil B. "Thomas Wolfe Fifteen Years After," *South Atlantic Quarterly*, LIV (Oct., 1955), 523–37.

Wolfe, Fred W. "To the Editor," *Saturday Review*, XXXIV (Aug. 11, 1951), 23–24.

Wolfe, Julia E. "Letter from His Mother," *Carolina Playbook,* XVI (March-June, 1943), 13-14.

————. "Look Homeward, Angel," *Saturday Review,* XXIX (Jan. 6, 1946), 13-14, 31-32. [An interview transcribed by Ruth Davis.]

Wolfe, Thomas. THE STORY OF A NOVEL. New York: Charles Scribner's Sons, 1936. Reprinted in Geismar, ed., *The Portable Thomas Wolfe,* pp. 562-611; and Holman, ed., *The Thomas Wolfe Reader,* pp. 13-51, and *The World of Thomas Wolfe,* pp. 9-32.

Notes on Contributors

Edward C. Aswell (1900–1958) was an editor for Harper and Brothers from 1935 to 1947. In addition to his editing of Wolfe's posthumous major fiction, he has written articles on Wolfe.

Maurice Beebe, Professor of English at Purdue University, is the author of *Ivory Towers and Sacred Founts*. He is the editor of *Literary Symbolism* and coeditor of *All the King's Men: A Critical Handbook*. He is also the editor of *Modern Fiction Studies*. His articles on modern fiction have appeared in a variety of journals.

Edward A. Bloom, Professor and Chairman of the Department of English at Brown University, has written and edited a number of articles and books. Among his publications are *Samuel Johnson in Grub Street, The Order of Poetry,* and *The Order of Fiction.*

William Braswell, Professor of English at Purdue University, is the author of *Melville's Religious Thought* and coeditor of *Thomas Wolfe's Purdue Speech.* His articles on American literature have appeared in a number of journals.

Oscar Cargill is Professor Emeritus of English at New York University. Among his many articles and books on American literature are *The Novels of Henry James* and *Toward a Pluralistic Criticism.* He is coeditor of *O'Neill and His Plays: Four Decades of Criticism* and *Thomas Wolfe at Washington Square.*

Margaret Church, Professor of English at Purdue University, is the author of *Time and Reality: Studies in Contemporary Fiction* and a number of articles on contemporary literature. Currently she is working on comparative studies of continental novels.

Clyde C. Clements, Jr., Assistant Professor of English at Xavier University, New Orleans, is the editor of *Xavier University Studies.* He has had articles published in *The McNeese Review* and *Modern Fiction Studies.*

Bernard DeVoto (1897–1955), former editor of "The Easy Chair" at *Harper's* Magazine, wrote and edited many books on history, American literature, and conservation. His three books on Mark Twain are *Mark Twain's America, Mark Twain at Work,* and *Mark Twain in Europe.*

Leslie A. Field, Assistant Professor of English at Purdue University, is the coeditor of *All the King's Men: A Critical Handbook* and *Thomas Wolfe's Purdue Speech.* He has published articles on a variety of subjects.

Irving Halperin, Associate Professor of English at San Francisco State College, is the author of five articles on Thomas Wolfe. Currently he is doing a study on the "literature of the survivors"— those who survived the concentration camps and ghettos of W. W. II.

Lois Hartley, Associate Professor of English at Boston College, is the author of *Spoon River Revisited.* She has also written a number of articles on Edgar Lee Masters, and is now Managing Editor of *Literature East and West.*

C. Hugh Holman, Kenan Professor of English at the University of North Carolina, is the author or editor of many articles and books, including four books on Thomas Wolfe. His most recent works are *William Gilmore Simms as a Man of Letters* and *Three Modes of Modern Southern Fiction.*

Richard S. Kennedy, Professor of English at Temple University, is the author of *The Window of Memory: The Literary Career of Thomas Wolfe* and a number of articles on modern novelists. He is now editing the Thomas Wolfe notebooks.

Martin J. Maloney, Professor of Speech at Northwestern University, is in the Department of Radio and Television. He has published articles on speech, semantics, and television.

Bruce R. McElderry, Jr., Professor of English at the University of Southern California, is the author and editor of a number of articles and books. He wrote both *Henry James* and *Thomas Wolfe* for Twayne's United States Authors Series.

Maxwell E. Perkins (1884–1947) was an editor for Charles Scribner's Sons from 1914 until his death. A number of his letters to the authors he worked with have been collected as *Editor to Author.*

J. Russell Reaver, Jr., Professor of English at The Florida State University, is the author of *Emerson as Mythmaker* and coauthor of *Fundamentals of Folk Literature.* He is also coeditor of *The Humanities in Contemporary Life* and *The Humanistic Tradition,* and the author of several articles which have appeared in folklore and other journals.

Paschal Reeves, Associate Professor of English at the University of Georgia, has published articles on a variety of subjects, including four articles on Wolfe. He is now editing the Thomas Wolfe note-books.

Louis D. Rubin, Jr., Professor and Chairman of the Department of English at Hollins College, Virginia, is the author of *Thomas Wolfe: The Weather of His Youth* and *The Faraway Country: Writers of the Modern South.* He has written or edited eight other books, including a novel, *The Golden Weather.*

Robert C. Slack is Head of the Department of Humanities and Associate Professor of English at Carnegie Institute of Technology. He is the editor of the forthcoming collection, *Bibliographies of Studies in Victorian Literature, 1959–1964,* and he has published articles on Hardy, Robert Penn Warren, and Shakespeare.

Wallace Stegner, Professor of English at Stanford University, is primarily a novelist and short-story writer. He has written eighteen books, including *A Shooting Star* and *The Big Rock Candy Mountain.* Recently he edited *The American Novel: From James Fenimore Cooper to William Faulkner.*

Robert I. Strozier is Associate Professor of English at Armstrong State College, Savannah, Georgia. He has had poems and articles published in various journals.

Richard Walser, Professor of English at North Carolina State University, has edited, written, or prepared for publication about twenty books. His books on Wolfe are *The Enigma of Thomas Wolfe* and *Thomas Wolfe: An Introduction and Interpretation.*

Robert Penn Warren, author or editor of more than thirty-five books, is also Professor of English at Yale University. His novel, *All the King's Men,* won the Pulitzer Prize in 1946. His most recent novel is *Flood* (1964), and his latest book of nonfiction is *Who Speaks for the Negro?* (1965).

Floyd C. Watkins, Professor of English at Emory University, Atlanta, is the author of *Thomas Wolfe's Characters* and coauthor of *Old Times in the Faulkner Country* and *Yesterday in the Hills.* He is also the author of a number of articles on Wolfe, Faulkner, and Southern literature.

Index